Borough Market Cookbook: Meat & Fish

BOROUGH MARKET COOKBOOK

Meat & Fish

Writing **Sarah Freeman** *and* **Sarah Leahey-Benjamin**

Photography **George Nicholson**

Design **Catherine Dixon**

Illustration **Emma Lofstrom**

Publisher **Tobias Steed**

CIVIC books

To Sarah
Your dream made this a reality

Frontispiece *The Dexter, Northfield Farm*

Borough Market Cookbook: Meat & Fish
2nd edition
Published by Civic Books 2007

Civic Books
7 Peacock Yard
Iliffe Street
London SE17 3LH, UK

Tel (0044) 20 7708 2942
Email info@civicbooks.com
Website www.civicbooks.com

ISBN-13: 978 1 904104 92 6

British Library Cataloguing in Publication Data
A catalogue record for this book is available from the British Library.

Meat

Fish

The Ginger Pig

Silfield Farm

Farmer Sharp

Farmhouse Direct

Furness Fish Poultry & Game

Gamston Wood Ostriches

Seldom Seen Farm

Northfield Farm

Wyndham House Poultry

Oysterman

West Country Park Venison

Brown & Forrest

Applebee's Fish

Denhay Farms

Wild Beef

Shellseekers

Foreword

The Borough Market recently celebrated 250 years of trading on its current site at the foot of London Bridge. A market of one sort or other has survived in this area since Roman times and a recorded market place for at least a thousand years – a testament to how a market providing the finest of produce can be an essential focal point for a community and a hub of commerce. No longer the 'best kept secret in London' the Market is now known throughout Britain and renowned in continental Europe as a centre of food excellence.

The *Borough Market Cookbook: Meat & Fish* is a further example of that excellence. This is an essential tool for any chef, whether novice or professional, to prepare and savour dishes and meals with produce from the traders in the market. The provenance of their produce is unsurpassed and so are the team behind this cookbook. This is not the work of a single individual but a collective effort that reflects the Market and its collaborative and community driven ethos.

Former Chairman of the Trustees George Nicholson has travelled around the country visiting meat and fish traders in their own back yard to capture images of them at work, while Sarah Freeman, author of *The best of modern British cookery* has been interviewing the traders to understand the passion and process behind their livelihoods.

The cookbook features interviews with sixteen traders and around 150 recipes all of which can be prepared with produce available through the Market. This is the first of a series of cookbooks. George, with his photography, extracts the essence of the traders in their own landscape and maintains the dignity of the animals captured on these pages. Sarah Freeman through her interviews has seen the spirit with which these dedicated professionals have passionately pursued their work. The book is not only a true testament to the quality of the produce available through the Market, but with the fabulous recipes created by Sarah Freeman and Sarah Leahy-Benjamin an essential tool for all Market goers.

Simone Crofton
Chief Executive, The Borough Market

Introduction

The origin of the Borough Market cookbook

This book was the direct result of the 2005 Making Markets conference at Borough Market. Sarah Freeman, who is a food writer, went to it and was especially impressed by the role that markets play in bringing the countryside into the town. In a market, you could find out anything you wanted about a product, not with difficulty or having to read small-print labels, but as a social exercise and as part of the fun of the experience. A night or two later she was looking at George Nicholson's wonderful book, *Made in Southwark*, which features photographs of some of the traders in the Market and the idea for the cookery book came to life.

Early plans for collaboration grew into a collective adventure for a committed few sharing a creative vision. It hasn't always been easy – what worthwhile project ever is? – but it has always been exciting and inspiring, while the satisfaction in being able to offer a book very much our own is enormous.

The working collective came together gradually. As the then Chairman of the Market's Trustees, George Nicholson introduced Robin Knowles of Civic Regeneration. He helped recruit Tobias Steed, of Can of Worms Press who had produced *The Borough Market book*, and who was as enthusiastic as we were. By then, Sarah Leahey-Benjamin, one of the most talented and interesting young chefs around had joined us to help Sarah Freeman with the recipes (their contributions are indicated thus [SF] [SLB]), and Catherine Dixon, the best typographer we felt we could ever find. Rachel de Thample provided editorial guidance whilst in her final trimester, ably assisted by Laura Chastney.

Throughout the book the texture and interplay of country and town is key, sensitively handled from the outset in a cover illustration by Emma Lofstrom. Overall the effect we hope for is one of a cookbook that will pass the test of time, and eating, to become one of those well-loved, well-worn cookbooks to be referred to again and again – a cookbook to pass on through the generations. We've all learnt a lot, and plan to do it again; indeed a book on fruit and vegetables is underway. We hope that you enjoy using this cookbook as much as we have enjoyed preparing it.

Borough Market, 2007

Notes on photography Seeing the world in black and white

The recipes in this book are not illustrated with any 'glossy' photographs of the dishes described by the two authors. It is a deliberate decision. Instead, what is being offered, is a return to an earlier more descriptive tradition, where human senses, cooking skills and ingredients were the main focus. Of course, presentation is an important part of the process. I would argue, however, that it is not, nor should it be, the principal one. An analogy comes to mind of a preference for a rose with a scent, rather than one merely as a competition exhibit. Readers and users of the cookbook can however be assured, that if the final product is not so immediately evident, each dish has been well tried and tested by the authors – both distinguished cooks.

So what is the philosophy behind the photographs in this cookbook? The renowned photographer, Paul Strand stressed that; 'the photographer has a duty to come to know, to see, to understand what they see with a good deal of humility and respect'. It is an important challenge, and one that chimes well with a key element of the Borough Market. Apart from its long history, a feature of the market – one that I would argue provides the very foundation on which its recent renaissance is based – is the representation of a core of small producers from around the UK. To illustrate this pictorially, there are four distinct themes; Place; People; Process and Produce. This is to give the reader, a flavour of the incredible variety of the British countryside; to spotlight the people behind the products in the market and give a sense of their daily lives; to illustrate something of the craft skills involved; and most importantly, to focus on the animals themselves. This is not a sentimental journey, nor can or should it be, when we are describing commercial farming, albeit one where animal husbandry is to the fore. But treating animals with dignity is an important objective underpinning the photographs.

The photographs were all shot in black & white, which might at first seem a little at odds with a desire to present the cookbook as a serious contribution to modern cooking. I personally prefer the medium, adding as I think it does a richness of tone absent in colour pictures. That is a personal preference. In the event, I was very struck by the sheer number of animals I photographed that were black and white, whether in feather, skin colour or coat. The world is indeed more black and white than you think!

[GN]

Borough and the Bridge
A brief history of Borough Market

The crucial factor in the history of Borough Market is London Bridge. Until the eighteenth century, it was the only bridge over the Thames from London (which at that time didn't extend across the river). It was thus the only link between London and southern England. Its enormous importance was reflected by constant complaints about traffic congestion on and around it and the prominence over the centuries of Southwark. In 1295 Southwark was the only borough in England apart from the City of London itself to be represented by two Members of Parliament; similarly, 300 years later it paid the king a larger subsidy than any other English town or city except London. Its leading position was echoed by the wealth and influence of some of its citizens, without whose support the Market almost certainly wouldn't have survived.

The first incarnation of the Market was actually on the bridge. There may have been traders there earlier than 1014, but at this date reference was made to the sale of grain, fish, vegetables, and cattle, who in the days before the railways had to be transported on the hoof. They were enclosed in pens, which must have had much the same effect on traffic as the barricades round roadworks today.

In 1276–8 the Mayor of London introduced regulations limiting trade from outside the City boundaries, presumably in the attempt to stamp out 'foreign' competition. Not long afterwards, a couple of bakers were convicted of bringing underweight loaves into the City and sentenced to be dragged through the streets tied to a hurdle. Other traders were similarly tried and punished in various ways. This phase of the Market ended when, allegedly because of congestion, it was moved to the grounds of St Thomas's Hospital. At that time the Hospital was in Long Southwark, now Borough High Street, which is the continuation of the road over the bridge. In the thirteenth century, as the result of a fire, the Hospital moved to its present site on St Thomas's Street. The market went with it and continued there for several hundred years.

Two centuries after the original market moved, another was founded in Long Southwark, the upper end of which, including the approach to the bridge, had until then belonged to the county of Surrey. In the fifteenth century, Edward III transferred ownership of it to the City, with permission to hold a market three days a week. The area thereafter became known as the Guildable Manor.

As was usual until comparatively recently, the new Market was both wholesale and retail. A bell was rung at 10·30 am to mark the change-over to retail, and again at the close of business in the evening. The traders were grouped according to type of produce, with farmers selling lamb, veal, and bacon (the first two presumably on the hoof) at the end nearest the bridge, followed by their wives with butter, then fish-sellers, then bakers, then vendors of vegetables and grain, and finally butchers. The butchers were not allowed to bring live cattle into the market because they were 'soe wilde that they run awaie as often as it happeneth'. In the days before refrigeration, one of a butcher's main concerns was keeping his stock fresh. One punishment for selling bad meat was for the culprit to be pilloried and have to smell it as it was burnt in front of his nose.

This Market stayed in Borough High Street for nearly 300 years. Congestion was an increasing problem throughout the period. Early in the sixteenth century a Market House was built in the middle of the road, which must have been almost as obstructive as the cattle on the bridge. To reduce congestion (or, to put it another way, to discourage dalliance), women selling produce from baskets were not permitted to sit down or stop walking in the market, and had to cry their wares continually. Similarly, unmarried women living in the slums of Bankside were forbidden to enter the Guildable Manor unless they were going to the Market – which one presumes was intended to prevent loitering in the surrounding streets but sounds like an invitation to turn the Market into the local Red Light district. That it served such a purpose, at least after it moved to its present site, is suggested by the name of the pub, The Hoar's Nest, now renamed The Market Porter; Madam Elizabeth Holland's 'House of Obscenitie' was also nearby.

As well as the Market, an annual fair was founded which took place in September and was immensely successful: at one stage, it lasted for as long as a fortnight. Hogarth's wonderful, intricate drawing of it shows flags flying, a man crossing the street on a tight-rope, apparently also flying, a vast picture of the siege of Troy, people playing the trumpet, bagpipes, and a drum amongst a sea of bodies, and a woman displaying a magnificent pair of thighs. Although published over 100 years later, Wordsworth's verbal description of St Bartholomew's Fair paints much the same picture:

> Below, the open space, through every nook
> Of the wide area, twinkles, is alive
> With heads…
> With chattering monkeys dangling from their poles…
> With those that stretch the neck and strain the eyes,
> And crack the voice in rivalship, the crowd
> Inviting; with buffoons against buffoons
> Grimacing, writhing, screaming, – him who grinds
> The hurdy-gurdy, at the fiddle weaves,
> Rattles the salt-box, thumps the kettle-drum
> And him who at the trumpet puffs his cheeks…
> All moveables of wonder, from all parts,
> Are here – Albinos, painted Indians, Dwarfs,
> The Horse of knowledge, and the learned Pig,
> The Stone-eater, the man that swallows fire,
> Giants, Ventriloquists, the Invisible Girl…

The fair was abolished because of its rowdiness in 1762, just a few years after the Market in the High Street was also forced to close.

By the eighteenth century, the crush of carts and carriages on the bridge was such that pedestrians climbed on to the parapet to avoid being run over. Some of them ended up needing medical treatment, which had to be paid for by the parish of St Margaret's at Southwark. Discussions about moving the Market House were already under way when a great fire broke out and it was burnt to the ground. The City seized the opportunity to try to close the Market but was forestalled by the wily citizens of Southwark, who succeeded in prolonging its life in the High Street for another eighty years.

This Market was finally terminated by an Act of Parliament in 1755. The residents of Southwark, however, petitioned success-fully to start another, which was to be independent of the City and in a place conveniently accessible to (but not actually in) the High Street. They raised £6,000 and bought an area called The Triangle which, with additions, is where the Market is still held today. As described at the time, it didn't sound very attractive: it was situated 'on the backside of Three Counties court eastwards, Fowle Lane buildings in Rochester Yard and Dirty Lane north-wards; and towards Deadman's Place westwards'. Possibly Deadman's Place was so called because the Clink prison was just down the road. Stoney Street similarly is said to be named after the stony-broke debtors who were taken there.

A covered area for selling corn was built on the new site within a few years. In 1801 the whole market was covered over. By 1870 its appearance had been transformed by a magnificent Crystal Palace-style glass and iron structure with twin arches and a dome. By this time too, the South Eastern Railway had built the viaduct over the market which is still there today: at that date, however, it was neatly sandwiched in the space between the two arches. Before it was built, the Market Trustees had insisted on certain terms in their contract with the railway company: these included a ban on building work at times when it might interfere with the wholesale market, ie between 10 pm and 10 am, the provision of adequate lighting both during and after construction, the maintenance of the viaduct in the future, and payment of a fine of £50 for every day that the work exceeded the agreed date of completion.

Until then, everything sent to the Market (unless local) had either come from the south of England in a horse-drawn vehicle or from abroad in ships docking at the Winchester or St Mary Overie ('Over-the-water') wharves – which suggests that foreign as well as British goods were sold probably throughout its history. The arrival of the railway enormously widened its catchment area. On the other hand, it brought soot. A letter written to the Trustees by a group of traders in 1896 read:

> Gentlemen, we beg to draw your attention to the very dirty condition of the arches of the South Eastern Railway Co. running over our stands, which are positively black with dirt to such a thickness that it is continually falling and damaging our samples of fruit and other goods. We… suggest that you propose to the South Eastern Railway the desirability of painting the arches white or some other light colour…

The very next year the elegant Crystal Palace-style roof was sacrificed to the railway company's need to widen the line. After another year or so, the retail side of the Market was ended and with it the vigour and excitement which had kept it at the centre of Southwark life for so long. However, the Trustees faithfully continued to guard its interests throughout the twentieth century. Ted Bowman, the Chairman from 1981 to 2000, records its difficulties:

> When I first became Chairman in 1981, there were… vacant stands in the Market, something which accelerated over the next ten or so years until we reached a point in 1995 when things were really getting precarious financially.

His first initiative was to hold an architectural competition: the winner was appointed Market architect. Then the Trustees began to consider how to reintroduce retailing. George Nicholson, who took the photographs in this book, became Chairman of a Development Committee which set the ball rolling with Henrietta Green's Food Lovers' Fair of 1998. A number of the traders who came still attend regularly and form the present retail market's nucleus. From that moment, as customers don't need reminding, the Market has never looked back – indeed, after eight years it is so successful that it seems set to return to Edward III's three days a week.

250th anniversary: shoppers at the newly refurbished retail market

An illustrated history of Borough Market: 250 years, various authors, published by the Trustees of Borough Market, 2006

Canon T P Stevens. *Historic Southwark*, Southwark Borough Council

David Johnson. *Southwark and the City*, published for the Corporation of London by Oxford University Press, 1969

Mary Boast. *The story of the Borough*, Southwark Borough Council, 1980 and 1997

Fruit, vegetable and flower markets of England: Borough Market, London SE1, 1953–4 London: Showcase Publicity

Southwark Fair, William Hogarth (picture)

The Borough Market book: from roots to renaissance, various authors, published by Civic Books, 2005

William Wordsworth. 'Book VII', *The Prelude*, 1850

I want to thank Michael Freeman and David Szanto for help with research.

Shopping & kitchen notes

Markets versus supermarkets

Recently I went to a debate at which six speakers, including Dominic Lawson and Giles Coren, argued for and against the motion 'Long Live Tesco!' When asked, all of them admitted to having been to a supermarket in the past few days except Giles Coren, who apparently doesn't need to – perhaps partly because, as The Times restaurant critic, he always eats out.

As far as I remember, the most exciting thing that any of them bought was a bagel. We all go to the supermarket (except Giles) for everyday items such as washing-machine tablets and cooking-foil, dog-biscuits, sugar, perhaps tea and cheap wine, and that tragically degraded liquid known as milk, which is pasteurized, homogenized, and separated so that you can buy it with as much of the cream returned as your doctor advises. Often, the goods on the shelves can't be seen because of the packaging (not that this much matters if it's only cooking-foil). Nor are there any smells except for the occasional laboratory concocted whiff of baking which it is hoped will make us feel hungry. In the stores I go to, there's no piped music as yet – but it may come. Everything is predictable: great efforts are made to ensure that bakery products and prepared meals are always exactly the same and very little of the produce sold isn't available from somewhere or other all the year round.

Shopping in the Market is a completely different experience. For a start, you can't buy dog-biscuits or cooking-foil. The items for which you go to Borough are top-quality meat, bright-eyed fish shining with freshness, seasonal fruit and vegetables, special-ist cheeses, and real bread. Instead of the information on the packet, you have the trader, who will be delighted to answer all your questions (eg in relation to meat, what the animal ate, how much space it had, and how it was slaughtered). They're as keen to talk to you as you to them. The social aspect of the Market is part of its raison d'être.

Another aspect of the Market experience is sensory. Not only can you see the goods, you can smell and often taste them. You can inhale the aroma of hot venison-burgers, griddled chicken, and Flour Power's rosemary bread baking in its on-site bakery or try Todd Trethowen's Gorwydd Caerphillly or John Bourne's unique long-matured Blue Cheshire. The way to shop here is to come without a shopping-list, wander round, take a long look at everything, and choose whatever takes your fancy. Then, with help of this book, you can decide what to do with it and buy the rest of the ingredients (if any) accordingly.

Shopping at Borough is more like an adventure than a chore – a voyage of exploration, if you like. It's fun. It offers good value too. Lots of people complain that the Market is expensive, but they tend to forget the nature of what they're buying. The comparison they should be making is with Harrods, Harvey Nichols, or La Fromagerie rather than Tesco or Sainsbury's.

But there is also a political dimension to shopping in the Market. Every purchase you make is a vote in favour of sustainability, small production, and craftsmanship, or in the case of meat, careful husbandry and humane rearing. The British public's refusal to be pushed into accepting GM foods was an example of customers' power. And, as politicians regularly remind us, every vote counts.

Slow Food's Ark of Taste

Slow Food was founded by an Italian, Carlo Petrini, as a reaction to the opening of a branch of McDonalds in the Piazza di Spagna, in Rome. It was started simply to promote the enjoyment of slow (for 'slow' read 'real') traditional food in the face of competition from fast food. It began in Bra, a town in northern Italy, and has now spread to 65 countries, including the United States, Australia and Japan. There are well over 2,000 members in the UK, and the number increases every day. It has initiated a number of schemes and projects, one of the most useful and popular of which is the Ark of Taste. This is a file of traditional regional foods judged to be at risk of disappearing under the pressure of modern conditions. To qualify for acceptance on the Ark, items at risk have to be associated with a particular area, and sufficiently delicious to be worth saving. In a few instances, active steps are taken to promote the article and increase sales.

Four of these have so far been established in the UK, including unpasterised cheddar cheese made in its native Somerset, available from Neals Yard Dairy alongside the market. A number of other Ark products are sold in the market. Those featured in this book are Herdwick Mutton, Morecambe Bay Shrimps, Colchester Native Oysters and Kentish Cobnuts. All of them are marked in the text with an asterisk.

Kitchen equipment

Sarah Leahey-Benjamin's kitchen is small, mine large; hers tidy, mine strewn with books and papers in all the places not used for preparing food. One thing our kitchens do have in common, however, is that because we both favour a very hands-on, as opposed to turn-on-the-machine style of cookery, we use only basic utensils and relatively few appliances. Sarah's background is New rather then old England and her approach (as reflects the Market) multi-cultural: thus she prefers polenta to potatoes and is more interested in sauces than pastry. Her list of essential equipment therefore doesn't include a pastry board and rolling pin. It consists of just eight items or groups of items:

A powerful fan oven, capable of reaching high heat with and without the fan in operation.

A blender

A mixer, which she regards as her one luxury.

Three knives: a sharp chef's knife for meat, a smallish paring knife for vegetables, and a knife with a serrated edge for bread. These three, she says, are all that you will ever need.

Three thermometers, one for the oven, one for the refrigerator, and one to measure the temperature of meat as it cooks.

A rubber spatula for clearing out every last drop or scrap from a bowl.

A pair of tongs

An apron

To this, I would add another eight which, if not absolutely essential, are highly desirable:

A pair of scales, with both metric and Imperial measurements

At least one heavy-bottomed, largish casserole with a tight-fitting lid

Two or three stainless steel saucepans with lids and U-shaped handles which don't conduct heat (and therefore won't burn your hands). They're expensive, and the lids add to the cost, but they'll last a lifetime. Try Pages, 121 Shaftesbury Avenue.

A good quality wok, preferably with a lid, which is lighter than a frying-pan and has the advantage that bits of food which brown too quickly can be pushed up the side.

A wooden or marble chopping board (wood is supposed to be bacteria-resistant).

A pestle and mortar

Sharp kitchen scissors, useful for trimming and dicing bacon.

A measuring jug

The only other items in my kitchen apart from cooking foil and kitchen paper are a griddle pan, baking sheets and trays, soufflé and pie dishes, a pepper mill, coffee grinder, sieve and colander, pastry-board and brush, rolling pin, perforated spoon, fish-slice, and wooden spoons.

Ingredients

We have included information about meat and fish in these respective sections. Details of all the other ingredients are given with the recipes except the following:

Organic or free-range eggs Please note that if you are using raw or partially cooked eggs, it is important that they should be very fresh and marked with the Lion Stamp as a precaution against salmonella. This will probably mean using free-range rather than organic ones, which seldom have the stamp. It is not advisable to give raw eggs to children, very old people, or anyone else who may be vulnerable to bacteria.

Unsalted or slightly salted butter

Fresh vegetables except where otherwise stated

Fresh as opposed to dried herbs I strongly suggest buying herbs in pots and, if you don't have a garden, keep them on the window sill.

Maldon salt When a recipe calls for sea salt we strongly recommend that you use Maldon sea salt, this comes in flakes and has a gentle, herbal flavour. You don't need a mill: the flakes are so soft that you can crush them with the back of a spoon.

Black pepper

Oven temperatures

Celsius	Fahrenheit	Gas Mark	Description
110	225	¼	*very slow and very cool*
130	250	½	
140	275	1	*cool*
150	300	2	
170	325	3	*very moderate*
180	350	4	*moderate*
190	375	5	
200	400	6	*moderately hot*
220	425	7	*hot*
230	450	8	
240	475	9	*very hot*

Please be aware various conditions and brands of oven will vary in their effectiveness and temperature accuracy.

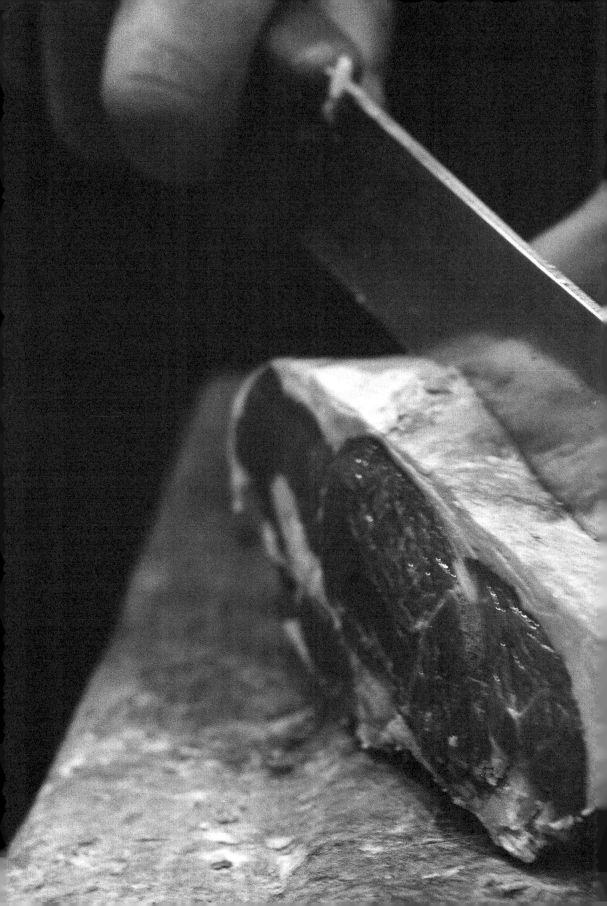

Meat

General notes on meat

Beef, lamb, mutton and venison

Fortunately, top-quality meat and happy animals go hand in hand. Other factors count too, but you can be pretty certain that superb beef or mutton with a deep, distinctive flavour led a pleasant life and certainly had a longer one than has become the norm.

In a nutshell, the quality of meat depends on breed, feed, and husbandry, which includes conditions of slaughter, and hanging. Opinions vary on the relative importance of breed and feed: some farmers emphasize the importance of the one, some of the other. Farmer Sharp put it this way: 'The breed is the genetic building-block of your meat, from which you can add or detract. With cattle, the more efficient they are as food converters, the faster they grow and the lower the quality of the beef' (he was careful, however, to stress that there are always exceptions). The traditional British breeds, which were once used for milk as well as meat, are slow-growing; among those represented in the market are Longhorn, Shorthorn, Dexter, Welsh Black, South Devon, Galloway, Belted Galloway (occasionally), and Highland.

Ageing

Now that the BSE restrictions have been lifted, beef can be sold at three or four years old or more: Tim Wilson of the Ginger Pig (page 166) is prepared to sell it aged as old as seven. Older age gives the animal more time to exercise and build up muscle, which makes for meat with a firmer texture and adds to its taste and character. Obviously, this doesn't happen, or only happens to a lesser degree, unless the animal is reared extensively and has plenty of space in which to move and graze. Space costs money and so does the extra food that it eats during a longer life: thus good beef doesn't come cheap.

The particular advantage of sheep is that they can adapt to the harsh conditions of mountains and moorland, which are otherwise useless in agricultural terms: thus seven-year-old Herdwick mutton from Cumbria is less expensive to produce than seven-year-old beef raised on good pasture in Yorkshire. The ability of sheep to survive in unpromising places is one of the reasons why they are never intensively reared. The other is that they refuse to eat if they are shut up and are also likely to catch pneumonia.

Their propensity to die is notorious: 'A dead cow is a disaster, a dead sheep a statistic'.

Red meats benefit from being hung, sometimes for as long as five weeks, partly to ensure tenderness and partly to allow the flavours to develop. Rather like the maturing of cheese, hanging demands a precisely controlled environment and constant supervision, which further increases costs, not only directly but indirectly, since it shortens shelf-life.

Slaughter

All of this, however, counts for nothing unless another, completely vital condition is fulfilled: humane, instant slaughter, carried out in such a way that the animal never knows that anything is happening. If it is frightened, as is likely if it has been herded into an overcrowded truck and driven a long distance without the people it knows, it will produce adrenalin, just as we do, which means that the meat will be tough however long it was hung.

To the question of how the customer can identify really good meat, there is no foolproof, easy answer. One indication is said to be marbling with fat, which is generally taken as proof that the animal has had plenty of exercise. By providing internal basting, as it were, it certainly helps to ensure tenderness and, since fat carries flavour, promises well for the taste. However, marbling can be created simply by feeding the animal high-protein cereal. Similarly, yellow fat is a sign of outdoor grazing but occurs only seasonally, since the colour comes from carotene in wet grass: when the cattle are fed on hay in the winter, the colour fades. In Farmer Sharp's words: 'If you want good meat, you should cherish your butcher.'

Pork, poultry and game

The case for happy meat is even stronger in relation to pork and poultry than mutton and beef, as anyone who has eaten the intensively reared versions will know. All the pork and almost all the chicken sold in the Market is free-range or, in the case of some of the chickens, organic. The recipes have been developed on this basis and will not taste the same if you substitute the industrial equivalent.

Unlike red meat and game, pork and poultry of all kinds, including farmed quail, goose and ostrich, should be eaten as fresh as possible. If eaten very young, the same applies to wild boar, but it should be hung for increasing lengths of time with

*Going to market —
country comes to town.
Farmer Sharp's stall,
Stoney Street*

age. Peter Gott's at Sillfield Farm is slaughtered at eighteen months old and hung for a week. Traditionally, pheasants and grouse used to be hung until they were 'high', with a strong gamy flavour, but now according to EU regulations all birds must be chilled within six hours of slaughter. This means that although they can still be hung, they will not acquire their characteristic tang. If you want pheasant as it used to be, you must either shoot it yourself or make a private arrangement. The pheasants at Wyndham House Poultry in Stoney Street and Furness Fish, Poultry and Game in the Market are hung for a week, like Peter Gott's wild boar, which gives them a gentle gamy tinge: you may like to add further flavour with a stuffing or by pot-roasting them with bacon and wine. Wyndham House stocks farmed rabbit, which is sold fresh; Furness has hare and wild rabbit hung for three or four days.

The future

Whereas the future of fish (unless farmed) is questionable, that of British meat looks bright. The ban on beef aged more than thirty months has been lifted; mutton, which not long ago was almost unobtainable, is now on the menu of every restaurant and gastropub of note; similarly, free-range or organic pork and chicken can be found not only at butchers and markets but supermarkets. Battery chickens will become illegal in the EU from 2012; legislation on broilers has not yet been approved by all the countries concerned but is on its way.

I believe that the future of British agriculture lies in the production of first-class animal produce, both dairy and meat, but particularly meat. Quantity can be supplied by other countries but only Ireland shares our damp climate and can match the excellence of our grazing. And please buy the top-quality product. If the sort of meat produced by Farmer Sharp or Tim Wilson of The Ginger Pig seems expensive, don't opt for a cheaper substitute, which is probably imported and will add to food miles: buy British but eat a little less of it or, better still, go for the cheaper cuts. Sarah Leahey-Benjamin and I have given lots of recipes for cheap cuts in which marinading and long, slow cooking produce far greater intensity of flavour than even the very best steaks or plain roast meat can give. The traders will be grateful too.

With thanks to Andrew Sharp and Tim Wilson

Meat recipes

THE GINGER PIG

GAMSTON WOOD OSTRICHES

FARMHOUSE DIRECT

FURNESS FISH, POULTRY & GAME

SILLFIELD FARM

Peter Gott *Kendal, Cumbria*

My early memories of Peter Gott have nothing to do with pork, pigs, or Borough Market. We first met when he was selling cheese at a fair in Alexandra Palace, North London. I was writing a book on British cheeses at the time and subsequently heard his name mentioned in connection with building cheese dairies, which he did on occasion either to help a friend or make ends meet.

However, Peter is first and foremost a pig-farmer, and in his brown Derby hat, red socks, checked shirt and striped apron, he has become an iconic figure at Borough. Nowadays, he has eight or nine people on his stand, all in similar uniform, but you'll easily pick him out from the rest if you watched the TV series *Jimmy's Farm*, in which he played the avuncular pig-rearing expert.

The Gotts come from the Lune Valley in Lancashire. His grandfather kept Cumberland pigs, Band Rock and Band Ruff chickens, and a pub called The Redwell Inn where guests staying the night could always be sure of ham and eggs for supper, and bacon, with eggs laid that morning, for breakfast. He inherited his flair as a salesman from his mother, who began with a market stall and ended up with half a dozen stalls, a string of seven shops, and a farm, on which Peter looked after the pigs until he was nineteen. Then he started his own career in retailing and was soon sufficiently successful to buy Sillfield, where he still farms today.

He and a neighbour, Les Salisbury of Furness Fish, discovered Borough Market through one of Henrietta Green's Food-Lovers' Fairs at a time when the only other regular traders there were Brindisa, selling Spanish products, and Randolph Hodgson of Neal's Yard Dairy. Immediately realising the market's possibilities, Peter leased not one but a number of stands and sublet all but two of them to farmers who shared his belief in first-class quality and the need to rear animals outdoors in conditions that are as natural as possible. (He recently said on BBC Radio 4 that if he couldn't allow his wild boar to wander at will in a wood he wouldn't keep them at all.)

Besides Les, the traders who joined him included Andrew (Farmer) Sharp selling mutton and beef, Ian Hartland, who sold Elizabeth King's Pork Pies, Peter Kent with Devonshire venison, and Jan McCourt with rare-breed meat from Leicestershire. Henrietta's Fairs had shown Peter how urgently small British

Peter Gott: Market trader,
pig farmer and inspiration

producers needed a showcase and he had intended that all his stands should go to British traders; however, he allocated one to Marco of Gastronomica, who sells Italian foods, because of his enthusiasm. 'He was so keen,' said Peter,' 'Or rather, he was so persistent!' He also kept a 'guest stall' for traders wanting to sell at the Market permanently in order to ensure that their produce met its standards.

Hearing the list of names, I couldn't resist asking where they all slept on Friday nights. 'In the refrigerator!' was the prompt response. This was indeed how it seemed to the other traders: however, he explained that he had built an extension to the back of his cold-store with bunks, washroom, and toilet, known to its fortunate inmates as 'The Boudoir'. It was fairly basic but 'bloody luxurious' compared to the alternative of spending the night in their vans. 'The only snag was the noise of the trains. You needed a lot of booze to sleep.' The booze came from The Wheatsheaf and The Market Porter across the road. This situation continued until a couple of years ago.

Even travelling at night, when there isn't much traffic, Borough is at least four hours' drive from Sillfield, although the farm has the advantage of being only a couple of miles from the motorway. It is in hillocky country rather than the Lakeland fells, on the edge of a shallow valley facing the wood where the wild boar roam. The house is a large but otherwise typical Beatrix Potter-style eighteenth-century farmhouse, still with its original heavy door made from just two planks of wood. Our visit was in February, when the fields were muddy and the trees bare, but it was still a delightfully pretty spot, with the varied shades of bark on the different trees adding warmth and colour to the landscape.

If Cumberland pigs had not been extinct, I have no doubt that Peter would have kept them: as it is, his stock includes six Middle White, eight Saddleback, five Middle White crossed with Saddleback and three Tamworth sows. Muddy as it might be, February was the best month to see them, since most of them were already surrounded by glossy, bouncy piglets. One Middle White sow who had not yet given birth trotted all the way across a field to greet Peter; a large Saddleback matron sank on to her side as soon as he approached, asking for a bellyrub just like a dog.

The wild boar farrow in Peter's wood, building nests with twigs and any bits of rag or sheep's wool that they can find: I didn't see any boar piglets, however, because at the time of my visit they weren't due for another month. Never having seen a wild boar at close quarters, I was surprised at how large and athletic-looking they are, with long snouts and thick brownish-grey coats which would make them extremely difficult to spot in the wild. During the mating season, the males tend to be aggressive, not only towards each other but males in general. At this time, therefore, Peter's partner Christine or another female has to feed them rather than Peter himself.

As well as the pigs and wild boar, Peter keeps a herd of Kendal Rough Fells sheep: hence the particularly delicious Sillfield Farm mutton pies on sale at his stand, which are made by Christine. Amongst the wide range of pork products, I especially recommend the haslet, which is made for him by a local farmer's wife, the bacon, and his excellent chipolatas, which show that real meat can transform even the humble British sausage into a genuine gastronomic experience.

Opposite In the wild boar woods at Sillfield Farm

Following (p. 35)
Wild boar and litter

BOROUGH MARKET COOKBOOK **Meat**

PETER'S WILD BOAR STEWED WITH ONIONS AND WHITE WINE

This is one of Peter and his partner Christine's favourite recipes. Since I first tried it, some time ago now, it has also become one of mine, not least because it is so undemanding both to make and to eat. It involves very little shopping: all you need besides the meat is a bottle of white wine, such as you probably already have in the cupboard, two or three onions, and a bouquet of fresh herbs, of which thyme is much the most important. As follows from this, not much preparation is needed either. For this reason, I can't quite understand why it takes me 40–50 minutes or more, but it does: at the last count, 55 minutes (including washing up). I think you'll have to assume that I'm just slow. The stew goes particularly well with Pink Fir-apple or baby baked potatoes. [SF]

Preparation time 55 minutes

Cooking time 2–2¼ hours

Serves 2–3, or 4 at a pinch

Season All ingredients available year-round

450 g diced wild boar
375 g white or mixed red and white onions (3 average-sized)
3 garlic cloves
1 organic or unwaxed lemon
2 or 3 large sprigs thyme
3 sprigs marjoram
2 bay leaves
2½–3 tblsp olive oil
Sea salt
Freshly ground black pepper
15 g plain white flour
Generous ½ tsp mixed black, white and pink peppercorns
½ bottle (375 ml) or possibly a little more dry white wine, such as Entre Deux Mers or Côtes de Gascogne
2 tblsp double cream

Unwrap the meat as soon as you reach home, put it on a plate, cover and leave in the refrigerator until needed.

When you are ready to make the stew, peel and finely slice the onions. Slice the garlic; then put it into a mortar and crush it into a rough paste. Wash and dry the lemon. Wash the herbs and leave them to dry.

Put 2 tblsp of the olive oil into a frying-pan, add the onions, and fry over medium to low heat for 12–15 minutes, until the onions are pale gold. Turn constantly, especially towards the end. Take them out of the pan and set them on a plate. Pour off and keep any surplus oil in the pan, wipe the pan clean if necessary, and return the oil.

Take the meat out of the refrigerator. Drain it if necessary, cut off any obvious pieces of fat and season it moderately with salt and a little more generously with pepper. Roll it in the flour, shaking off any surplus. Pour a little more oil into the pan, set it over moderately high heat, and add the meat. Fry it, turning continuously, until it is pale gold on all sides, adding a little more oil if the pan seems dry. Stir in the garlic and the mixed peppercorns, turn briefly, and take the pan off the heat.

Set the oven to 180°C / 350°F / gas 4.

Spread half the onions in the bottom of a small casserole. It is important that it should be small, or the wine will evaporate too quickly. Add half the meat, then the remaining onions, followed by the rest of the meat. Pare a couple of thin strips of peel from the lemon and place them on top of the meat with the herbs (whole). Pour in the wine and bake for 2–2¼ hours. Look at it after about 1½ hours to make sure that it hasn't cooked dry, and add more wine (or water) if necessary. Remove the herbs, stir in the cream, and if possible leave the stew to rest for 10–15 minutes, since it tastes better warm rather than piping hot.

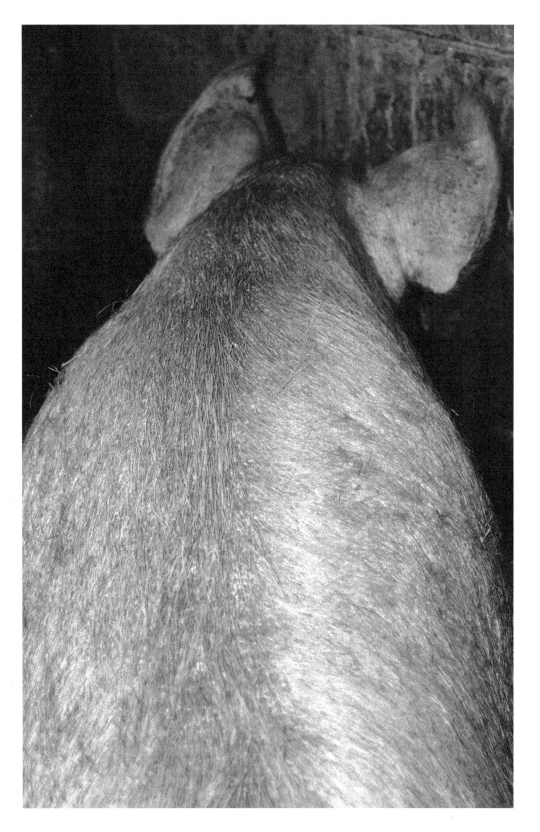

LANCASHIRE HASLET

Haslet is a kind of meatloaf intended to be eaten cold: variations used to be made in different parts of the country using local cuts of pork and the local breed of pig. Often, it would be taken into the fields and eaten with pickles as elevenses. I suggest that you eat it for lunch, especially for a picnic, or supper, accompanied by crusty bread.

Usually, Peter will have ready-minced pork on his stand: if he hasn't, buy a piece of loin and either mince or dice it at home. The haslet may not cohere so well with diced meat but if anything will taste even better. An egg will help to prevent it from being crumbly. On one occasion, I bought the pork but wasn't able to use it for several days: to preserve it, I marinated it in wine. I also, on impulse, added green peppercorns. The result was so good that I've made it that way ever since. [SF]

Preparation time 24–48 hours marinating, plus 3–4 hours minimum cooling time

Cooking time 2 hours

Serves 4–6

Season All ingredients available year-round

360 g minced pork or 400 g lean pork loin
1 medium free-range egg (if using pork loin)
2 large sprigs fresh sage
½ small red onion
1 tsp green peppercorns (optional)
85 ml Shiraz or similar full-bodied red wine
   (or water, if you prefer)
75 g stale white bread
Butter for greasing
Sea salt
Freshly ground black pepper
1½ tsp uncrushed sea salt

If you're using pork loin, it is best if you dice the meat and marinate it at least a full day before you plan to cook the haslet. To do this, trim off any large pieces of fat. There's no need to be too rigorous since a little will lubricate and add to the flavour of the meat, but it will melt during cooking and if there is too much, the haslet tends to shrink. Chop it into pieces about 5 mm thick and place in a large bowl. If using mince meat, simply place the mince in a large bowl.

Now, make the marinade: wash and finely chop the sage. Peel and very finely chop the onion. Measure the wine and the peppercorns (if you are using them). Add all of these ingredients to the meat and mix thoroughly. Cover the bowl with plastic wrap and put it into the refrigerator. Leave it for 24 hours; stir after 12 hours.

Before you're ready to cook, preheat the oven to 160 °C / 325 °F / gas 3.

Cut the crusts off the bread and grate it into fine crumbs (or you can use a blender). Line a 900 ml loaf tin or soufflé dish with cooking foil. Grease it thoroughly with butter. Add the breadcrumbs, salt, and a couple of generous grindings of pepper to the meat. If you're using diced meat rather than minced, lightly beat and add the egg. Stir the mixture very thoroughly and pack it down into the tin or dish. Smooth the top and bake it for 2 hours or until the top is gently browned. Allow to cool thoroughly and then chill for a few hours. Slice once it's completely cold – don't do this beforehand or the haslet will crumble.

Opposite Prototype no. 1
Cumberland Pig

PORK CHOP WITH FENNEL SEEDS AND MUSTARD SAUCE

The great challenge when cooking a pork chop is to crisp the crackling without overcooking the lean meat. It's an issue in America too but not, so far as I've observed, in France or Italy, where the fat is almost always carefully trimmed off. If you want to remove it for health reasons, please note that the sauce in this recipe is made with double cream. Partly for this reason, I have to admit that it perhaps goes better with a fatless chop than one with crackling; however, it's delicious either way.

Assuming that you're game for eating the crackling, you could follow Jamie Oliver's advice and cut off the fat in order to cook it for longer than the rest of the chop. I asked my husband what he thought about this and he replied that as far as he was concerned, it wouldn't seem like a proper pork chop at all. I'm afraid I agree. My solution is to ask for a thick-cut chop, rub the skin with salt as soon as I reach home, and bake it at high heat for just 37 minutes.

To make the crackling easier to cut at table, ask for the skin to be snipped at intervals — or do it yourself with a sharp knife of kitchen scissors. [SF]

Preparation time At least 4 hours for the salt to sink into the skin of the chop, plus a few minutes to season and trim the chop

---

Cooking time 37 minutes

Serves 1

Season All ingredients available year-round

---

1 thick-cut (just over 2 to 2·5cm) pork loin chop
Sea salt
Freshly ground black pepper
½ tsp Dijon mustard
1½–2 tblsp double cream (not extra thick)
½ tsp fennel seeds

Having rubbed the skin with salt, leave the chop in the refrigerator for at least 4 hours.

Set the oven to 220°C / 425°F / gas 7.

Wipe the chop all over, removing the salt from the outside as you do so, and season both sides very lightly with salt and moderately with pepper. Lay it on a rack or baking tray lined with cooking foil and bake for 35 minutes, turning once after about 20. Be warned: if it's thin-cut, it will be overcooked and dry. It really is essential that it should be thick.

While it cooks, thoroughly mix the mustard with the cream. Take out the chop, sprinkle it with the fennel seeds, and pour the mustard mixture over the top. Bake for another minute or two, until the cream is bubbling and slightly coloured at the edges.

Serve with an astringent vegetable, such as green or (in spring) purple sprouting broccoli.

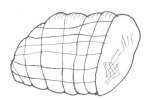

Pork

JAMAICAN JERK WILD BOAR LOIN CHOPS WITH AVOCADO AND MELON SALAD

Don't be put off by the long list of ingredients for the marinade, as you probably have them lurking in the back of your pantry. Peter Gott's boar chops have enough flavour to stand up to this classic Caribbean dish. Each of the chops has a bit of the loin, along with a piece of the boar fillet. These chops are delicious served with roast sweet potatoes — or better yet, roast sweet potato buttermilk cornbread. [SLB]

Preparation time 15 minutes, plus minimum 4 hours marinating

Cooking time 25 minutes

Serves 6

Season With the melon, fresh coriander and mint, this is best made in July when melons from Spain are ripe and juicy and the herbs most vibrant.

6 wild boar chops (bone-in)
1½ tsp ground allspice
1½ tsp dried thyme
¾ tsp cayenne pepper
¾ tsp freshly ground black pepper
½ tsp freshly ground nutmeg
½ tsp cinnamon
3 garlic cloves
Sea salt
1 jalapeno chilli
5 spring onions
1 lime (juice only) plus 1 or 2 more (enough for 3 tblsp juice)
50 ml olive oil plus 1 tblsp
50 ml soy sauce
2 oranges (enough for 120 ml juice)
1 large avocado
⅓ cantaloupe melon
1 small red onion
15 g fresh mint
15 g fresh coriander

Begin by marinating the loin chops. Mix the dried herbs and spices together in a small bowl. Peel and crush the garlic cloves with a little salt with a pestle and mortar. Wash and blot dry the chilli and spring onion. Cut the chilli in half and remove the seeds. Chop off the root end and peel off the outer layer of the spring onions. Slice both the chilli and spring onions and add to the pestle and mortar with the garlic, pounding the three ingredients together into a paste. Add to the spice bowl. Squeeze the oranges and lime and add the juice to the spice bowl along with the olive oil and soy sauce. Place the boar chops in a glass baking dish and pour over the marinade. Cover and refrigerate for a minimum 4 hours but preferably overnight.

To cook the boar loin chops preheat the oven to 180°C / 350°F / gas 4.

Heat a little oil over a medium flame in a large ovenproof frying pan. Add the chops to the frying pan (you will have to do this in two pans or in batches) and cook until golden brown, about 2 minutes. Flip and transfer the pan to the oven. Bake until the chops are crisp on the outside and thermometer inserted into the meat registers 65·5°C / 150°F – about 18–20 minutes.

Once you have the boar in the oven, dice the flesh of both the avocado and melon. Peel and finely chop the red onion. Wash the mint, remove the leaves from the sprigs, and chop finely. The skinny stems of coriander are fine to add to the salad, but make sure that you clean the coriander thoroughly as it can be a bit sandy. Combine all these ingredients together with the 3 tblsp lime juice and 1 tblsp olive oil, plus a good seasoning of salt and freshly ground black pepper.

Serve the chops on warm plates with a little salsa on top.

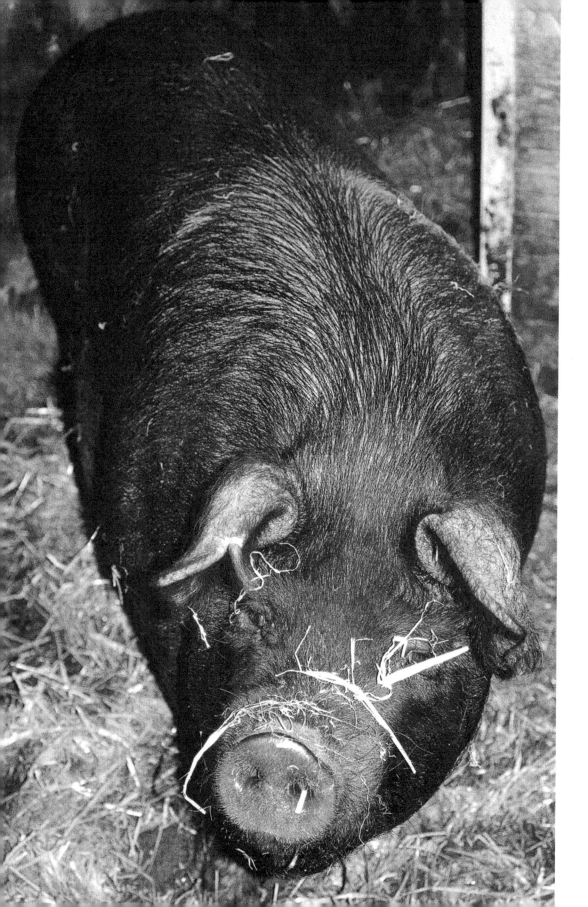

'3 AND DOWN' HONEY GLAZED PORK SPARE RIBS WITH CHINESE SPICES

I first served these ribs at a café in Notting Hill. It was difficult to watch people trying to eat them with a fork and knife: please don't, they are much better when eaten with your hands! Just ensure you have plenty of napkins at the ready. They are sticky, sweet, and lightly spicy. Star anise and garlic when cooked together smell absolutely amazing.

'3 and Down' refers to the size of the ribs; ribs under 3lb in weight have a much more tender flesh, making the job of producing succulent tasty ribs a snap for the home cook. [SLB]

Preparation time 15 minutes,
  plus minimum 1 hour marinating

Cooking time 1 hour and 15 minutes

Serves 3

Season All ingredients available year-round

1·3 kg pork ribs
3 tblsp runny honey
3 tblsp oyster sauce (or a light soy sauce or
  tamari will do)
4 garlic cloves
Sea salt
1 level tsp red chilli flakes
1 level tsp ground star anise
1 unwaxed and/or organic orange
¼ tsp freshly ground black pepper

If your ribs are in one piece, cut through with a sharp knife to separate each rib. To make the marinade, spoon the honey and oyster sauce into a glass baking dish. Peel and crush the garlic with a good pinch of salt in a mortar and add it to the dish, along with the chilli flakes, star anise and black pepper. Wash and dry the orange, then grate the zest, making sure that you remove the bright orange skin and not the pith underneath. Squeeze half the orange and pour the juice into the marinating dish. Season with sea salt. Rub the ribs in the marinade. Cover and refrigerate for an hour, or preferably overnight – they will be all the better for it.

Roast the ribs at 180°C / 350°F / gas 4 for about 1 hour for small ribs and 1 hour and 15 minutes for larger ribs. Keep an eye on them and turn them occasionally. After the specified cooking time, remove one of the ribs to see whether it is ready. They should be soft, but not falling off their bones. The sauce will have reduced slightly to coat the ribs.

Serve hot. The ribs are delicious with coriander chutney from Mrs Bassa's stall in the Market.

Opposite A Berkshire/
Saddleback cross

POLENTA AND WILD BOAR PROSCIUTTO BAKED EGGS

I envy the people who live close to Borough Market. Every Saturday morning around 10·30am you start to see the people who stayed up a little too late on Friday evening trickling in to the market buying breakfast. By the time I get home from market, I have been out of my pyjamas way too long to convince myself it's still breakfast-time. But it's never too late for brunch – especially when you have just brought a packet of Peter Gott's award-winning wild boar prosciutto. Although eating this tasty dish late morning has to be my favourite time, it can be served for breakfast or as a light supper. [SLB]

Preparation time 10 minutes

Cooking time 15–18 minutes

Serves 2

Season All ingredients available year-round

1 tsp unsalted butter
4 slices of thin wild boar prosciutto
    (you can also use Parma ham)
2 eggs
25 g Gruyère cheese
1 tblsp double cream
1 sprig tarragon
Sea salt
Freshly ground black pepper
2 tblsp polenta (coarse cornmeal)
1 spring onion
25 g Parmesan cheese
1 tsp unsalted butter

Preheat oven to 170°C / 325°F / gas 3.

Grease two ramekins with unsalted butter and line with the prosciutto – ensure you cover the base and the sides of the dish, with the ham rising up slightly to form a small collar around the top rim. Crack one egg into the centre of each ramekin. Grate and sprinkle Gruyère cheese over the top and drizzle with a bit of double cream. Wash the tarragon, blot dry, remove the leaves from the stems and divide between the two ramekins. Season well with salt and pepper. Transfer the cups to a roasting tin. Pour enough hot tap water (not boiling) into the tin to come halfway up the sides of the ramekins. Place the roasting tin into the preheated oven. Bake until the egg whites are set, about 15 minutes.

While the eggs are baking, pour 90 mls of water into a small saucepan, season with sea salt and pepper and bring to the boil. Gradually whisk in the polenta. Reduce the heat to low and simmer until thick and creamy, stirring occasionally, about 5–6 minutes. Meanwhile, peel the outer layer of the spring onion and discard. Wash and thinly slice both the green and white parts. Grate the Parmesan. Once the polenta has achieved the desired consistency, stir in the butter, grated Parmesan cheese and spring onion. Checking seasoning and set aside until ready to serve.

When the eggs are just set, cautiously remove them from the oven, being careful not to spill any hot water on yourself. Divide the polenta between two plates. If it's too stiff, simply add a few tablespoons of boiling water to loosen it. Run a sharp knife around the edge of the ramekins; tilt the cups and slide out the Prosciutto wrapped egg onto the warm polenta and serve.

A zesty lemon and tarragon dressed salad is a delicious accompaniment if you want to serve this dish as a light supper.

Cook's note The polenta can be made the evening before and refrigerated. For easy serving, line two more ramekins with cling film. Spoon the cooked polenta into the cling film lined ramekin and chill. When ready to eat, remove from the ramekin and unwrap. Toast in a grill pan to warm through before serving.

Wild Boar and Iron Age pig cross

FARMER SHARP

Andrew Sharp *Lindal-in-Furness, Cumbria*

Borough Market has been pivotal to Andrew Sharp's career – and, in turn, to the rising fortunes of the Herdwick breed of sheep. It may be that the first thing to catch your eye on his stand is a row of enticingly marbled Galloway or Galloway crossed with Shorthorn fillet steaks, but for some time now Herdwick lamb and mutton have been his leading lines, especially mutton, which recently started to outsell his lamb.

The first known reference to Herdwick (the name means 'sheep pasture') was made as early as the twelfth century. Over the years, the sheep have developed characteristics enabling them to survive on the higher ridges of the Cumbrian fells, in particular the fact that they are 'heafed', as it is locally known. This means that the lambs are born with an instinctive knowledge of their own particular territory, which enables them to graze in safety where other sheep could not and to which they always return. Beatrix Potter, understanding this, bequeathed the three

Andrew Sharp: Master Butcher and Herdwick champion

farms she owned to the National Trust on condition that the sheep should be treated as an inseparable part of the land.

As protection from the harsh winters, the Herdwicks also have exceptionally coarse, oily wool. Their appearance changes with age: if you go up into the hills around Ulpha or Coniston Water in the spring, for instance, you will see a mixture of grey and white sheep accompanied by new, completely black lambs. The lambs first develop white spectacles and then, by the end of their first summer, have white faces and pale grey legs. Thereafter, they become paler with each succeeding year so that, by the age of six or seven, they are completely white. They are listed by the Rare Breeds Survival Trust and in addition have been boarded on to the Slow Food Ark of Taste (see page 17).

Andrew's forbears have been farmers or shepherds in the Lake District for five generations. His grandfather's uncle was Beatrix Potter's shepherd and his father had a farm on the coast, just outside Barrow-in-Furness. At least in terms of investment, however, Andrew himself is more a butcher than a farmer. He not only raises Herdwick sheep and Galloway cattle but dresses the carcases of a co-operative of some forty farmers in the area. For this purpose, he recently spent £250,000 on a cutting-plant and air-drying room in which to hang preserved meats – a tribute, you could say, to the selling-power of Borough, which today accounts for ninety per cent of his turnover.

He originally heard about Borough through Peter Gott, and at first didn't want to go. 'I'd just got divorced and didn't want to leave my children, but Peter badgered me so much that eventually I went, and realised at once that it wasn't happening in Cumbria. My third customer said, "I'll see you next week," and I thought, well, maybe you will.'

He has a longer drive from Lindal-in-Furness than Peter, but enjoys the buzz of the city. 'You get the London bit without having to live there.' As for the children he didn't want to leave behind, the Market has solved the problem: he met a beautiful Polish girl there, married her, and as well as a mother for his first family now has a remarkably pretty new daughter.

Whereas the traditional age of mutton used to be five years old, his sheep are often left on the fells for longer: sometimes, his mutton is aged as old as seven. Like the other farmers selling meat in the Market, he has a deep feeling of fondness and respect for his animals which translated into the quality of the meat. In particular, he is emphatic about the importance of stress-free

Herdwick country.
Langdale, Cumbria

slaughter. 'You can raise the most wonderful rare breed meat, feed it perfectly – and spoil the whole effect if the slaughtering process distresses the animal.' Many farmers complain about the number of small slaughterhouses which have closed; however, he is fortunate in having one only a few minutes' drive away from his farm.

His mutton is hung in his cutting-plant at 2°c for around three weeks (the exact length of time depends on the weather). By the time it reaches the Market, it is exceptionally tender, despite the age of the sheep, with a fine-grained texture and distinctive, slightly gamy flavour. If you roast it, you should treat it like beef and use a very hot oven so that the outside is deliciously crisp but the centre still pink. Until its present renaissance, mutton had a reputation for being fatty, as some of it still is, but the rigour of life on the fells helps to ensure that Herdwick is unusually lean.

Besides fresh lamb and mutton and the Galloway beef on his stall, which he rears on his farm, Andrew has developed a range of preserved meats which includes air-dried mutton and beef, mutton prosciutto, and salami. The air-dried meat is prepared with a simple dry cure of sugar and salt and hung for three or six months; the mutton tastes a bit like jerky, with a positive flavour which goes particularly well with Flour Power's spelt and rye bread (which is baked directly next door). You may also like to try either of the air-dried meats or the prosciutto in salads.

Perfect balance:
Geoff Edmonson – shepherd,
sheep and dogs

HERDWICK LAMB STEWED WITH KIDNEYS AND PEARL BARLEY

Despite its very British ingredients, this is not a traditional dish but originated from George Nicholson's remark, made soon after we embarked on this book, that he loves anything which includes pearl barley. Here, the plenteous, wonderfully rich, vinous gravy is thickened by the barley so that the result is half way to soup, rather like risotto. With the barley, you don't need potato: serve simply with a traditional vegetable such as broccoli and crusty bread.

I've recommended using shoulder, which is streaked with tendons and fat. Somewhat unusually, this stew loses some of its kick and liveliness if kept until the following day, which means that you can't skim off the fat after chilling. As Herdwicks are notably lean, this is less of an issue than with most other breeds of lamb. [SF]

Preparation time 30–35 minutes

Cooking time 4 hours

Serves 4

Season Lamb is in season from May until December

450 g shoulder of lamb, diced
4 lambs' kidneys
1 medium red onion
6 garlic cloves
175 g button mushrooms
Large sprig rosemary
2 tblsp olive oil
Sea salt
Freshly ground black pepper
4 anchovy fillets
50 g pearl barley
600 ml Shiraz or Shiraz blend

Pick over the lamb and remove any large pieces of fat. Peel and slice the kidneys, throwing away the tough cores. Peel and finely chop the onion. Peel the garlic but leave the cloves whole. Trim, wash or peel the mushrooms, and cut any fairly large ones in half. Wash and blot the rosemary dry. Pull off the leaves (drag downwards) and chop them finely.

Set the oven to 150°C / 300°F / gas 2.

Measure half the oil into a wok or frying pan and add the onion. Fry it over medium to low heat, turning constantly, for 5–7 minutes or until soft. Put it into a casserole dish with a tight-fitting lid.

Add the second tablespoonful of oil to the wok or frying pan, season the pieces of lamb very lightly with salt and moderately with pepper, and stir-fry them over fairly high heat until they are seared on all sides, adding a little more oil if necessary. Put them into the casserole.

As with the lamb, season the kidneys with a very little salt, but rather more pepper, and sear them over fairly high heat. Add them to the casserole with the mushrooms, garlic, and rosemary. Finely chop and add the anchovy fillets. Rinse the pearl barley, stir it in and thoroughly toss together the contents of the casserole. Pour in half the wine and 150 ml water, cover and bake for 4 hours.

Look at the meat after an hour and add a little more wine; repeat after the second and third hours. Add the rest of the wine about half an hour before serving.

DAUBE OF GALLOWAY BEEF
WITH BACON AND SHIRAZ

You will have some idea of how delicious this is from the smell which emanates from the oven as soon as it starts to cook.

It's an example of a dish made with top-quality meat but a cheap cut, and even with the wine costs surprisingly little. You only need 300 ml of wine for cooking, and as Shiraz or a Shiraz blend usually keeps fairly well, you can use some for marinating the meat and drink the rest with it the next day.

Galloway beef is the ancestor of Aberdeen Angus and has a similar deep, rich flavour: if you can't buy Galloway from Andrew Sharp, you could use Aberdeen Angus instead.

The meat should be cut across into slices about 3 cm thick. The amount you need will probably mean three slices, which is inconvenient if there are four of you: however, the dish doesn't work so well if the slices are thinner. Don't chop it more than is necessary, as the idea is that each person has one or two pieces like steaks.

Serve with mashed or baked potatoes to mop up the sauce, or alternatively pasta shells or gnocchi. A good choice of vegetable would be green or purple sprouting broccoli and/or broad beans, which pick up the smokiness of the bacon. [SF]

Preparation time Overnight marinating, plus 20–25 minutes the next day. You will also need about 5 minutes to sieve and reduce the sauce before serving

Cooking time 4½–5 hours

Serves 4

Season All ingredients available year-round

550–600 g shin of Galloway beef,
    cut into 3cm slices
6 garlic cloves
12 peppercorns
300 ml Shiraz or a Shiraz blend
2 rashers smoked bacon (streaky or back)
1 medium onion
1 medium carrot
1 leek
1 tblsp olive oil
Sea salt
Freshly ground black pepper
2 cloves (optional)
2 bay leaves
Large sprig rosemary

Beef

Bacon

The day before you plan to serve the daube, wipe the slices of beef with damp kitchen paper and cut them into four or five pieces. Put them into a pudding basin or other deep bowl. Peel and add the garlic, leaving the cloves whole, plus the peppercorns and the wine. If necessary, press the meat down so that as much as possible is submerged; any parts which stick up should be rearranged at half time. Cover the bowl with cling film and leave it in the refrigerator for 24 hours.

The next day, cut the rind off the bacon and dice it using scissors. Peel and finely slice the onion. Peel and slice the carrot. Trim the leek; peel away the outer layer, chop the stem into slices, and then rinse to remove any earth which may be trapped inside.

Fry the onion and bacon over low or very low heat in the oil for 12–17 minutes, until they have turned pale gold; stir frequently. Streaky bacon especially will run fat; however, this tends not to happen until near the end of cooking, so you may need to add a little extra oil.

Heat the oven to 120°C / 250°F / gas ½.

Take the meat out of the marinade and spread it on a plate. Season each piece on both sides with a little salt and a rather more generous amount of pepper. Put half in the bottom of a small casserole, ideally 18cm in diameter and 9cm high.

Spread it with half the onion, bacon and pre-pared vegetables. Add the rest of the meat and then the remaining bacon and vegetables. Pour in the marinade with the peppercorns, tuck the cloves of garlic round the meat and, if you are planning to use them, drop in the cloves. Finally, wash and lay the bay leaves and rosemary over the top. Bake for 4 hours.

Then turn up the oven to 150°C / 300°F / gas 2 and bake for a final half to one hour. If you want to split the baking time between two days, cook for 3 hours at 120°C / 250°F / gas ½ on the first day, allow to cool and refrigerate over night, and continue to bake for 1½–2 hours on the second day, starting at 120°C / 250°F / gas ½ and turning up the heat after the first 1¼ hours. When ready, the meat should be very, very tender but not yet quite falling apart.

Take the casserole out of the oven but don't turn off the heat. Throw away the herbs on top of the meat and put the meat on a plate; scrape off any bits of vegetable and put them back into the dish. Set a sieve over a smallish saucepan and pour the juice, bacon and vegetables from the casserole into it; don't worry if there are also a few fragments of beef. Wash or wipe the casse-role clean, replace the portions of beef in it, cover, and return it to the oven while you finish the sauce. Press as much of the vegetable mass as you can through the sieve: there will be sev-eral tablespoons left. Set them aside. Bring the liquid in the pan to the boil over moderate heat and boil it for 5 minutes or until it has been reduced by about a fifth (if you turn the heat too high, it may spit in your face). Pulverize the pulp in the sieve with the back of a spoon and return it to the reduced liquid to make a thick, rough sauce. Don't use a blender, since you may find that the pulp foams – and in any case, the sauce isn't supposed to be smooth. Pour it over the meat and ensure when you serve that everybody has a fair share. If necessary, you can keep the daube hot in the oven (at 120°C / 250°F / gas ½) for quite some time.

If you leave the dish as a stew and eat it over two days, reheat it at 180°C / 350°F / gas 4 for 25–30 minutes or until it has bubbled gently for at least two minutes.

CHEZ LOUISETTE'S MUTTON STEW WITH MADIRAN

Chez Louisette is a restaurant in Barèges, in the Pyrenees, which specializes in dishes made with mutton from the local sheep. Our photographer, George Nicholson, has a house in the area and often eats there. This is one of his favourite dishes. You could call it the French equivalent of Irish stew, although it could hardly be more different.

You should set the stew to marinate 4 days before you plan to serve it. You might therefore call this a mid-week recipe, since if you shop on Saturday it will be ready on Tuesday or Wednesday.

You can use middle neck of mutton rather than best end, but the bones tend to disintegrate, which means being careful when you eat the stew.

According to the French recipe, this should be served with fingers of toast.

Madiran is a heady red wine from the region; it is available from Cartwright Bros in the market. [SF]

Preparation time 4 days

Cooking time 17 hours on the third day plus a total of 55 minutes on the fourth

Serves 4

Season Mutton is in season from October to March

200g carrots
1 medium onion
6–8 garlic cloves
150g lean smoked gammon
1kg best end of neck of mutton, cut into chops
14 juniper berries
½ tsp black peppercorns
600ml Madiran
2 good-sized sprigs thyme
2 bay leaves
Sea salt
Freshly ground black pepper
35g butter
35g plain white flour

Mutton

On the first day, peel and slice the carrots. Peel and quarter the onion. Peel the cloves of garlic but leave them whole. Wash, dry, and dice the gammon into small strips. Put the chops and all the prepared ingredients into a medium-sized heavy, preferably deep casserole with the juniper berries, peppercorns and wine; this should just cover the meat. If it doesn't, turn the chops at intervals throughout the marinating period so that they are all submerged some of the time. Rinse the herbs and lay them on top. Cover and put it into the refrigerator and leave the contents to marinate for two days.

On the third day, set the oven to 150°C / 300°F / gas 2.

Remove the herbs and gently stir the contents of the casserole. Season with a little salt and (despite the peppercorns) a moderate grinding of black pepper. Replace the herbs, cover, and cook for 45 minutes.

Turn down the oven to 120°C / 250°F / gas ½ and bake for a further 3¼ hours. Leave it to cool to room temperature and put it into the refrigerator until the following day.

On the fourth day, set the oven to 180°C / 350°F / gas 4. Take the stew out of the refrigerator about an hour before you want to serve it and skim off the fat, which will have collected in a solid layer on top. You may have to dig a little to free it from crevices between the ingredients. Be as gentle as you can: if you use too much force, the meat may fall from the bone, which doesn't really matter but spoils the look of the dish.

Bake the stew for 40–45 minutes, by which time it will be bubbling gently and smell wonderful. Take it out of the oven and turn down the heat to 120°C / 250°F / gas ½. Transfer the chops from the casserole to a plate. Pour the liquor with the gammon and the remaining ingredients of the stew into a jug or bowl through a sieve. Remove the herbs and onion from the sieve and put them back into the stew plus the juniper berries and peppercorns if you like (personally I prefer to include the juniper berries and peppercorns in the finished dish since they add texture to the sauce).

Return the chops and contents of the sieve to the casserole, discarding any bones from which the meat has fallen, replace the lid and put the casserole back into the oven to keep warm (even without its liquor, it won't dry out at this heat for the relatively short time that you'll leave it there).

Melt the butter over low heat in a medium-sized saucepan. When most but not quite all of it has melted, take it off the heat and add the flour. Stir until the mixture is perfectly smooth and pour in a little of the liquor from the jug. Return the pan to the heat (still low) and stir until the contents are smooth. Add the rest of the liquor gradually, stirring after each addition. By the time all of it has been incorporated, you will have a moderately thick sauce. Simmer it very gently, stirring constantly, for 14–16 minutes or until the taste of raw flour has disappeared, and pour it over the chops. Serve the stew with toast.

CASSEROLED MUTTON WITH RED WINE, CASSIA BARK AND ROASTED GARLIC

Shepherd's pies have always included a pinch of cinnamon to enhance the flavour. I've taken that idea one step further with the use of cassia bark to flavour our mutton casserole. Cassia bark has a black pepper edge to it that is more savoury than sweet. When blended with Herbes de Provence and roasted garlic this peppery-floral-earthy sweetness is the perfect match of mutton. The lengthy cooking provides plenty of time for the flavours to mingle and enhance one another. A good fruity red wine will help tenderise the meat whilst reducing into a luscious sauce without becoming overly tannic. This is a hearty casserole with warming spices to help see you through the winter months. [SLB]

Mutton

Preparation time 45 minutes

Cooking time 2 hours

Serves 4

Season Mutton is in season from October to March

2 tblsp olive oil
2 tblsp plain flour
650 g shoulder (bone-out weight),
    cut into large cubes
480 ml red wine, preferably a
    Grenache/Shiraz blend
240 ml chicken stock,
    home made or store bought
2 large carrots
1 large onion
1 tsp Herbes de Provence
2·5 cm–7·5 cm piece cassia bark
    (or a cinnamon stick)
2·5 cm–7·5 cm curl of orange zest
3 heads of garlic
25 g cold, unsalted butter, cut into 4 pieces
15 g fresh parsley
Sea salt
Freshly ground black pepper

Preheat oven to 170°C / 325°F / gas 3.

Heat 1 tblsp of the olive oil in a large frying pan over medium-high heat. Place the meat on a dinner plate and dust with flour. Shake off any excess to leave a very thin, fine dusting around each piece. Gently place ⅓ of the meat into the preheated frying pan and brown on both sides. Place browned meat into a high-sided roasting pan or a large casserole dish. Pour off any fat from the pan and stir in 55 ml of red wine, scraping up browned bits. Transfer the deglazing wine mix to the casserole dish and wipe the frying pan clean with paper towels and repeat procedure with remaining mutton and a portion of the red wine.

Place a small frying pan over medium heat. Peel and chop the carrots and onion into a fine dice. Add to the frying pan, along with 1 tblsp of olive oil. Gently sauté the vegetables until they soften. Sprinkle over the Herbes de Provence and fry to release their flavour, about 30 seconds. Spoon the sautéed vegetables over the chops in the casserole dish. Wash the orange and pare off a 7.5 cm curl of the zest. Tuck the cassia bark and the orange zest in amongst the mutton and pour over remaining wine and enough stock to nearly cover the meat. Place two sheets of foil over the pot and place the lid on top of the foil. Press to seal. Braise in the preheated oven for 2 hours, or until the meat is fork tender.

As soon as you have put the mutton into the oven, chop off the tops of the garlic to expose the cloves. Place on a piece of foil and drizzle with extra virgin olive oil. Season with salt and pepper and seal to close. Bake along side the casserole for about 1 hour and 15 minutes. The cloves will turn a rich brown and be extremely soft to the touch.

Once the mutton is meltingly tender, remove from oven and allow to cool. Extract and discard the cassia bark and orange zest from the pot. Using a slotted spoon, carefully take out the mutton and place it in a large dish. Set aside. Let the braising liquid sit for an hour at room temperature, when you should start to see the fat rising to the surface. Alternatively, refrigerate until the fat forms a skin on the top. Once separated, skim or scrape off the fat and discard.

Squeeze the heads of garlic you roasted earlier into the braising liquid. Whisk in the butter. Wash, dry and chop the fine stems and leaves of the parsley. Fold most of it through the braising liquid, but keep some for garnishing each portion.

As this dish is rather rich, serve with boiled and crushed or jacket potatoes.

Cook's note A few points to make here: Firstly I've used boned shoulder here, but on particularly lazy Sundays I have been known to throw the whole shoulder, bone and all, into the casserole. This makes for slightly more difficult serving but the added bone helps develop viscosity and flavour in the sauce. Secondly if your wine isn't very fruity the finish may be slightly acidic. This can be balanced with the addition of a sweetener. I like pomegranate molasses which has just enough sweetness with a mild tart edge to complement the dish. One tblsp should be plenty. Finally this past Christmas I turned this dish into a lovely canapé by first shredding the meat and then pulverising it into a coarse pate. There were definitely enough cooking juices to envelop the meat comparable to the classic fat-enriched rillette. If you don't have a food processor, pound the meat with the end of a rolling pin until roughly smooth. Before serving top with melted butter and a few chopped parsley leaves.

The morning dew – Langdale

TURKISH MUTTON PIZZAS

Yes, there are pizzas in Turkey and they are particularly beautiful when garnished with jewel-like pomegranate seeds. The minced mutton marinated in herbs and spices provides the perfect base to present an array of garnishes — try any combination of the ones listed below. Better yet, allow your guests to 'decorate' their own pizzas to suit their own taste buds. If making pizza dough isn't your thing, go to Flour Power for their delicious focaccia. Slice through the middle and assemble as directed. [SLB]

Preparation time 30 minutes,
    plus 45 minutes dough resting time

Cooking time 12–14 minutes

Serves 6 (makes 6 individual pizzas)

Season Mutton is in season from October
    to March

340 g plain or strong flour
2 tsp yeast
½ tsp caster sugar
180 ml warm water
Pinch of granulated sugar
½ tsp salt
2 tblsp olive oil
300 g minced mutton
Parsley (enough for 2 tblsp when chopped)
1 tsp coriander seeds
½ tsp caraway seeds (optional)
Pinch cayenne pepper
½ tsp fennel seeds
¼ tsp cumin seeds
½ tsp ground allspice
3 garlic cloves
1 medium egg (yolk only)
50 g coarse polenta

GARNISHES
Fresh pomegranate seeds
Toasted pine nuts
Barrel-aged feta
Fresh mint
Cucumber
Greek yoghurt

Preheat the oven to 200 °C / 400 °F / gas 6.

To make the pizza bases: sift the flour into a bowl and make a well in the centre. Spoon the yeast into the well. Pour over the water and sprinkle over the sugar. Allow to sit for about 5–10 minutes or until the yeast froths. Once frothy, add the salt and olive oil. Stir to combine. Turn the mixture out onto the counter and kneed for 10 minutes or until you have smooth, elastic dough. Place it in a bowl and cover with cling film. Allow to rest until it has doubled in volume, about 35–40 minutes.

While the dough rests, prepare the mutton. Place the mince in a large mixing bowl. Wash, dry and chop the parsley. Dry-roast the spices, then crush them in a pestle and mortar. Add both to the mince. Peel and add the garlic cloves with a pinch of salt to the same pestle and mortar and work into a paste. Separate the egg and add the yolk to the mutton. Use your hands to disperse the spices and create an even mixture.

Once the dough has doubled, punch it down with your fist. Separate into six small balls. Roll each one of these into an irregular pizza shape. Put them onto a baking sheet sprinkled with polenta. Top the dough with the mutton and drizzle a little olive oil over each one. Bake in the preheated oven for 12–14 minutes.

Once the pizzas come out of the oven, garnish at will with any combination of feta, Greek yoghurt, toasted pine nuts, diced cucumber and fresh chopped mint and finish off with the jewel-like seeds of the pomegranate.

MUTTON CHOPS WITH SEASONED YOGHURT AND FATTOUSH

Andrew Sharp's mutton chops were a real surprise. They are juicy, tender and full of good, clean flavour. Forget the gamy, over-strong tastes often associated with mutton – these chops are gorgeous. It is all down to the aging: Farmer Sharp's mutton is hung for three weeks before it hits the market stall. Andrew likens his mutton to a well-aged Barolo claiming that just as Barolo tannins need to be softened and strong fruit harnessed, mutton needs time for tenderising and to tame its ripe flavour.

This hanging allows a luscious crisp brown crust to develop, thus protecting the meat whilst cooking and making it a pleasure to eat. The chops are delicious on their own or with the accompaniments below.

Sumac is a dried, ground red berry that can be found at Café Arabica or Spices from Hell at Borough. If you can't find sumac, substitute it with ½ tsp of pomegranate molasses. [SLB]

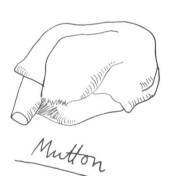

Mutton

Preparation time	20 minutes
Cooking time	15 minutes
Serves	2
Season	Mutton is in season from October to March

1 large pita bread
¼ large cucumber
1 punnet cherry tomatoes
½ small red onion
25 g fresh parsley
15 g fresh mint
½ an unwaxed or organic lemon
1 tblsp sumac
2 tblsp extra virgin olive oil, plus extra to rub into mutton before grilling
Sea salt
Freshly ground black pepper
4 tblsp Greek yoghurt
1 garlic clove
2 mutton chump chops,
    125–150 g in weight, 2·5 cm thick

Opposite Herdwick sheep

Preheat the oven to 180°C / 350°F / gas 4.

Prepare the salad, starting by tearing the pita bread into 2·5 cm pieces. Transfer to a baking tray and place in preheated oven for 5–10 minutes, until golden and crisp. Wash and dry the cucumber, tomatoes, onion, parsley and mint. Cut the cucumber in half, remove the seeds with a teaspoon and cut into 1 cm chunks. Quarter the cherry tomatoes. Peel and finely dice the red onion. Combine all the vegetables and the pita in a large bowl.

Finely chop the parsley leaves and fine stems. Remove the leaves from the mint stalks and thinly slice. Fold both of the herbs into the salad. Squeeze and add the lemon juice, sumac (and pomegranate molasses if using instead of the sumac) and olive oil. Season with salt and pepper. Set aside until ready to serve.

Spoon the Greek yoghurt into another small bowl. Peel and crush the garlic with a bit of salt in a pestle and mortar. Add the seasoned garlic, along with some freshly ground black pepper to the yoghurt. Stir to combine and set aside.

Heat a frying pan, or preferably a grill pan, over a medium flame. Rub a little olive oil onto the mutton and season with salt and pepper. Place in a medium-hot pan and cook for 6 minutes on each side. Transfer to a plate, cover with foil and allow to rest for 6–10 minutes. Serve with a good dollop of seasoned yoghurt and the fattoush salad.

ROAST LAMB WITH CHILLI DATE ALMOND PESTO

The cuisines of Persia and North Africa have been using the sweetness of dates to temper the full-flavour of lamb for centuries. The addition of mint combines these two cuisines in one dish. Spices from Hell and Cool Chile Co. sell both smoked paprika and chipotle chillies in adobo which will most certainly add a little authenticity to the dish.

I do want you to go home and make this delicious marinade yourselves but as we are all, on occasion, short on time, it's worth knowing that Café Arabica at Borough sells a sumptuously sticky and spicy date marinade, which works just as well in a pinch.

Butterflied leg of lamb works beautifully with the spicy-sweet marinade in this recipe. However, rack of lamb or even chump chops work equally well.

The cooking time given here allows the dates to take on a caramelised crust. [SLB]

Lamb

Preparation time 15–20 minutes, plus optional marinating

Cooking time 30 minutes, plus 8–10 minutes resting time

Serves 6

Season Lamb is in season from May until December

1 small onion
1 tblsp olive oil
1 tblsp medium-heat curry powder (or garam marsala)
½ tsp cinnamon
¼ tsp smoked paprika (optional)
1 small jalapeno chilli (or 1 tsp crushed chipotle chilli in adobo)
200g dates, pitted
50g almonds with skin
1 tblsp red wine vinegar
up to 2 tblsp water
15g fresh mint
15g fresh parsley
1kg boned leg of lamb
Sea salt
Freshly ground black pepper
240ml chicken stock or water (optional)

Preheat the oven to 200°C / 400°F / gas 6.

To make the spice paste, peel the onion and remove the tip and root end. Cut in half and slice into thin slivers. Pour the olive oil into a frying pan and place over a medium heat. Add the onion and cook for 3–5 minutes, or until it softens and is slightly tinged golden brown around the edges. Turn down the heat and add the curry powder, cinnamon and smoked paprika (if you are using it). Gently fry the onion with the spices until it becomes fragrant, about 30 seconds. Remove it from the heat and allow to cool.

Wash and dry the chilli and fresh herbs. Cut the chilli in half, remove the seeds and place in the bowl of a food processor or blender, along with the cooled onion-spice mix, pitted dates, almonds and vinegar. Process until you have a thin paste. The texture of the marinade should be thick enough to stay on the lamb but thin enough to coat the entire leg. If it is too thick, add up to 2 tblsp of water to the processor, one tblsp at a time. Chiffonade (a mixture of finely cut herbs) the mint by removing the leaves from the stem and stacking them in a neat pile. Roll them up, and using a sharp knife cut across in to very fine slivers. Chop the leaves and fine stems of the parsley. Transfer the blended spice paste to a small bowl and stir in the freshly chopped herbs. Add a good seasoning of salt and pepper.

A cook's best utensil is their own pair of hands, so dig in and spread the mixture all over the leg of lamb. The lamb can either be cooked straight away or it can be prepared up to this point in advance: anywhere from 2 to 24 hours marinating would certainly develop the overall flavour and tenderness.

Arrange the lamb in a roasting tin in a fairly even layer. Cook until the internal temperature registers 58°C / 135°F for medium rare – this usually takes about 30 minutes. Remove the lamb from the oven and transfer to a rimmed cutting board to allow it to rest. Cover with foil.

It is worthwhile to note that lamb continues cooking whilst resting. If you like your meat on the pink side, remove it from the oven 5 minutes earlier than recommended. You may have some nicely browned bits of marinade and lamb caramelised to the bottom of the roasting tin. If you wish, pour in about 225 ml of chicken stock or water and use the back of a wooden spoon to gently incorporate them into a sauce. Having the roasting pan over a burner whilst mixing will make lighter work.

Once the lamb is rested, cut it in half and turn each half 90 degrees to the right or left and then slice across the grain of the leg (doing this will make for a more tender bite). Serve with barley couscous and garnish with fresh herbs.

WEST COUNTRY PARK VENISON

Sue & Peter Kent *Hatherleigh, Devon*

We are sitting in an idyllic Devon garden on a perfect summer's day eating Sue Kent's homemade scones with raspberry jam and Devonshire cream. Did I say an 'idyllic' Devon garden? Well, it isn't quite because there are no roses. Sue can grow catmint, lavender, and spiny plants such as acanthus and pyracantha, but all her roses and rhododendrons have been eaten by the deer — of which, however, there has so far been no other sign.

Then, suddenly, they appear as if from nowhere, bounding and leaping over the turf in front of the house, just as Peter is explaining the slightly blurred difference between farmed and wild game. Peter's deer are indisputably wild. The nearest you can approach them is about 130 metres: any closer and, with a flash of their tails, they run away. At the moment, with the seasonal increment of fawns, Peter has 500: normally, it's only 400, which is as many as his 100 acres can comfortably support. They roam free over woods and open parkland and are not interfered with in any way apart from being fed with hay in the winter.

Compared with red deer, they are surprisingly small, certainly no larger in terms of body-size than sheep, with absurdly long necks and enormous eyes. They can be black or white (we later spotted both a black and a white fawn) but most of Peter's are pale *café au lait* dappled with white. Often, the dappling is surrounded by a white border which from afar makes them look as if they're wearing a rug. Some also have a black V on the rump.

The herd which first came into view was entirely male. In the summer, while their antlers are growing, the males never associate with the females, who at this time of year are bringing up their young. The does made their appearance about an hour later, accompanied by their fawns, who can run almost as fast as their mothers at three days old. Despite their consumption of roses, the deer live mainly on grass, although all the bark on the trees in the park has been eaten as far up as they can reach. Their instinct to browse is perhaps explained by the fact that they are not indigenous to Britain but originally came from southern Europe and the Middle East, notably Iran, where grass wasn't always available.

Peter's involvement with them began directly after he had finished university and took a job with the Forestry Commission. There, he was shown some antlers by a ranger, which fired his

Fallow country, Devon

imagination. He then went to work in the oil industry but spent every weekend helping the ranger with the deer on Commission land. He finally left the industry with the wish to take up farming of some kind, and settled for deer not only because he wanted to but, as he explained, because he knew nothing about any other kind of animal.

He and Sue started with the optimistic belief that people would seize on venison as a wonderfully lean, healthy alternative to beef. However, they soon found that the reality isn't like that, since only a tiny proportion of the public eats game of any kind and customers didn't quite know what to expect. In an effort to popularise the meat, they tried selling ready-to-eat sausages and burgers, which proved a hit, not only with regular market-goers but people working in the offices around, who now buy burgers for lunch every Friday.

His feeling for his stock is as deep and earnest as Andrew Sharp or Peter Gott's (pages 44 and 30). His particular concern is how it is slaughtered – which is also the commonest source of worry among his customers, who are always pleased to know that, as game, the deer are not sent to a slaughterhouse but shot. Peter always shoots them in the head so that they have no knowledge of what happens. 'To me, part of the responsibility of rearing an animal is to kill it in the most humane way possible,' he declared. (I should remind readers that the shyness of the deer means that he has to shoot from a distance of 130 metres.)

The Kents butcher not only their own meat but (to justify the cost of the equipment) that of eight other herds from parks nearby. Eighty per cent of their output is sold at Borough but they also supply a number of top restaurants including Pied à Terre and The Square, both in central London, and the leading hotel and restaurant Gidleigh Park at Chagford in Devon, not far from their park. As well as fresh meat, they produce smoked venison, which they sell in the summer when the fresh is out of season and I hope that one of these days they will try their hand at jerky, which used to be made by the staff at Aviemore in the Highlands as a way of passing the time during the Scottish long, dark winter evenings.

SUE KENT'S SMOKED VENISON SALAD WITH ROSY GRAPEFRUIT

You can eat the Kent's smoked venison at almost any time of day: in particular, it makes a splendid instant lunch with rye bread and a scattering of rocket or watercress and cherry tomatoes. However, the following scarcely takes longer and as well as lunch makes an unusual first course for dinner. It's a lovely combination: with the bitterness of the grapefruit, the venison tastes surprisingly sweet and the avocado unexpectedly creamy.

It's important that the grapefruit should be fairly sharp. For this reason, I've suggested using an organic one, which in my experience tends to be bitterer and more intensely flavoured than the (often) larger conventional ones. [SF]

Preparation time A few minutes

Cooking time Nil

Serves 2

Season All ingredients available year-round (smoked meat has a shelf life which means that it is available when fresh venison is out of season).

---

2 tblsp extra virgin olive oil,
    preferably peppery-tasting
½ tblsp red wine vinegar
Sea salt
Coarsely ground or roughly crushed
    black pepper
1 small organic grapefruit
1 avocado
80 g smoked venison

Make the dressing. Put the oil, vinegar, a little barely crushed sea salt and a generous sprinkling of very coarse, freshly ground or crushed black pepper into a cup and beat it vigorously with a fork.

Cut the peel off the grapefruit with a sharp knife. It's important to remove all the pith. Then, rather than dividing the fruit into segments, use the knife to cut the flesh into bite-sized pieces. Do this on a plate so that you can keep the juice. Peel and cut the avocado into pieces of about the same size.

Arrange the slices of venison down the centre of the serving plates, scrumpled, or as you will. Put the avocado pieces down one side and the grapefruit down the other. Beat the dressing again and pour it over the salad. Finally, pour over the rest of the grapefruit juice. Serve at once.

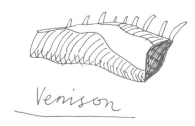

Venison

COUNTRY TERRINE

Terrines are great in the summer time and they are the perfect make-ahead food. They're convenient to pack for picnics, make a quick and easy snack or starter, and they freeze well. Once completely cooked and cooled, they will keep in the refrigerator for up to 4 days. They even get better with a day or two of 'aging'.

The recipe calls for allspice and juniper berries. Please try to purchase them whole and crush or grind them yourself. Unlike most dried spices, they quickly lose their strength when ground. Herbes de Provence lend a floral element to this recipe – you can find them in most good supermarkets. If you don't have any on hand, add a few lavender buds to a mixed herb blend – just make sure your lavender hasn't been sprayed with any type of growth treatment. [SLB]

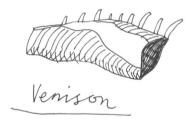

Venison

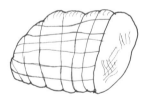

Pork

Preparation time 30 minutes prep time, plus overnight marinating and a further night's refrigeration once cooked

Cooking time 1½ hours, plus 1 hour cooling

Serves 8–10 as a starter

Season All ingredients available year-round

1 small red onion
3 garlic cloves
575 g minced venison
575 g minced pork
(preferably pork belly mince)
1 rounded tsp allspice berries
1 rounded tsp juniper berries
¾ tsp Herbes de Provence
1 tblsp tomato purée
1 tsp salt
1 tsp freshly ground black pepper
5 tblsp brandy
5 tblsp red wine
2 medium eggs
50 g fresh breadcrumbs
8–10 pieces streaky bacon to line the mould
1 bay leaf
3 sprigs thyme

Peel and finely dice the onion; peel and mince the garlic. Combine the minced meats, onion, garlic, freshly ground juniper and allspice berries, Herbes de Provence, tomato purée, salt, pepper, brandy and wine in a glass bowl and mix well. Cover with cling film and marinate overnight.

Before you're ready to mould and cook the terrine, cut a piece of cardboard that will fit inside a 1½-litre pâté mould or similar-sized loaf tin. Wrap the cardboard well with cling film and foil and set aside.

Preheat the oven to 150°C / 300°F / gas 2.

Lightly beat the eggs and stir into the minced pork along with the breadcrumbs. Place the streaky bacon in between two sheets of baking paper. Using a rolling pin, lightly pound the meat to make the pieces slightly thinner. Line your pâté mould with the bacon, covering both the base and sides. Press the meat mixture into the mould and seal by wrapping any overhanging bacon over the top. Cover any holes with additional pieces of bacon. Wash the bay leaf and thyme place them on the top and cover with foil and a tight fitting lid if you have one.

Place the pâté into a large roasting pan. Pour enough warm water into the roasting pan to come halfway up the side of the pâté mould. Bake in the preheated oven until the juices run clear when pierced with the tip of a small knife, about 1½ hours. The internal temperature of the pâté should be at least 60°C / 140°F. Upon removal from the oven the internal temperature will continue to rise by about 10 degrees Fahrenheit.

Take the mould out of the pan of water and remove the foil. Allow the pâté to cool for at least an hour at room temperature. Place the foil-lined cardboard on top of the pâté and then weigh the pâté down with a can or a brick wrapped in foil. Refrigerate the weighted pâté overnight.

Remove the weight and cardboard. Run a knife around the pâté and invert it onto a serving plate. Wipe it of excess cooled fat or jelly. Slice into 0·5 cm slices.

Serve with toast, pickles, and Dijon mustard, boiled new potatoes and seasonal vegetables.

Above The Fallow herd

VENISON AND PORK BELLY CHILLI

Warm spoonfuls of lightly spiced venison mingling with sweet pork will take the chill off any autumnal day. Serve in deep bowls so hands can cradle the chilli, inhaling the fragrant steam, nourishing the soul as well as the belly!

Many chilli con carne recipes are laden with spices which mask the flavour of the meat. I have pared the aromatics down to the bare essentials so that the flavour of the lean venison is enhanced rather than masked by the heat of the chillies.

This recipe easily doubles and freezes well. In a pinch, it can also be made with minced venison and sausage meat. Cool Chile Co. at Borough sells the most wonderful selection of dried chillies, all with heat gradients on the front of the package. Ancho chillies are fairly mild. So, for those of you who like it spicy add a jalapeno chilli to the mix. If you can't make it to Borough they are more than happy to deliver through online orders. [SLB]

Preparation time 1 hour, plus soaking the beans overnight

Cooking time 2 to 2½ hours

Serves 6–8

Season The venison season runs from late October until March

BEANS

225 g dried red kidney beans
   (found in gourmet or health food stores)
½ tblsp whole coriander seeds
3 garlic cloves
1 bay leaf
½ tsp sea salt

CHILLI

4 dried ancho chillies
120 ml boiling water
1 small green pepper
1 small onion
2 garlic cloves
800 g lean venison, cut into 1cm cubes
340 g pork belly with rind removed
2 tblsp olive oil
¾ tsp dried oregano (Mexican preferably,
   again sold at Cool Chile Co.)
1 tsp ground cumin
¾ tsp sea salt
¾ tsp freshly ground black pepper
600 ml water
440 g tin crushed tomatoes
2 tblsp tomato purée
Fresh coriander and sour cream
   for garnishing

Begin by preparing and cooking the beans. Place them in a large bowl and cover with water. Allow to sit overnight at room temperature. In the morning, wash the beans, place them in a large stockpot and cover with water. Crush the coriander seeds with a pestle and mortar and add to the pot along with three peeled garlic cloves and the bay leaf. Bring the water to a boil, reduce the heat to a simmer and cook the beans for 1 hour or until tender. After an hour, drain the beans, and discard the bay leaf and garlic cloves and return the beans to the pot. Stir in ½ tsp sea salt.

While the beans are cooking, prepare the remaining ingredients. Begin by placing the dried chillies in a large heatproof bowl and cover with 120 ml boiling water. If your chillies have been sitting in your pantry for quite some time, dry-toast them in a small frying pan for 30 seconds to reawaken their flavour. Let them stand for 20 minutes in the boiling water, until soft, then de-seed and remove their stems. Chop the chillies, along with the green pepper and onions, into a fine dice. Peel and crush two garlic cloves with a pinch of salt with a pestle and mortar.

Cut the venison and pork belly into small cubes, about a 2·5 cm square. Place a large casserole over medium-high heat and brown the venison and pork in 1 tblsp of oil. Transfer the meat to a plate and spoon off the excess fat.

Add the green pepper and onion, along with dried oregano and cumin. Season well with salt and pepper. Add the remaining tablespoon of olive oil if needed sauté the vegetables until softened.

Add the meat to the vegetables in the pot and pour over 600 ml of water, the tinned tomatoes and the tomato purée. Bring the whole mixture to a soft boil. Reduce the heat to low and cook, partially covered – with the lid slightly propped on the side or with a loose covering of foil – for 1½ hours. During the last half hour of cooking add the cooked beans to the pot and gently fold through.

Once cooked, ladle the chilli into bowls and serve with chilled sour cream and some chopped fresh coriander.

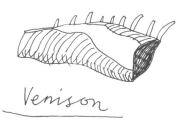

Venison

Pork

VENISON LOIN WITH MOLE SAUCE

The difficulty in this dish is in the preparation of the sauce. However, it can be made ahead of time and it freezes well. The ingredient list is lengthy but well worth the effort. Mole, pronounced 'mollie', is a classic Mexican sauce. There are probably as many different mole sauce recipes as there are houses in Mexico. This one utilises pasilla pepper, mulato and ancho chillies — otherwise known in Mexico as the holy trinity. Classically, mulato chillies make up about half of the mix. I have chosen to match the gamy venison with the more sweet-raisin-like heat of pasilla instead. The spice of the dish is tempered by bitter dark chocolate, which also adds a delicious viscosity and shine to the finished sauce. [SLB]

Preparation time 45 minutes

Cooking time 45 minutes for the sauce, 20 minutes for the venison

Serves 4

Season The venison season runs from late October until March

6 pasilla peppers (bought from Cool Chile Co. or ordered from their online shop)
3 ancho chillies (as above)
3 mulato chillies (as above)
5 tblsp vegetable oil
1 small onion
3 garlic cloves
¼ tsp cumin seeds
1 tsp coriander seeds
½ tsp dried oregano
8 prunes
2 tblsp almonds
2 tblsp sesame seeds
2 tblsp pumpkin seeds
225 g tinned chopped tomatoes
2 pints chicken stock
2 bay leaves
1 tblsp masa harina (or 2 tsp corn flour)
28 g bittersweet chocolate (above 70% cocoa content), finely chopped
500 g venison loin
Sea salt
Freshly ground black pepper

The moment of truth,
Peter Kent and customer

Soak the peppers and chillies in a bowl filled with warm water for 30 minutes.

Meanwhile, warm 3 tblsp of the vegetable oil in a large casserole dish. Peel and finely dice the onion. In a mortar, work the garlic into a paste with a little salt and add to the pot. Cover and cook over a low heat until the onions are soft.

Combine all the dried spices together in a pestle and mortar; crush to break open the coriander seeds and then add the spice mix to the casserole with the onions and gently fry. Once fragrant, after about 30 seconds, add the prunes, almonds, sesame and pumpkin seeds.

Remove the peppers from the water, pat them dry and pull out their stems. Add the peppers to the spicy onion mixture, along with the tomatoes. Give the whole mix a good stir and cook for 5 minutes or until the tomatoes and peppers start to break apart.

Pour over the stock, wash and tuck in the bay leaves and cook for 30–35 minutes on a low heat stirring occasionally. Season the sauce with sea salt and black pepper. Allow to cool before puréeing in a food processor. The sauce can be served as is, or can be passed through a sieve and returned to a clean saucepan.

Sprinkle over the masa harina and cook for 5 minutes to thicken slightly. If you can't find masa harina (also available from Cool Chile Co.), corn flour will work. Remove from the heat and stir in the chocolate until melted. Set the sauce aside in a warm place while you cook the venison.

Preheat the oven to 180°C / 350°F / gas 4.

Rub the remaining 2 tblsp oil into the venison. Season with salt and pepper. Then sear in a hot frying pan for 1–2 minutes on each side. Transfer the meat to the preheated oven and cook for 10–15 minutes, depending on how you like it cooked – 10 minutes for rare, 15 minutes for medium. Allow the meat to rest for 5 minutes before slicing. While the meat rests, wash and dry some coriander sprigs and warm the mole.

The sauce should be a rich-brown colour. To avoid drenching the venison in sauce, pool the warm sauce on the plate and arrange thick slices of venison on top. Garnish with a few sprigs of coriander.

Cook's note Considering the number of ingredients and the fact that a bulk of the preparation time is allocated to the sauce I listed enough sauce ingredients for 2 times the recipe. As there is no dairy in the sauce it freezes well and reheats like a dream.

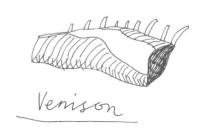

Venison

VENISON CARPACCIO WITH JUNIPER WHISKY CREAM

Here we are 'curing' the meat but we are doing so without the use of a liquid. Juniper, sea salt and caster sugar are crushed together and rubbed into the skin. As this mixture tightens and tenderises the meat some of the sea salt and sugar will be dissolved by the natural moisture from the venison during the cure thus allowing the juniper to infuse the entire loin with it's perfume. Remember to use a good quality whisky for the cream sauce. It is a prominent flavour in the finishing sauce. So make sure you try your whisky before you add it. The better the whisky the more you can use. When I was lucky enough to have a gorgeous, slightly syrupy Scotch whisky with a strong oak flavour, I added 120 ml to the cream sauce and it was delicious! [SLB]

Preparation time 15 minutes,
    plus 6–12 hours curing

Cooking time 25 minutes, plus cooling time
    and refrigeration – 1½ hours

Serves 8 as a starter

Season The venison season runs from late
    October until March

---

18 juniper berries
150 g sea salt
115 g caster sugar
500 g fillet venison
1 tblsp sunflower oil
120 ml double cream
115 g crème fraîche
60 ml Scotch whisky
Fresh watercress for garnish
Freshly ground black pepper

Begin by crushing 12 of the juniper berries in a mortar. Try to work them into a powder as best you can. Prepare the venison by removing any silverskin and connective tissue. Combine the salt, sugar, some freshly ground pepper to season and the crushed juniper berries in a glass bowl and mix well. Place the venison in the bowl and rub thoroughly to coat with the mixture. Wrap well in cling film and refrigerate for at least 6 hours, or anywhere up to 12.

Once cured, remove the venison from the mixture and rinse thoroughly. Pat dry with paper towels. Rub the oil over the venison. Place a frying pan large enough to accommodate the meat comfortably over a medium-high flame. Add the venison and cook for 2 minutes whilst continuously rolling the venison around in the pan. Keep the venison moving in the pan so that you don't allow a crust to develop – slicing will be easier without a thick crust. Transfer the meat to a shallow plate and allow to cool to room temperature. Once cooled, wrap the venison in cling film and refrigerate until cold – at least 1 hour.

Make the sauce by crushing the remaining 6 juniper berries with the side of a chef's knife and heating them in the double cream just until a thin skin forms on top. Infuse for 10 minutes; strain, and allow to cool. Combine the infused cream with the crème fraîche in a small bowl.

Pour the whisky into a small saucepan and gently bring to a simmer over a low heat. Once simmering, cook for about 30 seconds until, the alcohol burns off. Slowly pour the whisky into the cream sauce.

Once the venison has chilled, use a sharp knife to slice the meat as thinly as you can. Place 5–6 slices of venison on each plate. Either drizzle the cream sauce over the venison or serve it alongside, with a few leaves of cleaned watercress as a garnish.

VENISON STEAKS
WITH THAI VINAIGRETTE

Not all cuts of venison require lengthy cooking times. Venison steaks are one of these cuts, making them perfect for weeknight suppers. Being exceptionally low in fat, the lean tender meat requires only a few minutes in a hot pan to seal in perfection. Fallow deer has a light gamy flavour with a texture similar to lean beef.

Juniper berries, redcurrants and red wine are ingredients traditionally paired with venison. Yet, I've found the combination of tongue-tingling lime juice, fresh herbs, chilli and lightly toasted peanuts a near perfect match for the rich venison, if not a dieters dream. 'Rich' when used to describe food is often associated with fat. Fat melts and bastes the meat throughout cooking giving a depth of flavour and 'richness' to the finished product. Not so with venison. Lean venison meat has a richness all it's own and this vinaigrette merely enhances the rich meat by balancing it with bitter lime juice, fresh herbs and a little spice. [SLB]

Preparation time 10 minutes

Cooking time 6–8 minutes to cook,
   5 minutes resting time

Serves 2

Season Late October until March.

---

2 small shallots or 1 large banana shallot
1 garlic clove
Sea salt
½ red jalapeno chilli pepper
2 sprigs fresh mint
4 sprigs fresh coriander
4 tblsp roasted peanuts (optional)
2 limes (enough for 50 ml lime juice)
2 tblsp fish sauce
2 tsp caster sugar (or palm sugar)
2 venison steaks
   (about 2 cm thick, 150 g each)
1 tblsp olive oil
Freshly ground black pepper

Make the vinaigrette before cooking the venison steaks. Peel and finely dice the shallots. Peel and crush the garlic with a pinch of salt in a mortar. Wash the chilli, cut it in half and remove the seeds before finely dicing. Wash the fresh herbs and blot dry with kitchen paper. Remove the leaves from the stems and finely chop. Roughly chop the peanuts if you are using them. Combine all of the above in a small bowl. Squeeze the limes. Add 50 ml of lime juice, along with the fish sauce to the bowl and stir to combine. Sprinkle over the sugar and check for seasoning. Set aside until ready to use.

Rub the venison steaks with olive oil. Season well with salt and pepper. Preheat a frying pan over a medium flame for a minute. Add the steaks to the hot pan, cook for 3–4 minutes on each side. Transfer to a plate and rest the steaks for 5 minutes.

Serve the venison with some of the vinaigrette spooned over the top. Rice noodles tossed with grated carrot and cucumber are a delicious (and equally nutritious) side dish to help soak up some of the venison juices and vinaigrette.

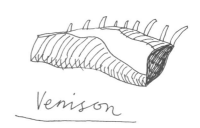

Venison

WILD BEEF

Richard & Lizzie Vines *Chagford, Devon*

In producing 'wild' beef (for 'wild' read 'traditional' or 'old-fashioned') Richard Vines is living out a dream. He began his career in the Army and was then employed for some years by the pub and hotel chain Grand Metropolitan. His ideal, however, had always been to go into farming. Eventually, he took the plunge and bought a small farm on the edge of Dartmoor, favouring Dartmoor because he wanted to keep cattle and the climate in Devon is particularly suitable for them. The moor was also seminal to his ideas on nutrition: the land is not only organic but permanent pasture, which means that it hasn't been ploughed and sown with grass as part of a crop rotation. Besides the advantage in terms of quality that he believes this confers, it provides a much more varied menu than usual, since there are many sorts of grass plus heather, bilberries, blackberries, bracken, and even ivy, which cows seem to like (in very small doses) if they feel ill.

His first cattle were two pedigree cows of the local copper-coloured South Devon breed, from whom he hoped to build up a herd. However, they made a bad start: one died, and so did the calf of the other. Instead of more Devons, he then bought four pedigree Welsh Blacks from Cerney in Gloucestershire. The bossiest, who became the herd leader, was called Cerney Ann. Her descendents all have names ending with Ann after her and still supply the herd leaders.

Richard's original plan had been to breed pedigree cattle rather than produce meat, and with this in mind he was careful to keep the two breeds pure. At the same time, he had become aware that even in Devon, the heart of cattle country, it was virtually impossible to find really good beef – added to which, as he said, he had to live. He therefore started to sell his own meat, using a small slaughterhouse which he trusted on the other side of Exeter, near Ottery St Mary. The hotel Gidleigh Park, which is near his farm, was his first customer.

Soon afterwards, he married Lizzie, who had formerly worked at Sotheby's but loves the cows and threw herself into the work of the farm as if born to the job. In 1998, like Peter Gott of Sillfield Farm and others, the Vines were introduced to Borough Market by Henrietta Green's Food Lovers' Fairs. By this time their herd was fast outgrowing the space at their farm, and

Lizzie Vines with Annie
'The Matriarch'

with the prospect of increasing sales at the Market, they leased a
second one at Ottery St Mary, near the slaughterhouse, to which
they transferred most of their cattle. They have since moved them
again, this time to an organic farm in Wiltshire where the pasture
is permanent, as on the moor, and the farmer a conservationist
with an especial interest in flowers, so that the cows have
exchanged heather and bilberries for orchids.

Although he is hesitant in talking about it, Richard has
thought long and deeply about nutrition. His theory, put briefly,
is as follows. The fertility of the soil depends on the proportion
of fungus and bacteria it contains. Most of the farmland in the

Wild beef country –
Dartmoor

Western world has been exhausted by intensive cultivation, in particular constant ploughing and the rigorous application of fertilizers and pesticides. In consequence, plants have shallow roots which don't penetrate far enough to reach the minerals in the deeper layers of the soil. In his view, even people eating organically often suffer from malnutrition because of the lack of minerals such as boron in their diet.

In explaining this, he was careful to emphasise that his ideas are entirely his own, with no scientific backing. All he can offer by way of proof is that, despite his initial bad luck with South Devons, his cows seem to have exceptionally strong immune systems. For the purposes of this book, scientific corroboration scarcely matters, since the proof which concerns us here is in the eating – and his beef really is absolutely outstanding: succulent, full of flavour, and remarkably tender. Most of it nowadays is crossed, but Richard still keeps a nucleus of pure-bred cattle, including North as well as South Devons. However, he says that he doesn't think breed makes that much difference to taste: 'It's the feeding that counts!' (Is he thinking of orchids?) To do the taste justice, you should perhaps serve the beef plainly, ie roast or as steaks, but Richard also stresses the importance of using the whole of the animal: hence the recipe for Wild Beef Bolognese that follows.

WILD BEEF BOLOGNESE

Like the beef on which it is based, this is rich, heady, and yet subtle. Unlike true Bolognese, you don't use minced meat but shin, which is slow-cooked to the point where it falls apart on the fork. It's one of the cheapest cuts – and Lizzie Vines of Wild Beef will be delighted to sell it, since at the moment it isn't as popular as it deserves to be.

I acknowledge that there are a lot of ingredients in this recipe, but this doesn't mean that it's complicated: on the contrary, it's extremely easy. Nor will you need to do much shopping, since everything except the beef and perhaps the bacon are the sort of thing that you probably have around anyway.

I originally envisaged it as going with spaghetti, or possibly penne, but by the time it was perfected I realized that its natural partner is gnocchi, which you can buy from the Fresh Pasta Co. in the market or Italian groceries. Alternatively, if you can spare fifty minutes or so, you can make your own. [SF]

Preparation time 40–50 minutes

Cooking time 4 hours

Serves 4–6

Season All ingredients available year-round

2 largish onions
6 garlic cloves
150 g smoked streaky bacon
2 smallish (inner) sticks celery
1 medium carrot
3 sprigs thyme
2 bay leaves
450 g shin beef
Sea salt
Freshly ground black pepper
2½ tblsp olive oil
Small knob of butter
400 g ripe tomatoes (plum if available)
1½ heaped tsp soft brown sugar
3 tsp red wine vinegar
1 tsp brandy
1 scant tsp mixed peppercorns
2 tsp tomato paste
2 generous glasses Shiraz or other spicy,
    full-bodied red wine

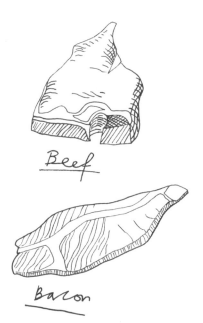

Beef

Bacon

Peel and very finely chop the onions. Peel the cloves of garlic. Snip the rind from the bacon and dice it finely (use scissors). Wash, dry, and dice the celery. Peel and dice the carrot; wash the herbs and leave them to dry. Chop the beef into chunks about 2·5 cm. As it's very lean, you won't need to trim off much fat; you can also leave tendons, which after long cooking will add to the richness of the sauce. Season the meat lightly with salt and rather more generously with pepper.

Heat 1 tblsp of the oil over fairly high heat and sear the meat just until it is pale on all sides. Lift it out of the pan and put it on a plate. Leave any oil and meat juices in the pan.

Put the butter and another tblsp of oil into the pan, add the bacon and prepared vegetables and fry them over low heat for 15–20 minutes, until they are reduced in volume and the onions begin to change colour. Turn them from time to time for the first 10 minutes or so and more frequently thereafter; add a little more oil if the pan seems dry.

While the vegetables fry, peel the tomatoes (immerse them in boiling water for 30 seconds and their skins will then peel off easily). Chop them into smallish pieces and, unless they are the plum variety, which has very little core, throw away the hard centres.

When the vegetables are sufficiently cooked and reduced, stir in the tomatoes along with the sugar, whole garlic cloves, vinegar, brandy and peppercorns.

Set the oven to 150°C / 300°F / gas 2.

Put half the beef into the bottom of a small casserole. Add half the bacon and vegetables. Spread with the rest of the meat and finish with the remaining vegetables. Beat the tomato paste with a little of the wine and pour it in with the rest of the wine. Bury the bay leaves and lay the sprigs of thyme over the top. Cover with a close-fitting lid and bake for 2 hours.

Then turn down the oven to 120°C / 250°F / gas ½ and bake for a further 2 hours, by which time the meat will almost have disintegrated into the sauce. Remove the stalks of the thyme and serve on top of the gnocchi.

OSSO BUCCO

The very first step in this recipe is to ensure that the veal shanks are thoroughly browned all over. This extremely important step not only makes for a delicious, full-flavoured dish, but also a sauce with depth and complexity.

I've given a basic tomato sauce with this recipe. It is added work but well worth the effort. Layering flavours within dishes is a good restaurant trick that many of us should be doing more often at home. It is a delicious tomato sauce to have on its own or used as we do here. At home, I often make up two or three times the amount of the tomato sauce below and store it in the freezer.

Normally, I would say you could use either red or white wine for most braises. However, please stay with white for this recipe. The white wine won't mask the delicate flavour of the veal. Look out for Chill Baked Cannelinni Beans in our next book the Borough Market Cookbook: Fruits & Vegetables – it is the perfect accompaniment.

Recently British veal has received a lot of press. The ban on exporting calves was lifted last year and this has brought back into the limelight the pros and cons of eating veal. I hope to encourage people to support British farmers who are embracing high animal welfare rearing systems for male calves of dairy herds, which will help to spare these animals the inhumane practice of the live export trade. British dairy farmers pride themselves on their standards of animal welfare for both the milk producing mums as well as male offspring. Male calves are now allowed room to grow and mature for 6 months in suitable buildings or over pasture land. They are given a varied diet producing rose-coloured flesh and the practice of using 'foster' cows is not unheard of for newborns. Six months may not seem like a full life, but these calves will live twice as long as a chicken, longer than most lambs, and have an equivalent maturation period of a good pig. [SLB]

Preparation time 35 minutes to make the tomato sauce

Cooking time 2 hours, 17–20 minutes to cook the meat

Serves 4

Season All ingredients available year-round

2 tblsp extra virgin olive oil, divided
30 g unsalted butter, divided
4 large veal shanks,
    cut 7–8 cm thick (about 1·6–1·8 kg in total)
Sea salt
Freshly ground black pepper
1 medium carrot
1 celery stalk
1 small brown onion
2 sprigs fresh thyme
½ tsp dried chilli flakes
240 ml dry white wine
240 ml chicken stock,
    homemade or store bought
240 ml tomato sauce (recipe below)

TOMATO SAUCE

2 tblsp extra-virgin olive oil
1 small brown onion
2 cloves garlic
1 small carrot
4–5 sprigs fresh thyme
900 ml tomato passata
Sea salt
Freshly ground black pepper

ORANGE GREMOLATA

15 g fresh parsley
2 level tblsp pine nuts
1 unwaxed and/or organic orange
Sea salt
Freshly ground black pepper

For the basic tomato sauce, heat the olive oil over low heat in a large casserole. Peel the onion and garlic. Slice the onion in half through the root and crush the garlic clove with the side of your knife. Add to the olive oil and cook until soft and lightly browned. Peel and grate or shred the carrot and add to the onion. Cook until the carrot is quite soft, about 5 minutes. Wash the thyme and tuck the sprigs in around the onion and add the tomato passata. Bring the sauce up to a simmer and cook until it has the consistency of porridge, about 30 minutes. Season with salt and pepper.

Preheat the oven to 150°C / 300°F / gas 2.

For the veal shanks, set a casserole over medium heat, into which they will fit in a single layer. Add 1 tblsp of the olive oil and 15g of the butter. When sizzling, add two of the shanks. Cook, turning carefully, until deeply browned all over, about 10–12 minutes. Remove the shanks to a plate and season with salt and pepper. Repeat with the remaining shanks, olive oil and butter.

Wash, peel and finely slice the carrot and celery. Peel the paper skins from the onion and finely

dice. Add all of the aromatic vegetables to the casserole and cover, reduce the heat to low, and cook in the olive oil/butter remaining in the casserole until the onions are soft, about 7 minutes. Wash the thyme and remove the leaves from the sprigs. Roughly chop the leaves with your knife. Lift the lid, and add the chopped thyme and the chilli flakes. Using a wooden spoon, scrape up any browned bits which may have stuck to the bottom. Pour over the wine and chicken stock and reduce the mixture by half. Mix in the tomato sauce and give the whole mixture a good stir. Gently lower the veal shanks into the liquid. Cover with a tight fitting lid and place in the oven for about 2 hours.

For the gremolata, wash and dry the parsley. Chop the leaves and fine stems and place them in a small bowl. Lightly toast the pine nuts in a moderate oven until just brown and allow to cool. Then, chop them finely and add to the parsley. Wash the orange and finely grate the zest. Fold the zest into the parsley mix, stirring thoroughly to disperse. Season with salt and pepper.

Serve the veal shanks with plenty of sauce and a teaspoon of gremolata on top of the bone.

Beef

THE ULTIMATE STEAK

Rump and rib-eye are the cuts for true steak-eaters. Each has a definitive texture with a little marbling which benefits from slightly more cooking than say a sirloin or fillet. The marbling needs to have that extra time to render it down, enrobing the meat and giving it flavour whilst protecting it from the extreme heat.

Wild Beef's native breeds are allowed to grow slowly to maturity before being humanely slaughtered and the meat is hung for four weeks. This attention to detail comes through in the taste, resulting in a deep, full-flavoured steak with extraordinary tenderness. Some things are best left unadorned. A good steak cooked to perfection is a recipe everyone should have in their repertoire. This is more a 'how to cook' rather than a flavour combination recipe. The only ingredients are: a little sea salt, freshly ground black pepper and olive oil. Simply serve with a side of strong mustard and sweet balsamic-dressed salad of baby lettuce leaves. We had a lovely Spanish red wine from the Priorat region, earthy and robust, which complemented the beef perfectly. [SLB]

Preparation time 2 minutes

Cooking time 13–15 minutes

Serves 2

Season All ingredients available year-round

---

2 tsp extra virgin olive oil
1 x 225–280 g rump or rib-eye steak, about
    2·5 cm thick
Sea salt
Freshly ground black pepper

Rub a tsp of olive oil onto one side of the steak. Season well with sea salt and freshly ground black pepper. Give the same treatment to the other side.

Heat a large frying pan, preferably with ridges, over a medium-high heat. Test the heat of the pan by adding a flicker of water: if it sizzles, the pan is ready for the steak. Place the steak into the pan and do not move it around or press it down with a spatula. Cook over a medium–high flame for 4 minutes. Flip the steak over and cook for another 4 minutes for a steak cooked to medium. If you like your meat rarer, cook for 3 minutes after flipping.

Transfer the cooked steak to a plate and cover lightly with foil. Allow to rest for 5 minutes before serving. This will give you just enough time to arrange some washed salad leaves over two plates and spoon out some mustard.

Obviously, this recipe can be doubled or tripled. The only word of advice I have about cooking steak is not to overcrowd the pan: a large frying pan is the right size for two steaks. Remember, steaks retain their heat for quite some time and are also perfectly delicious when served at a warm room temperature, so cook in batches if necessary.

*Opposite A pedigree
Welsh Black stare*

WILD BEEF BRAISED WITH RHUBARB, HONEY AND SAFFRON

This recipe has its origin in both Irish and Persian cookery. A traditional Irish recipe combines corned beef with a rhubarb mustard sauce, whilst Persian-Jewish recipes often combine beef with tart-sour fruits, sometimes in the form of a dried lime. Here we are using rhubarb for our tart-sour element combining it with a spice blend not far from a traditional corned beef recipe. Wait for the stronger outside-grown rhubarb for this recipe rather than the delicate champagne or forced rhubarb. Don't worry about the strong rhubarb flavour, the honey will temper the tartness and allow the rhubarb to cook down with the meat juices and the spice blend to create a lovely savoury warm, fruit chutney-style sauce to serve with the meat at the end of cooking.

Using shin of beef will make for easier serving straight from the pot whilst brisket holds together well during cooking and can be sliced. Cooking times for these two cuts of meat are generally the same. [SLB]

Beef

Preparation time 15 minutes, plus refrigeration overnight to let the meat absorb the spices

Cooking time 3½ hours

Serves 4–6

Season Outdoor rhubarb is in season from late March until May

1·8 kg shin of beef, beef brisket, or top side
2 rounded tsp coriander seeds
1 rounded tsp black peppercorns
8 allspice berries
½ tsp ground mace
1 tsp mustard seeds (black or yellow)
1 tsp sea salt
1 unwaxed orange
2 tblsp olive oil for browning the meat
50 g unsalted butter
1 large onion
1 rounded tsp plain flour
250 g outdoor rhubarb, pre-trimmed weight
1 small piece of ginger, about 2 cm when peeled
2 bay leaves
1 pinch saffron thread (0·4 gm)
100 g raisins
2 tblsp runny honey
175 ml white wine

Trim any large pieces of fat from the beef shin or brisket; a top side cut will be fairly lean. Be careful not to trim too much fat from beef shin as you want the meat to hold together whilst cooking. Either cut the meat into large-ish cubes or leave whole. When preparing meat for a casserole I generally cut the meat into 5cm by 3cm cubes, which I think makes for a cleaner presentation. Using a pestle and mortar pound all the spices into a coarse powder. If your spices have been in the cupboard for a while, dry roast them in a small frying pan to re-awaken their flavour before pounding them. Wash the orange, grate half the zest and combine with the spices. Sprinkle the spice blend over the meat and gently rub it in with your fingers. Place the meat in a bowl, cover and leave it overnight in the refrigerator.

Preheat the oven to 170°C / 325°F / gas 3.

Heat half the olive oil and unsalted butter in a large casserole dish. Gently lower half of the spiced meat cubes into the sizzling fat and brown on all sides. Remember, if you overcrowd the pan you will steam the meat rather than caramelise and brown the edges. If you are at risk of steaming the meat, brown it in batches. Transfer it to a plate when cooked and set aside. Leave the juices in the bottom of the casserole.

While the meat is browning, peel the onion and cut it into fine dice. Add to the casserole in which you browned the meat. Cover and reduce the heat to low. Cook for 5 minutes. Sprinkle over the flour and work into a paste with a wooden spoon incorporating any onion juice and fat from the pan. Scrape up any brown bits or spices which may be stuck to the bottom of the pan.

Prepare the rhubarb stalks by washing, trimming and cutting them into 1cm slices. If the rhubarb stalks are particularly thick, use a vegetable peeler and shave off the outer stringy-fibrous layer and discard. Set aside. Peel the ginger and add to the casserole along with the bay leaves, saffron, raisins and honey. Pour in the wine and bring the whole mixture up to a simmer. Add half the rhubarb and stir into the braising liquid.

Gently lower the meat back into the casserole with any juices that may have accumulated on the plate. Cut out a piece of parchment slightly larger than the circumference of your casserole dish. Place the parchment over the ingredients in the dish, followed by a tight-fitting lid so you end up with a ruffle edge of parchment around the outer rim of your casserole dish. This will help to lock in and circulate steam more efficiently during the long cooking time in the oven. Transfer the casserole to a preheated oven and cook for 1 hour and 30 minutes.

Carefully remove the casserole from the oven. Turn the meat in the liquid and add the remaining rhubarb. Return to the oven and cook for another 1 hour. Check to see if it is ready, the meat should be extremely tender: if not, continue cooking for another 30 minutes.

When cooked, remove the casserole from the oven and spoon off any clear liquid fat which may be on the surface. Taste the braising liquid. If it's too tart, add a little more honey. Spoon onto warm plates and serve with sautéed savoy cabbage.

'It's the feeding that counts'

BILTONG DATE AND CHEDDAR SALAD WITH HAZELNUT SHERRY VINAIGRETTE

When you're dealing with ingredients that have vibrant, wild flavours, a little bravery and a macho attitude are needed to tame them. Biltong, prepared in a true South African tradition, is one of these ingredients. I like to serve this wild beef, which is preserved with vinegar and salt, before it's dried in the sun to concentrate its flavour, in a simple salad with sweet dates, salty cheese and a bed of peppery rocket leaves dressed with fragrant hazelnut vinaigrette. With very few components, it is extremely important to get quality ingredients. Mejool dates and Montgomery's Cheddar are musts, as is a good oak-aged sherry vinegar. If you can't get to Neal's Yard for Montgomery's Cheddar, try a well-aged Parmesan Reggiano. [SLB]

Preparation time 15 minutes

Cooking time 5–10 minutes

Serves 2

Season Mejool dates are best in December

1 packet air-dried wild beef, (about 100 g)
50 g hazelnuts
1 tblsp sherry vinegar
Sea salt
Freshly ground black pepper
3 tblsp hazelnut oil
    (or a fruity extra virgin olive oil)
100 g Neal's Yard Montgomery's Cheddar
100 g rocket leaves
6 large Mejool dates

Preheat the oven to 150°C / 300°F / gas 2.

Place the air-dried beef and hazelnuts on two separate baking trays and lightly toast in the oven to re-awaken their flavours. The wild beef will fill your kitchen with the amazing aroma of a roast dinner. When the beef starts to crisp up and release some of its fat, remove it from the oven and set aside to cool. As the papery skins of the hazelnuts start to darken and flake, remove them from the oven and allow to cool.

Rub the slightly cooled hazelnuts between your hands to release their skins. Transfer the nuts to a cutting board. Roughly chop them, making sure to cut every nut at least in half. Transfer to a small bowl and pour over the vinegar. Season well with salt and pepper. Pour over the olive oil and lightly whisk to just combine the ingredients rather than emulsify them. There are so few ingredients in this dish and it is nice to show what each ingredient is and how it interacts with the others on the plate.

Cut the cheese into large shards. Break it up into crumbly pieces with your fingers and set aside. If there are large pieces of beef use a knife to give them a rough chop. Wash and gently dry the rocket leaves and scatter them over the plates. Build up the salad with the dates and cheddar cheese. Crumble the wild beef over the top and spoon over the nutty vinaigrette. Make sure to collect any hazelnuts which have sunk to the bottom of the vinaigrette bowl.

This feast for the senses is a great starter for any Spanish or Argentinean meal.

Cook's note If you can't find air-dried wild beef, try using an Italian bresola dried in the oven until crisp on a paper-lined baking tray.

DENHAY FARMS

Amanda Streatfeild *Broadoak, Dorset*

Anyone who thinks that rural England is no more should spend an afternoon lost in the Dorset lanes. Roller-coaster-style, you go up and down hills whose tops are bathed in brilliant sunlight and the bottoms shaded almost to blackness by thick woods. The roads twist and turn between high banks, making every bend blind, and are wide enough for only one car. There are passing-places, but you hardly need them. We drove for an hour and a half, not knowing where to go, before we finally met a delivery van. Instead of backing until it was able to pass, we asked the driver the way. The road was blocked for at least twenty minutes while (with difficulty) he worked out a route. We kept peering anxiously behind us but he was completely unconcerned. It never seemed to cross his mind that anything might come.

Once we had arrived, I was immediately struck by the similarity between the histories of Denhay Farms and Quickes in Devon, an hour's drive to the west. Both were originally mixed farms with dairy herds. When the economics of farming forced them to specialize, both of them used their milk for cheese and fed the whey to pigs, which was traditionally held to give the pork a particularly sweet, delicate flavour. At the time of writing, Mary Quicke doesn't process the meat but still keeps the pigs (though perhaps not for much longer). The Streatfeilds, conversely, produce ham and bacon but eventually felt obliged to give up their pigs and source their meat from elsewhere.

The original farm was bought shortly after the war by Amanda Streatfeild's father-in-law and a partner called Alexander Hood, a banker whose financial expertise (and subsequently that of his family) has been invaluable to the Streatfeilds over the years. They started making the farmhouse Cheddar for which Denhay is perhaps best known in 1958 and introduced the pigs a few years later. By the late 1980s they had built up a herd of some 500 breeding sows. Until then, like the Quickes, they had simply sold the carcases, but at this point, in Amanda's words: 'We looked at the business and decided to concentrate on value-added products from the pigs – and started with the most expensive that I could think of, which was an air-dried ham like Parma ham.'

By way of research, they went on a 'brilliant' holiday to Italy and concluded that, although they couldn't copy it exactly, they

could produce a very good English variation. Their next step
was to hire a technologist and develop a recipe: the one they settled on was based on a ham produced by a neighbouring farmer
which was wet-cured in cider and smoked in his chimney
throughout the winter. The final version, perfected in a double
garage at their home, uses apple sauce, local herbs, and honey.
As they predicted, it isn't the same as the Italian version, but delicious in a different way: it has a softer texture and is less smoky
but much sweeter, perhaps because of the apple.

Three years later, they introduced their award-winning dry-
cured bacon; then they finally, sadly, resolved that the pigs must
go. They were given plenty of space but were not free-range, less
for the farms' convenience than their own, since the soil in this
part of the world is rich clay and they would have generated a sea
of thick, heavy mud. 'It wouldn't have been fair,' said Amanda.
Customers, however, didn't understand this and by 2002 the
Streatfeilds felt that they had to comply with the demand for free-
range produce (which shows how far public opinion has swung:
a decade ago, free-range ham and pork were almost unknown).

The Streatfeilds now buy their pork from a farm in Norfolk
where the pigs are 'extremely' free-range. They are fed on corn
and maize (guaranteed GM-free): Amanda and her husband

George agonized somewhat over whether the lack of whey in their diet would affect the meat, but George says that he hasn't noticed any change at all.

Partly thanks to the Hoods' financial guidance, Denhay today is a flourishing company which owns not just the one but five farms. At present, its business is split about equally between pork products and cheese; it is also in balance, which means that according to conventional business wisdom, it is ripe for expansion, although in which direction has yet to be decided.

In the meantime, if you can't always find the Denhay stall at Borough, it's because Amanda only comes once a month – but she values her visits all the more: 'I couldn't do without them! They're my most valuable means of keeping in touch with my customers!'

Tastings in the Green Market

ROAST GAMMON
WITH MAPLE BOURBON GLAZE

There are as many ways of preserving gammon as there are butchers in this country. These days gammon has a very mild cure compared to the time before refrigeration. For this reason I have chosen not to soak or boil the gammon. Ask your butcher how he or she has prepared the joint. If you are concerned about a salty cure flavour in the finished dish, a general rule of thumb is to soak joints overnight in cold water. Unsmoked gammon traditionally has a stronger cure than smoked. Smoked or unsmoked joints can be boiled for 15 minutes per pound and then browned in the oven for 5 minutes per pound plus an additional 15 minutes.

If you are not going to boil the joint, I would recommend keeping the skin on to protect the meat during roasting and ask your butcher to make a diamond pattern through the skin. Cook a 2·2 kg gammon joint with skin for about 1 hour and 45 minutes to 2 hours, with 20 minutes resting time. [SLB]

Preparation time 20 minutes

Cooking time 2 hours,
      plus 20 minutes resting time

Serves 6

Seasonality All ingredients available
      year-round

2·2 kg gammon joint, smoked or unsmoked
180 ml fresh orange juice
90 ml pure maple syrup
2 tblsp bourbon
2 tblsp light brown sugar
1 tblsp dried mustard powder
2 tblsp soy sauce
Pinch cayenne
Sea salt

Place the gammon in a saucepan and cover with cold water. Bring up to the boil; reduce the heat and simmer for 1 hour and 15 minutes.

Meanwhile, put all the remaining ingredients in to a small saucepan over medium heat, whisking to combine. Bring to a simmer and cook, stirring occasionally, until the mixture has thickened and reduced by about one-third, around 10 minutes. Let it cool.

Once the gammon has boiled, use a paring knife to remove the skin from the flesh, leaving a thin layer of fat over the ham.

Pre-heat the oven to 240 °C / 475 °F / gas 9.

Sprinkle the joint with sea salt and using a pastry brush, coat the joint all over with half cooled maple-bourbon mixture. Transfer to a roasting tin and place in the preheated oven. Immediately turn the heat down to 180 °C / 350 °F / gas 4 and cook for 40 minutes in total, basting every 10–15 minutes with the remaining maple-bourbon mixture and any pan juices which may have accumulated.

Once it is cooked, give it 20 minutes resting time, covered with foil. Serve the gammon carved in slices with spiced apple chutney.

What to do with leftover roast gammon:

1 Make a basic focaccia bread dough and sandwich ham slices with fontina cheese.

2 Crush an avocado with lime juice, coriander, minced red onion and a good seasoning of salt and pepper. Spread on a slice of bread and top with slices of gammon.

3 Mash 225 g of shredded gammon with 115 g of clarified butter. Season well with mace, salt and pepper. Pack into a small ceramic pot and refrigerate. This is good mid-week sandwich filler. Serve with honeyed mustard or simply on toast wedges.

WHITE BEAN SOUP
WITH DENHAY BACK BACON
AND ROSEMARY

This is a soup I crave from time to time. There is something special about the earthy white beans cooked slowly with the pine fragrance of the rosemary. It is a labour of love to wait patiently for the beans to soak and then cook but truly worth the effort. Below I've listed a tin of tomatoes as an optional ingredient. Sometimes, depending on whether or not I have a full-flavoured chicken stock on hand, I may add the tomatoes to the pot at the end of cooking. Let your own taste buds be your guide. Adjust seasoning to suit yourself at the end. Remember that the back bacon have a fair amount of seasoning. However, beans do need a healthy dose of both salt and pepper to bring out their flavour.

This soup is even better the next day as the flavours develop and mature further. But it will thicken as it sits, so you may have to add another cup or two of water or stock to loosen it before serving. [SLB]

Bacon

Preparation time 15 minutes,
   plus minimum 6 hours soaking

Cooking time 1 hour 45 minutes

Serves 6 as a starter, 4 as a main course

Season All ingredients available year-round

200 g Denhay dry-cured back bacon
500 g dried haricot or navy beans
1 tblsp extra virgin olive oil
1 large onion
2 carrots
1 celery stalk
1 large potato
3 garlic cloves
1 tsp Herbes de Provence
3 large sprigs fresh rosemary
900 ml chicken stock,
   homemade or store bought
440 g tin crushed tomatoes (optional)
½ head of Savoy cabbage (optional)
Shavings of Montgomery Cheddar or
   Parmesan

Pour the dried beans into a large bowl and cover with plenty of water. Allow to sit overnight or for at least 6 hours before cooking.

Stack the slices of back bacon and cut into small matchsticks. Transfer to a large pot or casserole and place over a medium heat. Drizzle olive oil over the bacon and stir to coat. Lightly cook while you prepare the vegetables. Drizzle with olive oil. Peel and cut the onion into a small dice. Peel the carrots and cut into fine dice by chopping into matchsticks first, then into small 'squares' and repeat this technique with the potato. Wash and finely dice the celery. Once the bacon is tinged brown around the edges and has started to release some of its fat, add the vegetables. Cover and sweat the vegetables together with the bacon for about ten minutes or until they soften and start to become slightly translucent.

Chop the garlic finely without any salt – salt will toughen the surface of the beans, thus causing them to need a longer cooking time. Add the garlic and Herbs de Provence to the casserole and gently fry to awaken their flavour.

Drain the beans and add to the pot. Rinse and add the whole rosemary sprigs. Stir to coat both the beans and the rosemary in the fragrant oil. Pour in the chicken stock and bring to a simmer. The beans will take about 1½ hours in total to soften.

You can, however, allow the soup to carry on cooking slowly beyond this time, as long as the beans don't catch on the bottom of the pot. Cooking for longer will allow them to break down a bit and the soup will thicken. Check for seasoning. If you want to add the tomatoes or cabbage, do so toward the end of cooking, allowing 10 minutes or so for the flavours to settle and cabbage to cook. Sometimes a fresh acidity is just what the beans need to give them a lift.

Before serving, fish out the sprigs of rosemary, leaving behind any leaves that may have fallen off. Ladle into bowls and top with a drizzle of extra virgin olive oil and a good seasoning of black pepper. A few shavings of aged sharp cheese are always a good addition for garnish.

ZITA TAGLIATA (PASTA PIPES) WITH DENHAY BACON AND BRUSSELS SPROUTS

This is convenient in two ways: not only can you knock it up fairly quickly, but you will probably have most of the ingredients in your kitchen already. The only items you're likely to have to buy are the Denhay bacon and the pasta itself. The Denhay bacon is the main point of the dish: the sprouts and fennel seeds point up its clean, sweet, distinctively porcine flavour and the dry cure ensures that the fat will be crisp while the lean remains meaty and tender. If you can't make it to the market on a Denhay weekend, either buy it by mail order or use bacon from Sillfield Farm or The Ginger Pig instead. [SF]

Preparation time 20 minutes

Cooking time 15 minutes or as long as it takes to bring a pan of water to the boil and cook the pasta (De Cecco takes 11 minutes)

Serves 2

Season September–February (but Brussels sprouts are better before Christmas than after)

140–150g Denhay Farms, or other dry-cured smoked back bacon (with Denhay Farms' bacon, you need 5 rashers)
175g small Brussels sprouts (enough for 100g prepared weight, or 14–16 sprouts)
3 cloves garlic
30g Parmesan cheese
Sea salt
160g zita tagliata or similar shortish pasta pipes
1 tblsp plus a little more extra virgin olive oil
½ tsp black peppercorns
1½ tsp fennel seeds
2 generous tblsp double cream

Trim off the bacon rind if necessary and cut the bacon into 2–2·5cm squares (use scissors). Set it ready in a wok or deep frying-pan in which you can toss the pasta later. Peel the sprouts and garlic. Chop the cloves of garlic into slices and put them into a mortar. Grate the Parmesan.

Put a large saucepan of water on to boil for the pasta. At the same time get the sprouts and bacon going as described further below. When the water has reached a rolling boil, add a good pinch of salt (there's no need to crush it) and the pasta. After the water has come back to the boil, stir and cook it according to the instructions on the packet. Start testing it to see if it is ready at least two minutes before the time given. Drain it as soon as it is tender enough for your taste. You don't want it to be hard, but there is nothing more depressing than overcooked, soggy pasta. It should be *al dente*, *ie* soft but still with plenty of 'bite'.

Just cover the sprouts with water. Add a little salt and set them over brisk heat when you put the pasta on to cook. They will take only a few minutes. You will need to test them often to catch them at just the right point: they should be just but only just soft, rather like the pasta, with a crisp point in the centre and plenty of 'bite'. Don't worry if they're ready before the tagliata, since they'll be re-heated at the end, when it is tossed.

You should also start frying the bacon when you put the pasta on to cook. As with the sprouts, it won't matter if it is ready too soon since it will be re-heated before serving. Add 1 tblsp oil to the wok or deep pan in which you put it and set it over medium to lowish heat. Turn frequently and remove it from the heat when the fat is crisp and golden and the lean tender (but not browned).

In the intervals between turning the bacon, add the peppercorns to the mortar and crush them to a rough paste with the garlic and a little oil. Put the fennel seeds and cream conveniently to hand near the hob. As soon as you have set the pasta to drain, turn up the heat under the bacon to medium high and add the contents of the mortar. Turn the bacon and add the fennel seeds. Continue to turn for a few seconds, until the aroma rises. Add the sprouts and pasta and turn gently but thoroughly. Add the cream and take the pan off the heat. Toss, add some of the cheese, toss again and serve with the rest of the cheese either sprinkled over the top or on the side. To ensure that the pasta stays hot at the table, serve it on heated plates.

Dry curing the hams

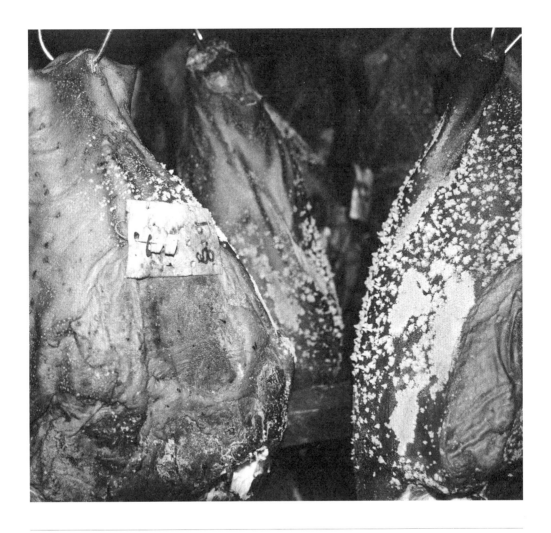

GOOD BACON SANDWICH WITH OVEN ROASTED TOMATO CHUTNEY

I am probably making purists scream with my addition of tomato chutney and use of streaky bacon here but there is rhyme and reason to such madness. There are many good producers of back and streaky bacon at Borough but Denhay Farms' dry-cured streaky bacon cannot be beaten when paired with Flour Power's deliciously chewy and tangy wholewheat sourdough bread. I know I'm tempting fate with the addition of tomato chutney, but its sweet-spicy acidity works wonders with the sour bread and smoky bacon. Of course, plenty of butter is also needed making this an irresistible sandwich.

The recipe for tomato chutney gives more than you need, but keeps wonderfully and makes excellent little gifts. And, it is gorgeous with air-dried ham as well as fresh and mature cheeses. If you're going to make the chutney, note that you'll need to do this weeks in advance (at least two) as it needs time to mature. [SLB]

Bacon

Preparation time Hardly any, excluding chutney

Cooking time 10 minutes

Serves 2

Season Ingredients available year-round. However, to make the best tomato chutney, buy your tomatoes from late June to mid-August, when their flavours are most concentrated.

6–8 slices Denhay dry-cured streaky bacon
1 tsp of sunflower oil
Butter for bread
4 slices Flour Power wholewheat sourdough bread
2 rounded tblsp oven-roasted tomato chutney (recipe next page)

Place a large frying pan over a medium flame. Pour in the sunflower oil. Brush or swirl to coat the pan. Lay the bacon into the pan and allow to cook slowly until tinged golden brown around the edges. Once crisp and brown, transfer from the pan to a paper towel-lined plate.

Lightly toast the bread, enough to keep the bacon warm and melt the butter. Spread one side with tomato chutney, arrange the bacon evenly over the top and cover with a second piece of buttered sourdough bread. A bacon sandwich with a cup of strong Monmouth coffee: I can't think of a nicer way to start the day.

OVEN ROASTED
TOMATO CHUTNEY

Preparation time 1 hour,
  plus minimum 2 weeks to mature

Cooking time 4 hours

Serves Makes 3 litres

Season British tomatoes are at their best
  from late June to mid-August, this is when
  their flavours are most concentrated.

2 kg tomatoes, preferably plum
500 g tart green apples (about 4 large,
  Granny Smith, Bramley work well)
3 medium onions
6 garlic cloves
1 tblsp dried mustard powder
5·5 cm piece fresh ginger
1 level tsp dried red chilli flakes
1 rounded tsp crushed coriander seeds
¼ tsp ground cloves
2 bay leaves
1 pint cider vinegar
500 g light brown sugar
Sea salt
Freshly ground black pepper

Preheat your oven to 130°C / 250°F / gas ½.

Wash and slice the tomatoes and arrange on a roasting pan fitted with a rack. It's important to use a rack to lift the tomatoes off the bottom of the tray so there's no colouring, only concentrating of the tomato juices, during the lengthy cooking time. Sprinkle the tomatoes with salt and freshly ground black pepper. Put into a preheated oven and cook for 3 hours. The tomatoes will shrink and their sweetness will concentrate as their natural water content reduces. For greater flexibility with your schedule, you can also reduce the oven temperature to its very lowest setting and cook the tomatoes for 5–6 hours.

While the tomatoes are drying, peel and core the apples. Grate the apples using the coarse side of a box grater. Peel and finely dice the onions. It is worthwhile spending a little time cutting the onions into very fine pieces because onions, no matter how long you cook them, will never break down. So, the size of the onion you put into the sauce or chutney at the beginning will be the size you get out at the end. Peel and crush the garlic with a little salt in a pestle and mortar. Measure out your spices and have them ready alongside the cider vinegar and brown sugar.

When the tomatoes have finished cooking, pulse them in a food processor just to break them up. Depending on the size of your processor you may need to do this in 2 or 3 batches. Wash and dry the bay leaves. Combine the tomatoes with all the remaining ingredients in a large saucepan and mix well. Bring to a boil, then reduce the heat and cook slowly, uncovered, for about 1 hour. The mixture will be quite soft and pulpy. When properly cooked you can drag a spoon across the bottom of the saucepan and leave a trail which will stay for a moment or two before disappearing. While still warm, spoon into clean, sterilised jars (either mason jars or ones with plastic-coated metal lids which will prevent any interaction between the vinegar and metal) and leave to mature, anywhere from 2 weeks to 3 months before serving. Makes about 7 jars (approximately 3·0 litres).

SELDOM SEEN FARM

Robert Symington *Billesdon, Leicestershire*

Probably like almost everyone else visiting Seldom Seen Farm, one of the first questions I asked when we arrived was why it has such an unusual name. 'We didn't call it that,' Robert Symington replied. 'The name was handed down to us. I suppose it's because it's in such an out-of-the-way spot that no one ever went there.'

The Symingtons have changed that. Long before rearing the geese for which they are chiefly known, they turned some of their land over to Pick-Your-Own and even on a wet, windy Monday afternoon there were a number of cars in the car-park and people could be seen returning from the picking-fields with baskets of strawberries, raspberries, and red currants. For exhausted pickers and the lazy, there is a shop and tearoom which looks out over a wide sweep of Leicestershire, a reminder of how pleasing and utterly, quintessentially English this part of the country is. In the tearoom you can choose from several traditional English cakes such as fruit and chocolate cake, which are specially made for the farm by a local cook called Julie.

Robert Symington

Most of the market garden is given over to soft fruit but in the shop we also saw broad beans and tiny new carrots. The strawberries for sale were so red and impeccable that at first I looked at them with suspicion, thinking that they looked exactly like those in my local supermarket: however, Robert gave each of us a punnet to take home (George Nicholson, the book's photographer, and his partner Julia were there too) and I can only say that they brought back youthful memories which I had long since dismissed as fictional. They were wonderful: firm but juicy, intensely sweet and yet sharp. Robert attributes their excellence to the not very rich soil, which he feeds liberally with manure. 'If I can avoid using chemicals, I certainly do.' However, he isn't quite organic, nor wants to be because he disapproves of the premiums often charged. 'Quite a lot of people can't afford organic food.... Some of the prices the supermarkets charge are outrageous.'

Like the Vines and others at Borough, Robert isn't descended from a long line of farmers. His father, however, bought the farm when he was eighteen, which has given him plenty of time to gain experience and learn how to use his land to the fullest advantage. Originally, the farm was mixed with cows, sheep, and pigs: the sheep are still there but the cows and pigs went years ago. The fruit was introduced as soon as the Symingtons arrived, when there was only one other Pick-Your-Own in the area. It was so successful that they bought a second farm which they kept for as long as the fruit was their mainstay: this role, however, has now been taken over by the geese.

The geese, far from being planned, were the result of a mistake. Claire, Robert's wife, had said that she would like two or three to wander round the farmyard. Robert bought her a pair as a Christmas present but there were another thirty in the van delivering them: hence their first year's sales. Today, reflecting the enormous recent rise in the popularity of goose, the Symingtons now rear a total of 4,500, of which 3,000 are kept at Seldom Seen and the rest on a farm with a similar soil-type in Wiltshire.

Geese, as market-goers probably know, are the only species of poultry which doesn't lend itself to manipulation: they can't be intensively reared, which is certainly one reason why they have become fashionable, nor can their natural breeding-season be modified. Robert's, which are Embdon/Toulouse crosses, aren't hatched at Seldom Seen (poultry-breeding is a specialised business) but arrive as day-old chicks in three batches. At the time we were there, in early July, the youngest were two weeks old and

the oldest nine weeks. They are fed on corn but also eat whatever else they can pick up in the fields (traditionally, geese were reared in the East Midlands because corn was grown there and they were fattened on the stubble after the harvest).

I had glimpsed a flurry of white on the way down the drive to the farm but wasn't prepared for the sight of the whole huge flock. They're dignified, beautiful, blindingly white once their feathers have grown, and move with astonishing speed and grace, although (sadly, as it seems to me) they're too heavy to fly far. Watching them, I suddenly understood the origin of the term 'goose step'. They all march together in perfect formation, arrow-shaped behind their leader, never stepping out of line or being left behind, even at the age of only two weeks. I've often thought about them since, and it occurs to me that the number of words and expressions in the English language which include 'goose' (eg gooseberry, goose-flesh, 'Don't be a goose!') are indicative of how deeply ingrained in our culture geese are.

The Symingtons don't come to Borough throughout the year, but only in the autumn and spring. The geese are sold from the end of October to early December: customers will be happy to know that they are slaughtered as humanely as possible, on the farm by having their necks wrung, which produces instant death. As Robert put it, 'It's OK.' In the spring, Seldom Seen sells made dishes and game such as quail – really, as Robert admits, 'just to maintain a presence.' The dishes are made by a team on the farm under Claire's direction. The best known dish is a three-bird-roast consisting of a goose stuffed with a chicken stuffed with a pheasant (which, however, isn't made in the spring but when the geese are ready, before Christmas). It's so popular that it accounts for nearly half their flock.

I only wish that they would maintain their presence in the summer as well as spring and autumn by selling strawberries.

ROAST GOOSE WITH BREAD SAUCE AND A CHOICE OF THREE STUFFINGS

In the past, goose was traditionally eaten at Michaelmas (29 September), a custom said to have been introduced by Queen Elizabeth I. In Mrs Beeton's words: 'Her Majesty happened to dine at the table of an English baronet when she received the news of the discomfiture of the Spanish Armada. In commemoration of this event, she commanded the goose to make its appearance at table on every Michaelmas.'* By the time Mrs Beeton was writing however, goose was already popular at Christmas: she describes how, before the coming of railway transport, huge flocks were driven on foot from Lincolnshire and Cambridgeshire to be fattened by London poulterers after their journey.

Let's be clear: a goose is not as economic as a turkey. A 3·75–4 kg bird will feed only six; a 4·5 kg one is enough for eight. Geese are fattier and much more difficult to carve than turkeys. When you taste them, however, you realise that none of this counts. Nigella Lawson doesn't agree, but as far as I'm concerned, goose beats turkey hands down. [SF]

*Household Management, facsimile of 1861 edition, paragraph 968

Preparation time 30–40 minutes, this includes the gravy and potatoes

Cooking time 2 hours 50 minutes (including 15 minutes while it rests)

Serves 8

Season Goose is available from Seldom Seen Farm's Market stall from the end of October until early December

4·5 kg oven-ready goose, with neck and innards
Stuffing of your choice
Sea salt
1 smallish onion
1 stick celery
50 g unsmoked streaky bacon
5 cloves
6 peppercorns
90 ml port
1·75–2 kg floury potatoes
Freshly ground black pepper
Bread sauce for serving (see page 135)

goose

To cook the goose

Preheat the oven to 225°C / 425°F / gas 7.

Thoroughly wipe the goose with damp kitchen paper; insert the stuffing. Don't force in more than will fit comfortably or it will escape during cooking. Put it in a roasting tray on a rack: the rack is important, as a great deal of fat will run. Prick the goose all over and season it moderately with salt. Roast for 20 minutes. Take it out of the oven and drain the fat and reserve it for later use.

Reduce the oven heat to 180°C / 350°F / gas 4. Cover the goose with cooking-foil, return it to the oven, and roast it for 1½ hours. After about thirty minutes, pour off the fat again; repeat this at least once. After the 1½ hours is up, remove the foil and cook the bird uncovered for a final 30 minutes, by which time it will be crisp and golden. Test it by sticking a skewer into the thickest part of the breast: if any pink liquid emerges, it isn't ready. When it is fully cooked, turn off the oven and leave it in the oven to rest for 15 minutes.

To make the gravy

Start making the gravy soon after you have put the goose into the oven. Peel and finely chop the onion. Wash, trim and finely slice the celery. Dice the bacon using scissors. As soon as you have drained the fat from the goose the first time, put 1 tblsp of it into a saucepan with a lid and fry the onion, celery and bacon in it (uncovered) over moderate heat for 6–7 minutes or until the onion is just starting to change colour. Turn frequently. Add the cloves and peppercorns and turn; then add the port. Allow it to heat for a few moments. Pour in 600 ml water. Take the neck of the goose and add it, curling it to fit into the pan. Bring the contents of the pan to the boil, skim thoroughly, cover, and simmer the gravy very gently while the goose cooks. Keep

an eye on it and if the liquid runs low, add a little extra water.

When you take the goose out of the oven and transfer it to a serving dish, skim off all the fat from the roasting pan but leave the juices behind. Pour the gravy into the roasting pan through a sieve. Scrape the bottom of the pan to dislodge any juice which has stuck, stir thoroughly, and return the gravy to a saucepan. Reheat it while the goose is carved.

To cook the potatoes

After preparing the gravy, peel the potatoes and cut them into moderate-sized chunks. If you like, boil them in lightly salted water for 2 minutes before roasting them: this will give them a creamier centre, but the difference when you're cooking them at moderate heat, as here, is relatively small. When the goose has been cooking for a little over an hour, pour a thin film of goose fat over the bottom of a baking tray large enough to take the potatoes in a single layer. Roll each chunk in the fat so that it is coated on all sides and set it in the tray. Try to ensure that none of the chunks touch each other. Season moderately with pepper and lightly with salt if the potatoes weren't pre-boiled; omit the salt if they were. Put them into the oven when the goose has cooked for an hour and a half.

To carve

Cut off the wings and the legs at the thigh joints and slice them separately. Draw the knife down the side of the breast-bone along the whole length of the bird before slicing the breast; repeat on the second side. Each person should have a portion of both breast and leg meat.

THREE STUFFINGS

Sausage, walnut & quince stuffing

Preparation time 15 minutes

Cooking time 15 minutes cooking to make raw stuffing (this doesn't include roasting time inside the bird)

Serves 8

Season Quince and walnuts both come into season, and are at their best, in October

1 quince
1 small onion
45 g butter
2 garlic cloves
3 sprigs fresh parsley
1 sprig fresh thyme
115 g walnuts
450 g sausage meat
85 g fresh breadcrumbs
90 ml single cream or full-fat milk
1 medium egg
Salt and pepper

Quince is a tricky fruit to work with as they are extremely hard to cut, so be careful during preparation. However, they do have a lovely honeyed sweetness and are well worth the effort. Peel the quince, then cut it into quarters. Carefully trim out the core and discard. Dice into 1 cm chunks. Put it into a small saucepan with a few spoonfuls of water – you want to steam the fruit, not boil it. Place a tight fitting lid on the pan and steam until soft, about 12–15 minutes. Set aside to cool.

Peel and dice the onion. Place the onion in a large frying pan over a low flame with the butter. Peel and crush the garlic with a little salt in a mortar. Add the crushed garlic to the onion and fry for another minute or until fragrant. Set aside to cool.

Wash and chop the leaves and fine stems of the parsley and thyme. Roughly chop the walnut and place in a large bowl with the sausage meat. Add the cooled quince, onion-garlic mixture, fresh herbs, single cream and egg. Mix well and season with salt and pepper.

Stuff mix into goose once ready to roast and cook according to the bird's size and weight. [SLB]

Sourdough, sage & onion stuffing

Preparation time 15 minutes

Cooking time 15–20 minutes cooking to make raw stuffing (this doesn't include roasting time inside the bird)

Serves 8

Season All ingredients available year-round

450 g loaf day-old sourdough bread
1 large onion
2 leeks
3 celery sticks
1 tblsp fresh sage
1 tblsp fresh chives
1 tblsp fresh thyme
1 tblsp fresh parsley
113 g unsalted butter
480 ml chicken stock,
    homemade or store bought
1 medium egg
Salt and pepper

Preheat the oven to 190 °C / 375 °F / gas 5.

Remove the crusts from the sourdough bread, and cut into 2·5 cm cubes. Place on a baking tray and gently toast for 15 minutes or until dry and lightly browned around the edges. Maintain oven temperature once you've removed the bread.

Peel the onion and cut into a fine dice. Slice the leeks in half lengthwise and rinse well under cold running water, along with the celery. Then thinly slice the leeks and celery and set aside. Wash and dry the herbs, removing the leaves from the sage and thyme, and finely chop enough to measure 1 tblsp of each. Heat a large frying pan over a medium-low flame. Gently fry the onion, celery and leeks with the butter for 10–15 minutes, or until the onion is translucent. Fold through the fresh herbs and remove from the heat.

In a measuring jug, mix the chicken stock and the egg and stir well. Make sure your chicken stock is at room temperature or cooler so you don't end up cooking the egg. Place the bread in a large bowl, spoon over the herb/onion mixture, and pour over the chicken stock-egg mix. Toss until all the liquid is absorbed. Season to taste.

Fill the cavity with the stuffing and roast according to the bird's size and weight or spoon the mixture into a baking dish and bake for 50–60 minutes, or until golden brown. [SLB]

Sourdough, chestnut & mushroom stuffing

Preparation time 15 minutes

Cooking time 50 minutes (this doesn't include roasting time inside the bird)

Serves 8

Season Chestnuts and wild mushrooms are at their best in the autumn months

450 g sourdough bread
115 g unsalted butter
1 large onion
2 celery stalks
2 garlic cloves
4 large sprigs fresh thyme

225 g mushrooms (preferably a mix of chestnut, shitake, black trumpet, chanterelle)
½ tsp ground nutmeg
425 g jar of chestnuts
Pinch saffron threads (0·4 g)
490 ml chicken stock
Salt and pepper

Preheat oven to 200°C / 400°F / gas 6.

Remove the crusts from the bread and cut into 2·5cm cubes. Divide the bread between 2 large baking sheets. Stir occasionally, bake until golden, about 15 minutes. Transfer to a large bowl.

Melt the butter in a heavy large frying pan over low heat. Peel and finely dice the onions and celery. Add to the pan and cook, stirring occasionally, about 20 minutes. Wash and remove the leaves from the thyme sprigs, and roughly chop to bruise the leaves and release their flavour. Peel and crush the garlic with a little salt in a pestle and mortar. Add to the pan with the thyme, and fry gently for a minute or two.

Brush off any dirt from the mushrooms with a dampened kitchen towel. Quarter the chestnut and shitake mushrooms and trim others as necessary to ensure they are all the same size. Add to the frying pan and stir until they begin to soften and release juices, about 5–10 minutes. Cook until all the mushroom juice has evaporated and they begin to fry.

Stir the mushroom mix into the bread cubes. Sprinkle in the nutmeg and season to taste with salt and pepper. Roughly chop the chestnuts and fold through the mix.

Heat the chicken stock with the saffron in a small saucepan. Allow to infuse and colour for a minute or two. Pour it over the stuffing mix and toss to coat until all the liquid is absorbed.

Stuff the mixture into goose and cook according to the bird's size and weight. [SLB]

LEFT OVER GOOSE RILLETTES

Everyone loves the idea of roasting a goose. However, geese are big birds and there are often leftovers. This is a delicious way to use them up. And, as it keeps well in the refrigerator if covered with clarified unsalted butter, you can have a few days off in between your roast goose dinner and the rillettes. I've chosen to use butter here purely for convenience. If you have saved any of the goose fat from roasting or possibly have some rendered chicken fat (if you have cooked a Label Anglais chicken you will definitely be able to collect some fat) blend the butter with the fat from either the goose or chicken and proceed as directed below. [SLB]

Preparation time 20 minutes

Cooking time 5 minutes

Serves 6

Season Goose is available from Seldom Seen Farm's Market stall from the end of October until early December

1 small onion
3 garlic cloves
½ tsp sea salt
2 tblsp extra virgin olive oil
1 level tsp freshly ground black pepper
Nutmeg
Meat from two goose legs
    (from a 4·5kg goose)
15g fresh parsley
2 tblsp Cognac
Up to 250g unsalted butter, softened

Peel and finely dice the onion. Peel and work the garlic into a paste with a little salt in a mortar.

Place a small frying pan over a low flame. Add the olive oil, along with the onions and garlic. Cover and cook for 5 minutes or until the onions become soft and translucent without colouring. Grate ¼ tsp of nutmeg and add it with the pepper and sea salt to the onion mixture; stir to combine.

Allow the mixture to cool slightly while you shred the meat from the goose legs as finely as you can. Place the onion mixture along with the meat in the bowl of a food processor. Pulse a few times to coarsely chop the meat and disperse the ingredients. This can also be done in the bowl of a standard mixer or by hand. If doing it by hand, a flat end of a rolling pin comes in handy when pounding the meat into a purée. Or, if you have a large pestle and mortar, that may work too. Wash, blot dry and finely chop the parsley leaves and fine stems. Add to the bowl. Sprinkle the cognac evenly over the meat mixture. Break half of the unsalted butter into chunks and dollop over the meat. Pulse chop in the food processor to bring everything together. If you are using a food processor, make sure you do not purée the mixture. The end result, whatever method you choose to use, should be that of a very coarse pâté or finely chopped meat. Taste for seasoning, adding a little more salt or butter depending on how lean your goose was to start with.

Pack the mixture into 6 small ramekins or into one larger ceramic dish.

To make the clarified butter, melt the remaining half of the butter over low heat. Simmer for a minute. Then, strain through a damp muslin cloth: the idea is to remove the white milky solids. Once you're left with a just-clear, yellowy liquid, pour it over the rillettes.

The rillettes will keep in the refrigerator for up to 1 week.

Opposite The latest hatch

NORTHFIELD FARM

Jan McCourt *Cold Overton, Rutland*

My first reaction to Jan was simply that I liked him: my second, a feeling of admiration for the way he has pulled his life together after two serious setbacks. As I write, he is in hospital after a third, which is perhaps too dreadful to call a mere setback: he has been run over by his tractor. Years ago, the same thing happened to a cheesemaker called Doug Campbell. Taking the cup to be half full rather than half empty – well, he's lucky to be alive and with every hope of a complete recovery.

When Jan bought Northfield, twelve years ago, he was an investment banker in the City. His plan had been to continue in the City for at least another ten years: in the event, he lost his job in three. He made no attempt to find another because, as he said, he wanted never again to be at other people's beck and call. Instead, he decided to follow his heart and produce rare breed meat in a traditional, sustainable way. It was 1997, when BSE was raging, which to him seemed the perfect moment to start a business of this kind. His watchword was responsibility. 'I wanted to say to everyone, "You should take responsibility for what you eat."' He isn't registered as organic, feeling that the word has been hijacked, but never uses chemical sprays or fertilizers on his land.

To start with, he stocked his farm with a small herd of Dexter cattle, a flock of Grey-faced Dartmouth sheep, and Gloucester Old Spot pigs. No BSE had ever been reported in a Dexter herd and he particularly likes the taste of the beef. In his view (which doesn't agree with that of Richard Vines) breed makes a very considerable difference to taste. 'I have customers who definitely prefer some breeds to others, and specify which they want.' He chose the grey-faced sheep because he had been told that they were the most biddable and easiest of all sheep to handle – adding: 'But they need to be shorn early because they get flies in their fleeces.'

He first went to Borough in 1999 and frankly acknowledges that without it, he wouldn't have a farm now. Thanks to him, the same probably applies to many other farmers in the area. Since he doesn't have enough stock to satisfy the Market demand, he also sells the meat of some forty or fifty other producers, who range from people with only two or three animals to fatteners with 400 or 500. All of them rear their meat according to sustainable

Rare breed – a White Park.
Delilah, the Matriarch of the
herd at Northfield Farm

principles. Not all of it is rare breed but he says: 'We have every rare breed coming through at one time or another' (which means that his stall offers a unique opportunity to judge for yourself how far breed affects taste). By now, he himself has added Shorthorn and White Park cattle plus Jacob and Shetland sheep to his stock. The cattle and pigs go to a small slaughterhouse forty to fifty minutes' drive away; the sheep travel only ten miles to Melton Mowbray.

While he was still working in the City, his wife managed the farm; thereafter, they ran it together for some years. Then she left him. Their daughter now lives with her, but they have two sons who have stayed with their father and love living on the farm as much as he does. In her absence, Jan is helped by a loyal team of assistants – whom he will certainly need while he recovers.

The farmyard is decorated with neatly trimmed bay trees in pots. On the day we went there was an energetic Dexter bull in one of the barns 'because we want to give the cows a rest'. Another barn has been transformed into an immaculate shop selling gammon, bacon, sausages, burgers, salt brisket, and jellied shin of beef, all produced on the farm by two or three chefs, plus cheese, chutney, local free-range eggs, and a selection of puddings made by the egg producer. Besides the shop and Borough (where he only sells meat) Jan supplies Roast at Borough and Tom Aikens, plus Hambleton Hall, which is nearby, and a number of other local restaurants.

Does it pay? 'Not really… But it's a passion.'

Opposite Dexters at Cold Overton, Rutland

Left Brendan Maguire, Northfield Farm stand, Borough Market

PORK FILLET MEDALLIONS WITH MANGO SALSA AND WATERCRESS SALAD

This main course salad is equally good with pork chops on the bone. To use pork chops instead of fillet, prepare as directed below. However, cook the pork chops by first browning on one side in an oven-proof frying pan, flip over and transfer to a preheated 180°C / 350°F / gas 5 oven and continue cooking for 18–20 minutes. Serve with mango salad as below. [SLB]

Preparation time 25 minutes

Cooking time 4 minutes

Serves 2

Season English watercress is at its best in May

350g pork fillet
Flour for dusting
85g fresh breadcrumbs
1 egg
1 bunch watercress
15g fresh coriander
½ jalapeno chilli
1 mango
1 small red onion
1 lime
2 tblsp olive oil plus more for frying
2 tsp toasted sesame seeds

Begin by preparing the pork. Cut the fillet into 6 slices. Place the slices in between two pieces of parchment paper. Gently bash the pork with a rolling pin to about 1cm thickness making sure to keep an even 1cm thickness all the way across the fillet piece.

Lightly beat the egg in a small bowl to break up the yolk. Place the flour and breadcrumbs on separate plates nearby. Dredge the pork in flour and then pat it to shake off the excess. Dip the floured pork into the egg and then into the breadcrumbs. Place on a plate and continue with the remaining pieces. Refrigerate until ready to cook. If the pork is left at this stage for 30 minutes in the refrigerator, the breadcrumbs will have enough time to be softened by the beaten egg coating thus resulting in a more crispy crust when cooked.

Begin preparing the salsa by washing the watercress, coriander and chilli. Blot dry with a kitchen towel. Peel and core the mango and cut into fine dice. The core of the mango is thin and wide so it is easiest to cut off the mango 'cheeks' then use your knife to detach any side pieces. Peel off the skin of the onion and finely dice. Cut the chilli in half and remove all the seeds and any white ribs. Finely chop the chilli and coriander leaves and combine with the mango and onion in a small bowl. Squeeze the lime and fold the juice into the mango mixture along with the olive oil. Season well with salt and pepper. Set the salsa aside, along with the watercress, until ready to serve.

Heat a frying pan over a medium-high flame. Pour the oil into the pan and swirl to coat the bottom. Gently lower in three of the pork medallions and cook for 2 minutes on each side. While the pork is cooking, divide the watercress between two plates. Arrange the cooked pork medallions over the cress and top with a few spoonfuls of mango salsa. Sprinkle with sesame seeds and serve.

LAMB LOIN CHOPS WITH BASIL AND ANCHOVY BUTTER

This is quick, utterly simple, and I suppose obvious — but nonetheless a winner. It's a very good way of serving rare breed meat because the flavoured butter can be served on the side rather than on top of the chop so that the diner has the option of tasting the meat by itself. The perfect accompaniments to it are new potatoes and peas, both of which go as well with the butter as the lamb itself. [SF]

Preparation time 20 minutes,
   plus optional chilling time for the butter

Cooking time 8–14 minutes

Serves 2

Season Lamb is in season from May until December

1 large garlic clove
20 fresh basil leaves
4 anchovy fillets
25 g unsalted butter
4 lamb loin chops
Sea salt
Freshly ground black pepper

Peel and finely chop the garlic. Place in a mortar. Wash, blot, dry and shred the basil leaves into small pieces. Put them into the mortar with the anchovy fillets (roughly chop before adding) and a tsp of the butter. Crush to a rough paste, adding the rest of the butter as you go. Store until needed in the refrigerator.

Set your oven to 200 °C / 400 °F / gas 6

Season the chops lightly with salt and coarsely ground pepper. Grill for 4–7 minutes on each side, until well browned on top but still pink in the middle: if you insert a knife into the meat, it will be cooked to this point when a little pink liquid emerges.

Serve at once with the chilled butter on the side.

Lamb

GRILLED BUTTERFLIED LEG OF LAMB WITH LEMON, DILL AND GARLIC

Butterflied leg of lamb can sometimes get a little unwieldy. To secure loose flaps of meat, run two long metal skewers lengthwise and two skewers crosswise through the leg, bunching the meat together. Securing the lamb this way will also help it cook more evenly. Here the lamb is cooked in a hot oven. But, it is even more delicious cooked on a barbecue. For outdoor cooking, give it 15–20 minutes per side, depending on the thickness. [SLB]

Preparation time 15 minutes,
   plus minimum 1 hour marinating
   (best if allowed 24 hours)

Cooking time 30 minutes,
   plus 15 minutes resting time

Serves 8

Season Lamb is in season from May
   until December

---

8 garlic cloves
1 tsp sea salt
2 tblsp dried dill
1 tsp freshly ground black pepper
Juice from 1 lemon
3 tblsp olive oil
1 x 3·2 kg leg of lamb, trimmed of all fat,
   boned, and butterflied by butcher
   (about 1·75 kg without bones)

Preheat the oven to 220 °C / 425 °F / gas 7.

Peel and crush the garlic in a mortar with the salt. Add the dried dill and black pepper, stirring to work into a paste. Juice the lemon and pour in along with the olive oil.

Put the lamb in a large glass or ceramic dish and with tip of a sharp small knife held at a 45 degree angle cut 1·5 cm–deep slits all over it, rubbing the herb mixture into the slits and all over the surface. Allow to marinate for at least 1 hour at room temperature or up to 48 hours in the refrigerator.

When ready to cook, place the lamb in a roasting pan and set in the middle of a preheated oven for about 30 minutes, or until an instant-read thermometer horizontally inserted into the meat registers 57 °C / 135 °F for medium rare. Remember the internal temperature of lamb continues to increase upon resting. So, if you like it on the pink side, remove it just before it is cooked to the point you want. Transfer the lamb to a cutting board. Let stand, loosely covered with foil, for 15 minutes. Cut it into slices and serve with any juices that have accumulated on cutting board.

Cook's note To serve this to a crowd, cube the lamb and arrange as kebabs for the barbecue. Preheat the barbecue to hot and brown the meat on all sides after which time the lamb will be perfectly cooked on the outside and pink and juicy on the inside.

Lamb

LAMB MEATBALLS BRAISED IN A SAFFRON TOMATO SPINACH BROTH

I love the simplicity of this recipe. I know, there is a lot of 'to-ing and fro-ing' with the chickpeas and with the browning of the meatballs. Although, the simplicity here comes from the few classic ingredients given time to develop and enhance one another. Please use dried chickpeas instead of drained tinned ones, as well as good bread. A French white sourdough had to be my favourite but a good quality stick worked well too. In a recipe where simplicity is paramount quality of ingredients should be your highest priority. We choose barley couscous to absorb all the sweet onion saffron tomato juices but leftover meatball-making bread functioned well as a 'mop' wiping the bowls clean! [SLB]

Preparation time Soaking the chickpeas overnight, 1 hour 15 minutes

Cooking time 1½ hours

Serves 4

Season Lamb is in season from May until December

125 g dried chickpeas
2 slices white bread
4 tblsp whole milk
2 garlic cloves
Sea salt
Freshly ground black pepper
1 medium egg (separated)
300 g minced lamb
15 g fresh parsley
Extra virgin olive oil
1 large onion
3 tblsp tomato purée
Pinch of saffron (0·4 g)
225 g fresh spinach

Place chickpeas in a large pot. Cover with water and soak overnight.

Drain the chickpeas and return them to the pot and cover with fresh water. Cook for 45 minutes, until they are partially cooked. Set a heat-proof bowl and a sieve in the sink. Drain the chickpeas through the sieve and reserve the cooking water. Set both the chickpeas and cooking water aside separately. By saving the chickpea water you will add body to the finished broth that is hard to achieve with water alone. However, saying that, if you do forget and discard the cooking water all is not lost. Continue the recipe as directed.

Remove the crusts from the bread. In a medium-sized bowl, soak the bread in milk for 10 minutes. Peel and crush the garlic with a pinch of salt in a mortar. Wash and finely chop the parsley. Add the garlic, along with the lamb, parsley and egg yolk to the bread. Use your hands to distribute the ingredients evenly. With oiled palms, roll the mince mixture into small balls. Place on a baking tray and refrigerate for half an hour until firm.

After half an hour, remove the meatballs from the refrigerator and brown them in a frying pan with a little olive oil. Set aside.

Heat 1 tblsp of olive oil in a large casserole dish over a low flame. Peel and finely dice the onion. Add to the casserole and cook without browning for about 5 minutes. Add the tomato purée and pour over 480 ml of the reserved chickpea cooking water and crumble the saffron over the top.

Gently lower in the meatballs and the partially cooked chickpeas into the pot. Cover with a tight fitting lid and simmer for 30 minutes.

Wash, drain and dry the spinach thoroughly and set aside. After the chickpeas and meatballs have been cooking for 30 minutes, remove the lid of the casserole and place the spinach on the top. Return the lid and allow the steam to wilt the spinach. Serve with barley couscous or crusty bread to soak up the cooking juices.

LITTLE LAMB SHANK PIES WITH PARMESAN PASTRY

Everyone feels special when a dish has been prepared as an individual serving – a little present just for them. Individual pies are the perfect 'presents' as there is the true element of surprise as to what lies beneath the rich pastry. Although in this recipe the protruding lamb shank bone (which also acts as a vent in the pastry) provides a clue, curiosity will still take over when you place these parcels in front of your guests. There will most certainly be a moment or two of silence which will rapidly be replaced with a low 'umm' as the first bite goes into their mouths. Both the lamb shanks and pastry can be made in advance. Once both components are well chilled they can be assembled ahead of time which makes them particularly suited to entertaining. Here, I have put them together in individual portions, however the below recipe works equally well in one large soufflé dish or individual French onion soup bowls. [SLB]

Preparation time 45 minutes

Cooking time 2 hours 25 minutes

Serves 4

Season Lamb is in season from May until December

Lamb

FILLING

1 tblsp olive oil
4 lamb shanks, preferably the larger hind
    shanks but smaller fore shanks will do
2 medium onions
2 large carrots
½ small celeriac
4 garlic cloves
3 sprigs fresh rosemary
480 ml chicken stock,
    homemade or store bought
600 ml red wine, preferably a
    Grenache/Shiraz blend
1 tblsp plain flour
1 tblsp unsalted butter, softened
Sea salt
Freshly ground black pepper

PARMESAN SHORTCRUST PASTRY

30 g Parmesan cheese
90 g cold butter
250 g plain flour
3 medium eggs
1 tsp white wine vinegar
2–4 tblsp cold water

Preheat the oven to 170 °C / 325 °F / gas 3.

Begin by heating the olive oil in a large casserole which can accommodate all the lamb shanks comfortably. Brown each lamb shank on all sides and transfer to a plate. Keep the residual oil and fat in the dish.

While the lamb shanks are browning, wash and peel the onions, carrots and celeriac and cut each into a small, equal-sized dice about 1cm in size. Add all the aromatic vegetables to the casserole, cover with a lid and allow to sweat for about 4 minutes – the moisture will exude out from the vegetables, which will help to loosen any brown bits stuck to the bottom.

Whilst the vegetables are cooking, peel and work the garlic into a fine paste with a little salt in a mortar. Wash and remove the leaves from rosemary and run your knife over them, roughly chopping and bruising them slightly.

Once the vegetables have softened, add the garlic and rosemary. Give the whole mix a good stir, allowing the garlic and rosemary to fry gently. Pour over the stock and bring the mixture to a boil. Using a wooden spoon, scrape up any bits that are still stuck to the bottom of the casserole and incorporate into the mixture. Reduce the stock by half before adding the wine. Season well with salt and pepper.

Return the lamb shanks into the casserole. Place a circular piece of parchment paper directly over the lamb shanks before covering with a tight-fitting lid. Place into a preheated oven and cook for 2 hours. In a small bowl, work the flour and butter into a paste and set aside for use later.

While the lamb is cooking, make the pastry. Finely grate the Parmesan and place it in a large bowl, along with the butter which has been cut into small cubes. Sift the flour into the bowl. Using your fingers work the flour into the butter, lifting the mixture as you work. Continue rubbing the mixture together until it resembles coarse breadcrumbs. Separate two of the eggs and lightly whisk the eggs yolks with the vinegar and 2 tblsp of water. Drizzle over the dough and gently work the mixture into a firm ball.

Cook's note The dough must not be too dry or it will be difficult to roll out. Wrap in cling film and refrigerate the dough for at least 30 minutes.

After two hours, check on the lamb. Remove the shanks from the casserole and set aside to cool. Add the flour-butter paste to the pot, bring to a boil and cook until the mixture reduces and thickens, about 3–4 minutes. Taste for seasoning and adjust as necessary. Remove from the heat and allow to cool.

Increase the oven temperature to 180°C / 350°F / gas 4.

Place each lamb shank into individual, oven-ready dishes. I like to use large, deep ramekins which could hold about 350 ml liquid, but dishes that are a little larger will do – you just want to make sure you have enough space for the shank, some vegetables and sauce. Spoon in some vegetables around the shank and underneath if there is room. Divide the sauce between the ramekins. Depending on how much the sauce reduced, you may have some left over.

Remove the pastry from the refrigerator and roll it out to about 7 mm thickness. Cut into circles large enough to cover each pie-cooking vessel. Cut a hole/slit for the shank bone. In a small bowl lightly beat the remaining egg. Brush one side of the pastry with egg and place the pastry egg-side-down over the shank bone. Gently press the pastry onto the edge of the cooking vessel to secure. Brush the top of the secured pastry with some of the remaining egg. Place in the preheated oven and cook for 20 minutes or until the pastry is golden brown.

CASEROLED BEEF PROVENÇAL

You may look at the recipe below and think there is a typo with the amount of wine — there isn't. Traditionally, Italians would separate the cooked meat from the braising liquid and serve the liquid as a sauce for a pasta first course possibly tossed with some wilted cavolo nero and shavings of pecorino or dollops of fresh ricotta. You find this style of cooking in Spain as well, with braised oxtails being pulverised into a coarse pâté and the cooking broth being served as a consommé tapa. Yet, however you choose to serve this dish, I can assure you it will be delicious. Have your butcher cut up the unsmoked bacon into lardons, or do it yourself, using a good, sharp pair of kitchen scissors. [SLB]

Preparation time 1 hour,
  plus minimum of 2 hours marinating

Cooking time 3 hours

Serves 6–8

Season All ingredients available year-round

---

1 head of garlic, plus two extra garlic cloves
6 sprigs thyme
Sea salt
Freshly ground black pepper
1·8–2·2 kg boneless beef chuck roast
120 ml cognac
225 g unsmoked bacon with rind,
  cut into lardons
3 tblsp plain flour
8–10 round shallots, or 4–5 banana shallots
2 carrots
1 celery stick
2 tblsp tomato purée
1 bottle red wine, a fruity Grenache-Shiraz
  blend works well
4 sprigs parsley
1 strip of orange zest
2 bay leaves
1 tblsp olive oil

Begin by washing and drying your fresh herbs and aromatic vegetables. Peel and crush the two garlic cloves in a mortar. Remove the leaves from three sprigs of thyme and add, along with a level tsp of sea salt and about a ½ tsp of freshly ground black pepper, to the mortar. Stir to combine and to gently bruise the thyme leaves to release their flavour. Set aside.

Place the beef in a large glass or ceramic dish and drizzle over the cognac. Rub the thyme/garlic mixture into the flesh. Cover and marinate the beef for at least 2 hours, in the refrigerator but preferably overnight.

When ready to cook remove the meat from the refrigerator so as to allow its internal temperature to rise to a cool room temperature before cooking. Preheat the oven to 150°C / 300°F / gas 2.

Using good sharp kitchen scissors, cut up the bacon (if your butcher hasn't already done it for you). Transfer to a casserole with a tight-fitting lid large enough to fit the entire roast. Drizzle with a teaspoon of olive oil and fry the bacon. Remove the bacon once it is slightly browned around the edges and transfer to a plate lined with kitchen paper.

Lift the beef from the dish. Reserve any residual cognac. Lightly coat the beef in the flour and gently lower it into the casserole with the bacon drippings. Brown on all sides. Using tongs and a fork, lift the beef from the casserole and transfer to a dinner plate while you prepare the rest of the ingredients. If there is a large amount of fat on the bottom, use a large, flat spoon to scoop some of it out – you want about 2 tblsp or enough to coat the bottom of the casserole in a thin layer.

Put the whole shallots (skins and all) in a bowl and cover with boiling water – this will make it easier to peel them. Leave them whole whilst you peel and chop the carrots and slice the celery. Then, peel the shallots but don't slice them. Place in the casserole along with the carrots and celery. Cover, reduce the heat to low, and cook for 5 minutes or until the vegetables have softened in the bacon fat and beef drippings.

Add the tomato purée and gently stir for a minute to caramelise and concentrate its flavour. Pour in the red wine with any remaining brandy from the marinade and bring the entire mixture up to a rolling boil. Cook to reduce the wine by a third, this should take about 15 minutes.

While the wine is reducing, tie the remaining three sprigs of thyme together with the parsley, orange zest and bay leaves with some kitchen twine. Add the herb bundle to the casserole. Slice the top off the head of garlic to expose the cloves. Gently lower the browned beef and the bacon lardons into the braising liquid and tuck in the head of garlic, making sure the cloves are covered with the liquid.

Cut a piece of parchment paper slightly larger than the circumference of the casserole. Cover the casserole with the parchment and place the lid on top of the parchment-covered casserole and press to secure the lid in place. This will help ensure that no steam can escape from under the lid whilst cooking. Cook in the preheated oven for 2 hours. Start checking the meat after 1½ hours. When poked with a fork, the meat should be tender but not falling apart. Once cooked, the casserole at this point will keep in the refrigerator for 2–3 days.

Cook's note In addition to the vast quantity of wine used in this recipe, it was also traditional to include a pigs trotter. Visually for some, this may be a difficult hurdle to overcome. Yet, I promise you it is well worth the effort. Have the butcher cut the trotter in half lengthwise. When you add the beef back and bacon back to the pot tuck in both halves of the pigs trotter. The collagen from the trotter will give a luscious viscosity to the sauce. If you are feeling brave, when cooked remove the trotter from the casserole and flake the meat from inside the cut trotter back into the wine sauce before serving for an unbelievably delicious depth of flavour (and texture) in the finished dish.

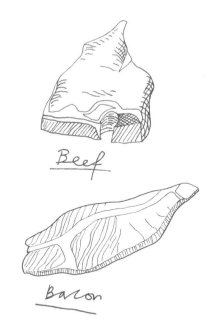

Beef

Bacon

INSIDE-OUT BEEF BURGERS

There is one thing I miss from my home in *America* and that is my parents' hamburgers cooked on the barbecue. They would choose a well-aged blade steak and have it minced, twice, by the butcher to order. It was then shaped by hand into thick patties and refrigerated before cooking, which allowed the meat to relax. Their only addition would be some salt and pepper. Seasoning meat, either before or after cooking, will bring on a heated discussion amongst chefs. I prefer seasoning throughout cooking so that the end result is mature, developed and well-rounded.

Below is another addition I have experimented with: compound butters. Now, I'm not brazen enough to think that this is an improvement on my parents' recipe: it's only an option. The 'inside-out' name is derived from the cooking process. Sometimes meat is basted with some sort of marinade while cooking. Here the burgers are self-basting. The butter is nestled in the centre of the burger during shaping. When cooking, the butter (and any flavours included in the butter) melts and bastes the burger from the inside-out, resulting in an exceptionally juicy burger. The butter recipes make more than you need for one batch of burgers, but they are great to have on hand. Wrap in parchment paper and shape into a log twisting the ends like a giant Christmas cracker. Put into the freezer and pull out at your next barbecue.

Here, in Britain, butter mince with at least 15 percent marbling is what I look for when making hamburgers. The percentage of fat may be high in some eyes, but is necessary. Cooking over a medium high heat will allow the fat to melt slowly throughout the cooking process, resulting in a tender interior enclosed within a crisp crust. With so few ingredients freshness of all the components is paramount. My mother wouldn't even think about not having a slice of mature sharp cheddar over the top, whilst my dad opted for the strict meat with salad, yet another heated discussion best left for another day! [SLB]

Preparation time 15 minutes

Cooking time 8–10 minutes

Serves 4

Season All ingredients available year-round, but best on a barbecue in the summer

BUTTERS
Rocket and goat cheese
115 g unsalted butter
115 g soft, fresh goat cheese
200 g or two large handfuls fresh rocket
Sea salt
Freshly ground black pepper

Stilton, fig and port
115 g unsalted butter
115 g Stilton
3 tblsp port
4 large figs
Sea salt
Freshly ground black pepper

Garlic and herb
115 g unsalted butter
1 large shallot, peeled
1 tblsp Dijon mustard
2 large garlic cloves
1 tblsp white wine (if you have a bottle open)
Leaves from 3 sprigs each parsley and thyme
Leaves from 1 sprig rosemary
Sea salt
Freshly ground black pepper

Lemon, anchovy, caper and tomato
10 semi-dried tomatoes
115 g unsalted butter
5 anchovies
1 tblsp capers, rinsed
1 tsp lemon juice
Zest of 1 lemon

For each of the butters, wash and dry all herbs. Blitz the ingredients in the bowl of a food processor. Spoon the mixture onto a piece of parchment and roughly shape into a log. Roll up and twist the ends in opposite directions so it looks like a Christmas cracker. Freeze until firm and slice off as necessary. If you don't have a food processor, all the butters can be mixed together by hand. However, remember to finely chop all components before folding into the softened butter.

BURGERS

700 g 'butter' mince
   (or combination of ground sirloin/chuck)
8 thick slices of wholewheat sourdough
   bread
4 slices of prepared flavoured butter of your
   choice, cut 7mm in thickness
Sea salt
Freshly ground black pepper
Extra virgin olive oil

OPTIONAL TOPPINGS

Tomatoes, thinly sliced red onion, lettuce, aioli, Dijon mustard or tomato chutney (see page 97)

Beef

Begin by setting up the barbecue for direct grilling, or preheat gas or electric grills to high.

Place both types of mince (if not getting 'butter' mince from the butcher) in a large mixing bowl, break up with a wooden spoon and combine thoroughly. Season well with salt and pepper: I usually use a level tsp of sea salt and then grind over about ½ tsp pepper. Avoid mixing the meat with your hands because your fingers will warm it. Wet your hands with cold water and divide the meat into 8 equal portions. Working quickly and with a light touch, pat each portion into a 0·5 cm-thick square-ish patty. Place a slice of butter on to the top of four of the patties. Top each with the remaining patties and seal the meat around the butter.

When ready to cook, brush each burger with olive oil and place on the rack. Cook according to taste, about 3 to 4 minutes per side for medium-rare. To see if it is ready, you can insert an instant-read meat thermometer through the side of a burger into the centre. The internal temperature should be about 63 °C / 145 °F for medium-rare. Only use a thermometer as a last resort, as once you pierce the meat, lots of the buttery juice will flow out.

Meanwhile, place the bread slices on the hot rack and grill until lightly toasted, 1 to 2 minutes per side. Arrange whatever deliciously crisp optional toppings you have chosen onto the bread and top with a hot juicy burger. Cover with another piece of lightly toasted bread and enjoy!

WYNDHAM HOUSE POULTRY

Lee Mullet *Stoney Street, Borough Market*
Nick & Chris Frederick *Temple Farm, Roydon, Essex*

The answer to the oft asked riddle 'which came first the chicken or the egg?' is undeniably the chicken when talking to Lee Mullet of Wyndham House Poultry. His shop facing the market in Stoney Street, sells a remarkably wide range of poultry and game including 'Label Anglais' chickens from Temple Farm in Essex, organic chickens from Springfield Farm in Hertfordshire, Barbary and Gressingham ducks, bronze turkeys for Christmas, and grouse, woodcock, partridges, pigeons, snipe and teal.

The market was a lifeline for Lee. After working for 20 years in the intensive chicken farming business he decided there had to be a better way to raise chickens. His path crossed with Chris Fredericks of Temple Farm who was wholesaling seasonal turkeys and experimenting with a continental breed of chicken. Chris and Lee worked together on the 'Label Anglais' and started in Borough on a stall down the Middle Road. On their first weekend they took £120. Today Lee has shops in Chelsea and Pimlico in addition to the Stoney Street shop he opened in 2002. Lee says: 'Borough has been critical and has provided the platform for expanding reach and availability. We try to provide an education to our customers about quality produced chicken. We started with whole 'Label Anglais', but ever mindful of our customers needs we now provide a broad range of everything poultry.'

For me, visiting Temple Farm turned out to be a trip down memory lane. My family lived a short drive away from their farm, in a part of Hertfordshire where, as in this corner of Essex, the Green Belt round London is still rigorously upheld. I pray that despite the need for new homes it may ever remain so. The countryside isn't spectacular nor even especially pretty, but pleasant and intimate, with small hills, secret pockets of woodland, and delightful place-names (Ugley, Mark Tey, Stanstead Abbots).

The farm isn't spectacular either but must surely come pretty close to chicken heaven. The birds are extremely free-range, with large fields in which to roam, peck for worms, or simply sit sunning themselves. To an outside observer like myself there seemed an awful lot of them, but by commercial standards there are very few: the Fredericks keep 25,000, split into hen-houses holding 800–900 each, in comparison to 50,000–100,000 on commercial farms. The condition of the land is maintained by moving the

Opposite The River Lea at Roydon, Essex

Chris Frederick

houses around the field and to a fresh field every year. Also, as slow-growing breeds, the chickens they rear enjoy not only an excellent standard of life but considerably more of it than usual having the same growth rate as sixty years ago, and are sold at 14 weeks. Ninety-nine per cent of birds for the table in Britain are Ross Cobs, who reach slaughter-weight in six weeks.

Most of them are an old-fashioned, chestnut-coloured breed called Cornish Red; the rest are a slightly more commercial, bigger-breasted white Cornish Red cross. Both are unique to Temple Farm in this country. Ironically, Chris and Nick found the Cornish breed on the Continent: this was an influence on the name 'Label Anglais', but the main reason was simply that it sounds more interesting than 'English Chicken' (though 'Cornish Chicken' has a certain ring). The white crosses are sold as 'Special Reserves'.

The full-bred Cornish Reds or 'Label Anglais' birds have a pronounced, distinctive flavour and firm but exceptionally succulent flesh, with a layer of golden fat under the breast which gives a deliciously crisp skin. Gordon Ramsay uses them in most of his restaurants, while Heston Blumenthal favours Special Reserves at his famously experimental restaurant, The Fat Duck at Bray – where lucky Chris was going for lunch the next day.

Like most others (all others, if one goes back far enough), Temple Farm was originally mixed. Nick and Chris's father started out with arable crops, sheep, ordinary farmyard hens and turkeys. Rearing bronze turkeys for Christmas, mainly Kellys, was the Fredericks' first speciality, the bronze variety was long out of fashion (because people were thought to prefer their turkeys with perfectly white skin). After forty-odd years of experience with turkeys (not that he is as old as this suggests, since he was only ten when his father started keeping them), Chris understands them better than chickens and, it seemed to me, rather prefers them: 'They'll follow a car if it comes, or a photographer, whereas chickens just run away!' I didn't see the turkeys because, like geese, they're seasonal and I visited the farm before the chicks had arrived. As you can see, however, by the time George took his photographs, they were very much in evidence.

Clearly Lee and Chris are doing something right, staff at the shops has increased from three to 35. And as for which came first, if you now walk down the Middle Road you can find eggs as well as chickens, and sizzling hot chicken-burgers straight from the griddle-plate on Lee's market stall where it all began, (if you don't know how to find it, just follow the delicious smell).

POULTRY PREPARATION

Boning, butterflying and carving poultry well takes practice. It is not hard to do but requires a sharp knife and some attention. The following steps may seem complicated, but learning to de-bone your poultry will not only save you money over buying pre-boned cuts, but it is also immensely rewarding in the cooking process.

To bone or butterfly poultry

The first step to boning a chicken is to remove the wishbone. This is the upside-down V shaped bone at the top of the breastbone and bottom of where the neck should be. This will make for easier removal of the breasts later on. Work with one side of the chicken at a time. Flip the bird over and carefully cut through the skin from the back of the neck down, tracing around the thigh. With the tip of your knife, make small cuts to remove the meat from the bone, gently scraping the bone as you go. Use your fingers to help loosen and pull the meat off the bone so that you can see what you are doing.

Then, use your knife to cut through the hip socket to expose the top side of the thigh. Begin to cut the breast meat away from the rib cage as well. Cut the breast meat away from the bone with long strokes of your knife, going over the ribcage until you get to the breastbone and the chicken tenderloin. Continue up to this stage with the other side of the bird.

At this stage your chicken carcass should be sticking up off your cutting board with breast meat and legs on either side. From here, carefully carve the breast meat off the breastbone.

Then remove the bone from the legs. To do this, follow the fat lines, which are creamy white lines in the leg meat. There should be one along the length of the thigh, one separating the thigh from the drumstick and another down the length of the drumstick. This will expose the leg bones and make for slightly easier bone removal.

Now you should have a completely boned chicken all in one piece. With a little practice this becomes much easier and will take about 15 minutes preparation time.

To carve poultry

Turn the chicken so the head section with the two wings on either side is facing you. Firstly remove the wings. Grab hold of a wing with one hand and hold your knife in the other. Place the blade about an inch into the breast meat attached to the wing you are holding. Insert, and cut down through the shoulder joint. This will leave a little breast meat on the wing. Repeat with the other wing.

Secondly, remove the legs. Keep the head section of the bird facing you. Cut through the skin to separate the drumstick from the breast. Grab a hold of the drumstick with one hand and with your knife in the other begin to cut down around the newly exposed thigh meat until you see the hip joint.

Pop the hip joint by pressing down on the leg and cut through the joint. Cutting down towards the backside, making sure you include the 'oyster' muscle at the top of the leg joint. From the oyster muscle release the bottom side of the thigh which is attached to the backbone and release the leg. Repeat with the other leg.

Thirdly, remove the breast meat. Turn the bird so the open cavity is facing you. Spread the skin taught over the breastbone with one hand. Holding a sharp knife with the other hand, cut through the skin, down alongside the breast-bone. You will hit the ribcage. With shallow long strokes cut the meat away from the rib-cage. By holding the bird in this manner you will work with the direction of the flesh and ribcage which makes for easier and cleaner breast meat removal.

Use the wishbone at the other end to guide your cuts. As you make the cuts, use your other hand to pull the breast meat gently away from the carcass.

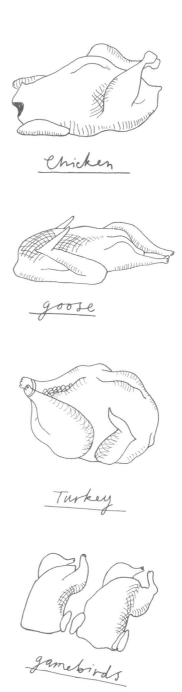

Chicken

goose

Turkey

gamebirds

CHRISTMAS TURKEY WITH CHESTNUT AND SAUSAGE-MEAT STUFFING

If you want to be conventional and serve a turkey at Christmas, Wyndham House can supply among the best you'll find. I cooked a twenty-four-week-old bronze one (a supermarket bird would be twelve to fourteen weeks) reared by Stephen Childerhouse at Whew's Farm, Attleborough, Norfolk, where the turkeys spend their time foraging in a wood. Bronze turkeys are a cross between the usual white ones bred to have large breasts and the old-fashioned, small-breasted Norfolk Blacks. They were first developed by Paul Kelly in Essex to combine the best of both, ie the flavour of the Norfolks with the plenteous breast-meat of the white breed. And they do: they have lots of breast (though the legs taste better) and a truly turkey-like, nutty, distinctively gamy flavour. I can't compare them directly with the original Norfolk Blacks because I haven't tried one: Wyndham House stocks them, not from Stephen but another Norfolk producer, James Graham, who also raises rare-breed Bourbon Reds.

Just as Christmas cake isn't Christmas cake without the icing, so the trimmings are an integral part of the Christmas turkey. As Christmas comes but once a year, I don't see the need to be original and am giving the recipe for the stuffing which has been our family favourite over the years. However, whereas once we used to spend nail-breaking hours peeling fresh chestnuts, I can now recommend ready-roasted vacuum-packed or tinned ones. As for the gravy, I've dubbed it 'Lazy' because you don't need to fry anything but can put all the ingredients straight into the pan to simmer. The result is deliciously rich and full-flavoured.

The stuffing can be made on Christmas Eve. You also need to leave the milk for bread sauce to infuse for 24 hours. The traditional vegetable to serve with the turkey is Brussels sprouts: if they're small and there are a lot of you, it's not a bad idea to peel them in advance too (just for once: in general, it isn't recommended because they leach nutrients). You can cook them while the turkey rests. [SF]

Preparation time Excluding stuffing and bread sauce but including potatoes and gravy, 20 minutes or more according to the number of potatoes

Cooking time 15 minutes per 450 g plus 15–20 minutes' resting time: this means 2½ hours plus 15–20 minutes for a 5 kg turkey

Serves A 5–5·5 kg bird is enough for at least 10 servings

Season 1 December–Christmas

Chestnut and sausage-meat stuffing (see following page)
1 turkey
Butter for rubbing over it
Freshly ground black pepper
Sea salt
As many rashers of lean smoked back bacon as there are diners (optional) plus two for the gravy
140 g (1 medium to smallish) onion
1 smallish carrot
Heart, liver and neck of the turkey
3 allspice berries
6 peppercorns
4 cloves
150 ml (1 small glass) robust red wine such as Cabernet Sauvignon or a Shiraz blend
900 g roasting or floury potatoes per 5–7 people
2 tbsp of olive oil or more as needed
Bread sauce for serving (see page 135)

Opposite Black & White, Bronze Kelly turkeys

STUFFING

Preparation time 15 minutes

Cooking time Outside the turkey, 10 minutes

Small handful parsley
   (enough for 2 tblsp when chopped)
3–4 sprigs thyme
135–140 g (1 medium to small) onion
75 g lean smoked back bacon
1 large unwaxed or organic lemon
200 g tinned or vacuum-packed unsweetened
   roasted chestnuts
3 garlic cloves
15 g unsalted butter
1 tblsp olive oil
300 g sausage-meat
Freshly ground black pepper
120 ml robust red wine, *eg* Cabernet
   Sauvignon or a Shiraz blend

Rinse the herbs and leave them to dry on kitchen paper. Peel and finely dice the onion. Trim off the rind and finely dice the bacon. Wash the lemon; roughly chop the chestnuts. Peel and crush the garlic to a rough paste in a mortar.

Melt the butter in the oil over low heat and fry the onion and bacon for 7 minutes or until soft but not brown, turning often. Add the garlic and fry for another couple of minutes; turn constantly. Remove the pan from the heat and allow the contents to cool.

Finely chop the parsley, including the finer stems, and pull the leaves off the thyme stalks (drag downwards). Put all the prepared ingredients into a bowl with the sausage meat. Grate in the zest of half the lemon, add a gentle seasoning of black pepper, and pour in the wine. Mix very thoroughly. Cover and store in the refrigerator until ready to use.

To cook the turkey

Turn the oven to 220 °C / 425 °F / gas 7.

Wipe the turkey all over, inside and out, with damp kitchen paper. Set the turkey breast upwards, untruss it and wipe it inside and out with kitchen paper. Insert the stuffing at both ends. Rub the outside with a little butter, season it moderately with pepper and very lightly with salt, and place it in a large roasting-tray breast-side down: this helps to ensure that the breast stays moist. Cook it for 30 minutes. Then turn down the oven to 190 °C / 375 °F / gas 5, and cover the bird all over with cooking-foil. Continue to roast it for 1½ hours if it weighs 5 kg or for the rest of its cooking time minus 30 minutes. For the final half hour, turn it breast-side up and remove the foil so that the breast can brown.

If you want to serve bacon rolls with it, trim the rind from as many rashers of bacon as there are diners, roll them up, and thread them loosely on a long skewer. Put them into the roasting tray with the turkey when the bird has 15 minutes left to cook. When you leave the turkey to rest, set them to finish cooking with the potatoes.

To check that the turkey is fully cooked, stick a skewer as far as it will go into the middle of the breast: if only clear liquid emerges, it's ready. A final precaution is to insert a meat thermometer into the centre of the stuffing. It should register 70 °C / 160 °F or over when inserted for 2 minutes.

To make the gravy

Set the gravy to simmer as soon as you have put the turkey into the oven. To make: dice the remaining two rashers of bacon. Peel and dice the onion; peel and slice the carrot. Chop the heart and liver of the turkey and put all the prepared ingredients plus the neck of the bird into a saucepan with the allspice berries, peppercorns, and cloves. Just cover with water and simmer gently until the turkey is turned breast-side up. If the water runs low, add a little more. After turning the bird, pour in the wine and continue to simmer until you take the turkey (and bacon if you are serving it) out of the roasting tray.

As soon as the turkey is dished up, pour off any fat in the roasting-tray but leave the juices behind. Remove escaped fragments of stuffing or bits of potato and pour the liquor from the saucepan into the tray through a sieve. Use a spoon or spatula to scrape up any juices which have stuck to the bottom. Return the liquor to the pan and boil it over high heat for 3–4 minutes. Taste it to see if any seasoning is needed (it probably won't be), pour it into a jug, and serve.

To cook the potatoes

Peel the potatoes after setting the gravy to simmer and cover them with water until needed. When the turkey has 50 minutes left to cook, cut them into pieces 3–4 cm square. For extra creamy centres, boil them in slightly salted water for two minutes before putting them into the oven.

If your oven is fan-heated, spread a thin film of olive oil over the bottom of a baking tray large enough to take all the chunks of potato in a single layer, preferably without touching, and roll them in the oil so that they are coated all over. Season moderately with salt and pepper if they weren't boiled beforehand (omit salt if they were), and set them to roast on a shelf underneath the turkey. If they aren't browning satisfactorily when you take the turkey out of the oven to rest, turn up the heat to 200 °C / 400 °F / gas 6.

With a non-fan-heated oven, cook as many as will fit round the turkey, rolling them as before in oil or turkey fat (if there is too much fat, however, you should drain off most of it). The rest can be cooked on a shelf underneath and changed over at intervals. If this applies to most of them, set them to roast a little sooner. Let them cook until the turkey is served; if necessary, leave it to rest for a few minutes extra.

Turkey

BARBECUED TURKEY

Turkey is not just for Christmas. In fact, I think it may be my parents' favourite way to feed a crowd at any time of year. My father has taken a liking to cooking turkey on the barbecue — not a boneless breast, but the whole bird! His method of choice allows people with small kitchens to leave their oven free for cooking side dishes and also prevents the kitchen from heating up. During a hot summer this cooking method may come in handy.

Smoking can impart both subtle and robust flavours of wood, tea and spice into a dish, depending on how long it is exposed to the smoke and what is used to create the smoke. Generally fish and meat are smoked and these smoked items pair beautifully with cream, cheese, grains, and natural syrups, like maple syrup. Chinese cookbooks often explain how to convert woks into smokers whilst Indian cooks employ a method called dhungar, which involves setting small bowls of smouldering charcoal inside casseroles of cooking food.

Barbecuing awakens some of the most primitive instincts in all of us. There is something in the combination of man feeding family and friends and an open flame which exudes bravado — this often results in a little backyard competition. For those die-hard barbecue fanatics I've included a number of steps to help with a little neighbourly one-upmanship. But it is worthwhile to note that cooking the turkey on the barbecue with only an orange and a drizzling of sesame oil is pretty hard to beat. Try this recipe with and without both the brine and glaze depending on your timetable (and ambition) to still yield fantastic results. [SLB]

Preparation time 30 minutes

Cooking time 4 hours, plus half an hour for resting, and 24 hours for brining

Serves 9–10 as part of a meal, or 15–20 if making into sandwiches

Season All ingredients available year-round

2 large brown onions
100 g fresh ginger (weighed after peeling)
250 g coarse sea salt
4 large bay leaves
4 whole star anise
12 whole black peppercorns
175 g light brown sugar (a mixture of any brown or white sugar will work too)
One 5 kg turkey, without giblets
1 large unwaxed or organic orange
3 tblsp extra virgin olive oil
2 tblsp toasted sesame oil
180 ml pure maple syrup
120 ml white wine
1 tblsp white wine vinegar
2½ tblsp Dijon mustard
30 g butter

Special equipment
250 g smoke chips, soaked in water 30 minutes and drained
1–3 disposable 23 x 15 cm (approximately) aluminium trays

Peel off the outer brown skin of both the onions and the ginger. Combine in a very large pan with the salt, bay leaves, star anise, peppercorns and brown sugar. Pour over 5 litres of water and bring the mixture up to a simmer, stirring to dissolve salt and sugar. Set aside and allow the brine to cool completely. Wash the turkey by blotting with a damp paper towel. Place the turkey in the brine, pressing to submerge. Chill overnight. If you don't have a pan or a deep pot which can hold the turkey and brine comfortably, it may sound a little crazy but a clean bucket will do quite nicely. Pour the brine over the turkey and cover as best you can with cling film. If you have any brine left over, refrigerate in a small container for another use. I've used this brine on duck breasts (without bones, brine 4 hours) and small chickens (brine 6 hours to overnight) with equal success.

If using a charcoal barbecue: Mound the charcoal in the barbecue and allow it to burn until light grey. Using tongs, carefully divide the hot coals into two piles, one pile at each side of the barbecue. Sprinkle each pile with a teacupful of chips if you are using them. Place an empty aluminium tray between the piles. Position the grill rack about 15 cm above the coals. Open the vents on the barbecue so that the chips smoke and the briquettes burn but do not flame (smoulder).

If using a gas barbecue: Preheat the barbecue with all the burners on high. Turn off the centre burner and reduce the temperature of the outside burners to a medium-low heat. Sprinkle a teacupful of chips in each of two disposable trays and place them over the two remaining lit burners. Place an empty tray over the unlit centre burner. The grill rack should be about 15 cm above the burners.

Remove the turkey from the brine and discard the brine. Blot the turkey dry with kitchen paper. Cut the orange into thick wedges and stuff in the main cavity. Drizzle the olive oil and toasted sesame oil over the turkey and rub into the skin. Set it breast-side up on the barbecue, centred above the empty tray. Cover and start cooking – the whole bird will take about 4 hours to cook through. During this time, ensure the barbecue temperature remains constant. To do this, add six lumps of charcoal (if using a charcoal barbecue) every 30 minutes. Once the new lumps of charcoal have a light ash coating scatter over a few more dampened wood chips over the new coal. After 2½ to 3 hours cooking, check the temperature of the bird by inserting a cooking thermometer into the thickest part of the thigh. The temperature you're after is 70 °C / 160 °F. Make sure not to touch any of the bones when taking the temperature. The juices should run clear when tested. If you don't have a thermometer, use a sharp knife to make an incision where the drumstick is touching the breast. There should be a collection of juices, and as above, when the bird is cooked they will be clear.

While the bird is cooking, place all the remaining ingredients together in a medium-sized saucepan and bring to a simmer. When the turkey has cooked for three hours and has reached the internal temperature of 70°C / 160°F, brush the glaze over the bird and continue cooking for another hour, or until the internal temperature reaches 80 °C / 175 °F. Keep an eye on the turkey and cover any parts of the bird which may be getting too dark with foil. Once cooked, transfer the turkey to a plate and tent with foil. Allow to rest for 25 minutes before carving.

ROAST CHICKEN
WITH ROAST POTATOES
AND BREAD SAUCE

Please don't buy an intensively reared chicken. From the gastronomic point of view, as I've said elsewhere, there's no point. In particular, it's a waste of energy to roast it. A free-range, slow-growing bird such as the Label Anglais Cornish Red, on the other hand, is an illustration of why chicken has been regarded as a delicacy down the centuries. You can cook it in any number of ways but it is also delicious plainly roasted, with no embellishment beyond a hint of rosemary and a dollop of creamy, slightly spiced bread sauce as an accompaniment.

Ever since reading the first edition of Simon Hopkinson's Roast chicken and other stories *(Ebury 1994), I've adopted his method of roasting, by which you put the chicken into a hot oven to start with and then turn down the heat to moderate. This encourages the fat over the breast to run quickly and ensures that the chicken stays moist and succulent.*

The potatoes I've used lately are an organically grown Pembrokeshire variety called Triplo, which have lots of flavour and come out of the oven deliciously crisp on the outside and melting within. Normally, I'd recommend boiling potatoes for a couple of minutes before roasting, but with these there's no need to bother. [SF]

Preparation time 20 minutes

Cooking time 1 hour

Serves 4

Season All ingredients available year-round

800–900 g floury potatoes
2 tblsp olive oil
2 kg Label Anglais chicken
Sea salt
Freshly ground black pepper
Sprig of rosemary
225 g smoked back bacon (about 8 slices)

Set the oven to 220 °C / 425 °F / gas 7.

Peel the potatoes and cut them into pieces 3–4 cm square. Choose a roasting tray large enough to take them in a single layer, cover the bottom with a thin film of oil (you may not need the full 2 tblsp) and roll each potato in it so that it is covered on all sides. Arrange the potatoes over the bottom so that they aren't touching and season them lightly with salt and moderately with pepper.

Wipe the chicken thoroughly with damp kitchen paper and lay it in a baking dish. Rinse the rosemary and stick it into the cavity. Rub the chicken very sparingly with oil, season it moderately over the breast with salt and pepper and put it into the oven with the potatoes. Leave it to cook for 15 minutes. Then turn down the heat to 190 °C / 375 °F / gas 5 and cook it for another 30 minutes. It doesn't need basting: the fat under the skin means that it bastes itself.

While it cooks, trim the rind from the bacon (use scissors) and roll up each rasher. When the 30 minutes is up, set the rolls of bacon round the chicken. Put the chicken back into the oven and cook for another 20 minutes. Check it is cooked through by sticking a skewer or sharp knife into the thickest part of the breast. If no pink liquid emerges it is ready. If necessary, cook for a further few minutes. Then turn off the oven and leave it to rest a final 15 minutes. This can be difficult if people are hungry, but is well worth it, since it allows the meat to settle and enormously improves the texture.

Nick and Chris Frederick advise cutting off the legs before carving the breast because this means that you can roll the breast in the buttery liquid which emerges.

Don't waste the carcass: use it for stock and make soup or risotto (see page 136).

BREAD SAUCE

This is a traditional accompaniment to roast pheasant and roast goose as well as chicken. You could also serve it with grouse or guinea-fowl.

It's important to use cloves from a bottle or package which hasn't been opened long or they will have lost their potency. Similarly, you need a strong onion. The last time I made bread sauce I used an organic onion from Wales which was so pungent that even with the protection of spectacles, my eyes streamed – but the sauce was delicious.

It's much easier to make the breadcrumbs from real bread such as you can buy in the Market than from supermarket bread, which is designed never to dry out and forms soggy lumps when grated. Usually, bought crumbs will have been dried, if not also fried, and won't melt into the milk. Soggy lumps aren't wonderful, but they'll do; fried breadcrumbs won't.

If possible, set the milk to steep 24 hours in advance.

Finely crush the cloves with a pestle and mortar. Peel and finely chop the onion. Bring the milk to a simmer with the cloves and onion and let it simmer slowly for 15 minutes. Take it from the heat, allow it to cool, and leave it in the refrigerator (covered) until the next day, or at least for some hours.

The next day, make the breadcrumbs (they need to be reasonably small but not very fine). About 25 minutes before the chicken is ready to come out of the oven, pour the milk into a smallish saucepan through a sieve. Throw away the onion. Add a fairly generous seasoning of pepper, a little salt and the breadcrumbs. Bring to a simmer and continue to simmer gently for 20 minutes; stirring constantly, especially towards the end when the sauce will be very thick. Just before serving, stir in first the butter and then the cream; finally, grate and stir in the nutmeg. The finished sauce should have the consistency of half-whipped cream.

Preparation time Exclusive of making the breadcrumbs, about 5 minutes to prepare sauce and 24 hours for steeping

Cooking time 15 minutes on the first day and about 20 minutes on the second

Serves 4–6

Season All ingredients available year-round

5–6 cloves
1 medium onion
   (enough for 100 g when chopped)
450 ml whole milk
75 g stale white bread, preferably about 2
   days old, weighed without crust
Sea salt
Freshly ground black pepper
2 tblsp double cream
25 g butter
½ whole nutmeg

chicken

ROAST CHICKEN STOCK

A few people will most certainly disagree with the roasting of chicken bones before making stock but I have found it practical for home cooking as it conserves time and effort whilst developing a fantastic flavour and viscosity which is unparalleled. Making your own stock doesn't take long, is easy to do and you can freeze any surplus.

The intense heat of roasting helps to break down the collagen in the joints and knuckles of the chicken which then meld effortlessly into the stock to create a luscious texture. By removing most of the fat, all the ingredients can be added to the stockpot at once, eliminating the job of standing over a steaming pot for a half hour skimming foaming 'scum' which rises to the surface. Actually, according to Herve Thes, a French gastronomic microbiologist, there is no impurity whatsoever in the foam which rises to the surface of stock. But it is fat-based and when boiled fat eventually breaks down and incorporates into the water it undoubtedly creates a cloudy end-product.

Here I have chosen to match the intense flavour of roasted chicken with sweet onions and plenty of carrots. While these aromatics will bring out the natural sweetness of chicken, the mushrooms (an unusual addition to chicken stock) add depth of flavour and an earthy back-note aroma. [SLB]

Preparation time 15 minutes

Cooking time 30 minutes roasting,
   3 hours simmering

Serves Depending on how rapidly your stock
   boiled during the 3 hours, you should end
   up with about 2 litres of cooked stock at
   the end

Season All ingredients available year-round

1 chicken carcass,
   preferably with leg bones as well
2 onions, paper skin left on
4 carrots
125 g close cap mushrooms,
   preferably chestnut
1 head of garlic
2 celery stalks (preferably leafy)
1 rounded tsp black peppercorns
2 bay leaves
3 cloves
4 sprigs thyme
2 sprigs parsley
4 litres water
Sea salt

Chicken

Pre heat the oven to 180°C / 350°F / gas 4. Roast the chicken carcass until lightly browned and some of the fat has dripped off, about 30 minutes. The carcass from a roasted whole chicken would be perfect. There is no need to re-roast the bones if the chicken has been cooked already as a whole.

While the carcass is roasting wash and prepare the aromatic vegetables and herbs. Cut the onion in half and discard any dirty paper skins. Try to leave at least one undamaged brown papery layer. Trim the tops and bottoms of the carrots and peel. Discard the trimmings and set aside. Wipe the mushrooms to remove any clumps of dirt. Try to avoid washing them. If you have particularly dirty mushrooms blot the dirt off with a damp clean cloth. Rinse and slice off the top of the head of garlic to expose the small cloves. Trim the base of the celery and rinse thoroughly.

Gather your fresh and dried herbs together and keep the leaves of thyme and parsley on their stems.

Remove the carcass from the oven and place in a large saucepan. Add all the prepared aromatics and pour over enough water up to cover the chicken and bring to a boil. Once the liquid is at a rolling boil, reduce the heat to low and simmer for 3 hours – any less and the chicken stock will be dominated in flavour by the aromatics; any more and it will taste slightly bitter. Season well with salt; I usually add about one and a half level teaspoons, but season to your own taste.

Leave the stock to cool to room temperature; then strain through a fine sieve. Cover with cling film and chill overnight in the refrigerator or until ready to use. Once thoroughly cold I usually portion out the stock into small plastic containers and put them in the freezer.

CHICKEN WITH WILD BOAR PANCETTA AND PERRY

This recipe brings together key ingredients from three of my favourite Borough Market traders: Wyndham, Sillfield Farm and New Forest Cider. Here I have braised chicken in a lightly reduced perry broth which is complemented by a full-flavoured wild boar pancetta. A few herbs scattered over the top and steamed vegetables round out a quintessentially early autumn meal; one which will certainly fend off an approaching winter chill.

Thus far we haven't mentioned New Forest Cider, but their stall is well worth a visit. Perry is a type of cider made with pears rather than apples. When cooked and reduced, it has a more mild fruity taste which is less sweet than even the driest of ciders. It is becoming a rarity, with many orchards being replaced or replanted with apples. Some of you might disregard this recipe as you may not like cider. But I urge you to re-consider as New Forest Cider is in a class of its own. Their cider is made from real fruit juice, not from concentrate. Their cider and perry are dry and crisp with minimal carbonation, unlike commercial brands. The people behind New Forest Cider are passionate about their products and are always up for a tasting: taking that into consideration, you may want to make it your last stop, as perry is pretty strong stuff! [SLB]

Preparation time 15 minutes

Cooking time 1 hour

Serves 4 as a main course

Season All ingredients available year-round

100g thinly sliced wild boar pancetta
2 tsp extra virgin olive oil
1·6 kg chicken, jointed
    (or approximately 8 thighs)
Sea salt
Freshly ground black pepper
½ tsp dried oregano
3 large banana shaped or
    6 small round shallots
1 pint perry
3 large sprigs rosemary
6–7 mixed root vegetables (parsnips, carrots, and/or turnips is a favourite mix of mine.)

chicken

wild boar

Preheat the oven to 180°C / 350°F / gas 4.

Slice the pancetta into thin strips. Heat a large deep casserole over a medium flame. Cook the pancetta with the olive oil, stirring occasionally, until most of the fat is rendered and it has started to brown nicely around the edges. Transfer the pancetta to a plate with a slotted spoon and set aside.

Season the chicken all over with salt, pepper, and dried oregano. Make sure your dried herbs are not stale – ie they still have vibrancy in colour and aroma. If they have been lurking in the back of your cupboards for 6 months they will be well worth replacing. Place the chicken skin-side down and brown, without disturbing, for a few minutes. Do this in batches. If you overcrowd the casserole you will only steam the chicken rather than render the fat and caramelise the skin. Once the skin side is nicely browned, about 4–5 minutes, transfer to a large plate and set aside.

Peel and cut the shallots into slivers. Add to the pan and sauté over a medium heat until lightly browned around the edges. Pour over half of the perry and deglaze the pan by scraping up the bits stuck to the bottom of the casserole as they will help flavour the sauce. Add the remaining perry and bring the mixture up to a rolling boil. Let the perry boil down until it is reduced to about 300 ml.

Arrange the chicken pieces in the liquid and sprinkle the crispy pancetta over the top. Wash the sprigs of rosemary and tuck them in around the chicken. Peel and cut the root vegetables into long thick sticks and place them on top of the chicken and pancetta. This layering technique will help with the appropriate cooking of each ingredient: the objective is to braise the chicken and bacon in the reduced perry whilst steaming the vegetables. Tear a circular piece of parchment paper about the size of your casserole. Place the paper on top of the root vegetables. If you don't have a tight fitting lid make the circle a little larger than the diameter of the casserole. Lay the paper on top of the casserole and press the lid onto the parchment securing it in place. This process with the paper, either on top of the vegetables or under the lid, will help circulate the perry steam and baste the chicken throughout the cooking process.

Cook in the preheated oven for 50 minutes. Check half way through whether the perry is boiling too ferociously. If so, turn down the oven by a few degrees. At the end of cooking, carefully remove the vegetables and place them onto a warm rimmed serving dish. Arrange the chicken over the top. Taste the sauce for seasoning. If it is too thin, bring the liquid up to a boil and reduce it slightly to thicken. Spoon the thickened sauce over the chicken and vegetables and serve.

CHICKEN AND MUSHROOM POT PIE WITH A PARMESAN-CHIVE CRUMBLE CRUST

This is a great make-ahead dish; it's also ideal for using up left over roast chicken — but you can, of course, use fresh. I have included instructions for both. However, keep in mind that it is a perfect recipe to feed a crowd from one chicken.

Label Anglaise chickens are not inexpensive, but they do have superior flavour. Here is a recipe to get the most for your money.

A few years back I set out on a mission to change the perception of stodgy, heavy chicken pot pies. Following many experiments with wines, pastry toppings and variations on vegetable additions, this one had to be my favourite. If you were hungrier than you thought and you don't have as much left-over chicken as the recipe calls for, just top up with some more aromatic vegetables. [SLB]

Chicken

Preparation time 30–60 minutes, depending on whether or not you are using pre-cooked chicken

Cooking time 30–35 minutes in the oven

Serves 6–8

Season All ingredients available year-round

15 g fresh chives
225 g self-raising flour
Sea salt
1 tsp baking powder
85 g unsalted butter
75 g Parmesan cheese
225 ml full fat milk plus up to tblsp
Freshly ground black pepper
30 g dried porcini mushrooms
680 g left-over roast chicken meat or equivalent amount of fresh boneless chicken
1½ tblsp olive oil
1 medium onion
2 carrots
340 g button or chestnut mushrooms
Freshly ground black pepper
4 sprigs fresh thyme
50 g plain flour
240 ml chicken stock, homemade or store bought
240 ml porcini hydrating liquid
15 g fresh parsley
4 tblsp butter
3 tblsp Marsala wine

Begin by preparing the ingredients for the topping. Wash, dry and finely chop the chives and set aside. Sift the flour, salt and baking powder into the bowl of a food processor or a medium sized mixing bowl. The butter can be incorporated into the dry ingredients by 'pulse-chopping' the flour-butter mixture into a fine crumb or by working the butter into the flour with your fingertips. If using a processor, transfer the mixture to a large bowl. Finely grate the Parmesan cheese and add, along with the chopped chives, to the mixture and fold to combine. Sprinkle the milk over the top and season with black pepper. Stir just until the mixture holds together. It will look like a wet scone dough when combine. Keep it in the bowl and put it in the refrigerator until ready to use.

Soak the dried porcini mushrooms in 480 ml of boiling water until soft, about 20 minutes. Lift the mushrooms from the liquid and strain the liquid, reserving 240 ml.

Preheat the oven to 180°C / 350°F / gas 4.

If you are not using left-over roast chicken, cook the chicken by poaching it in a small deep pan. Cover with water, bring to a simmer, and cook for 15 minutes for boneless breasts, 45 minutes for a whole bird. To check that it is fully cooked, insert a skewer into the thickest part. If no pink liquid emerges, it is ready. Transfer the meat to a large bowl.

Pour the oil into a large pot – if you cooked the chicken from raw use the pot you used to boil it. Peel and dice the onion and carrots. Slice the fresh mushrooms and re-hydrated porcini. Add to the pot and sauté until softened, about 5 minutes. Season well with salt and pepper.

While the vegetables are sautéing, shred the chicken (cooked or left-over) into small pieces. Transfer the cooked vegetables to the bowl with the shredded chicken.

Heat 4 tblsp butter over medium-high heat in the same now empty saucepot. Wash and remove the leaves from the sprigs of thyme and add to the hot butter. After about 30 seconds, when the sizzling subsides, add the flour. Cook the flour mixture for a minute until it darkens slightly in colour. Slowly pour in the chicken stock, reserved porcini hydrating liquid and the milk. Bring to a simmer, and continue to simmer until the sauce thickens. Again, season with salt and pepper. Then, add the Marsala.

Pour the sauce over the chicken and vegetables. Stir to coat. Wash, chop and add the parsley. Taste for a final seasoning and transfer to a large rectangular baking dish, about 33 x 23 cm in length. Using a large spoon, dot the surface with walnut-sized pieces of the Parmesan-chive crust. Try to create a slightly uneven finish; it will be more visually appealing once it comes out of the oven giving it a 'cobbled' effect. Place in the preheated oven and cook for about 30 minutes, or until the crust is nice and browned and the filling bubbling.

Cornish Reds in Essex fields

CHARMOULA CHICKEN

Charmoula is one of the most versatile marinades I know and it tastes equally fantastic with British lamb and mutton. Here, I'm using the oven grill to crisp up the chicken. However, if fair weather beckons, by all means, take it outside to the barbecue! [SLB]

Preparation time 15 minutes,
　　plus minimum 30 minutes marinating

Cooking time 25 minutes

Serves 4 as part of a main course

Season All ingredients available year-round

---

4 chicken legs (thighs and drumsticks)
1 pinch saffron threads (0·4g)
2 garlic cloves
Sea salt
½ red chilli
3 sprigs fresh parsley
3 sprigs fresh coriander
1½ tsp ground cumin
1 tsp sweet paprika
½ tsp smoked paprika or Cool Chilli Co.
　　chipotle chilli in adobo (use chipotle chilli
　　in place of not in addition to the red chilli)
½ tsp ground cinnamon
1 organic or unwaxed lime
3 tblsp olive oil
Freshly ground black pepper

Using a damp paper towel gently blot the chicken clean. Using a sharp knife, cut through the middle of the legs to separate the drumstick and thigh. There is a milky white fat line which separates the two, aim for that and you should be able to cut right through. Place the chicken in a large shallow glass or ceramic dish, skin side down.

Boil the kettle and pour 1 tblsp of boiling water over the saffron threads in a small dish and set aside to cool. Peel and crush the garlic with a little salt in a mortar into a smooth paste. Wash the chilli and cut it in half. Using only half of the chilli, de-seed and finely chop. Combine with the garlic either directly in the mortar or in a small bowl large enough to accommodate the entire marinade. Wash and chop the fine stems of the parsley and coriander and add to the bowl, along with the cumin, paprika and smoked paprika, chipotle chilli in adobo (if using), and cinnamon. Wash and grate the zest of the lime, making sure that you remove only the bright green skin. Squeeze out as much of the lime juice as you can into the bowl. Mix all ingredients for the marinade together with the olive oil and pour over the chicken. Season well with salt and pepper. Allow to marinate for at least half an hour in a cool room temperature. The chicken can be prepared to this stage well ahead of time but once in the marinade, place in the refrigerator until ready to cook.

Preheat your oven grill to its highest setting and place the chicken pieces on a baking tray fitted with a wire rack. Cook for 25–30 minutes or until the chicken is cooked through, turning occasionally. Check that the juices run clear by stabbing the thickest part of the thigh with a sharp knife. If the chicken legs are particularly big and getting too much colour, after 25 minutes, change the oven setting from grill to roast and cook for an additional 10 minutes or until the juices run clear.

This chicken can only be made better with the addition of a seasonal tabbouleh salad, followed by a fresh pomegranate juice jelly for dessert.

POMEGRANATE CHICKEN
AND BREAD SALAD

Make sure that you allow for the marinating time in this recipe. As there is no acid in the marinade it can be prepared two days in advance without a problem. When cooking the chicken, keep a watchful eye on the rate at which the skin browns. The combination of pomegranate molasses and honey will caramelise and crisp the skin rather quickly. Pomegranate molasses is available in most Middle Eastern grocery stores. I don't often recommend frying, but these bread croutons are simply divine. They are crispy on the outside and soft on the inside, not dissimilar to the texture of a roast potato. By drying them slightly in the oven they soak up some chicken juices and vinaigrette when served. This salad is a feast for all the senses: tasty, crunchy and visually stunning. [SLB]

Chicken

Preparation time 15 minutes to prepare the marinade plus 1 night marinating time, 30 minutes to prepare the salad

Cooking time 25 minutes to cook the chicken

Serves 4

Season All year round, pomegranates are best December through mid-March

2 garlic cloves
Sea salt
4 chicken breasts, with skin
1 rounded tsp cumin seeds
6 tblsp olive oil, plus an extra 60ml for the dressing
1½ tblsp pomegranate molasses
2 tblsp honey
Freshly ground black pepper
375g day-old bread, preferably a sourdough, crusts removed
180ml full-fat milk
1 lime or lemon
½ tsp harissa paste or chipotle chilli in adobo
1 bunch watercress
30g mixed fresh herbs (parsley, coriander, chervil, tarragon in any combination)
60g pine nuts
1 pomegranate (if available)

Begin by making the marinade. Peel and smash the garlic, and work into a paste with a bit of salt. Place in a bowl large enough to accommodate all the chicken breasts. If your cumin seeds have been in the pantry for a few months, gently dry roast them in a frying pan and add to the garlic. Pour in 2 tablespoons of olive oil, the pomegranate molasses, and 1½ tablespoon of the honey. Add the chicken breasts, season well with pepper and toss to coat. Cover and leave to marinate overnight in the refrigerator.

Preheat the oven to 200 °C / 400 °F / gas 6.

Cut or tear the bread into rough cubes and place in a small bowl. Drizzle with the milk to soften. Heat the remaining 4 tablespoons of olive oil in a frying pan. Add the bread cubes to the hot oil and cook until they are just browned around the edges. Transfer the crispy bread to an oven-proof frying pan or baking tray and continue cooking in the oven until browned all over, about 8–10 minutes.

Remove the chicken from the marinade. Warm a second oven-proof frying pan over medium-high heat. Fry the chicken skin-side down for 5 minutes in the pan without any oil. There should be enough olive oil from the marinade to keep the chicken moist and protect it from the intense heat. Flip the chicken over and place it in the oven for 10–12 minutes depending on the thickness of your chicken breasts.

Whilst the chicken is in the oven, make the dressing. Squeeze the lime or lemon, and mix the juice, the rest of the honey, harissa/chipotle chilli in adobo, and 60 ml extra-virgin olive oil. When the chicken is cooked, remove from the oven and allow to rest for 10 minutes.

Wash the watercress and mixed fresh herbs and blot dry. Place the watercress, herbs and crispy bread on a large platter. Remove seeds from the pomegranate (if you are using) and scatter, together with the pine nuts, over the watercress. Add any juices that may have accumulated from the chicken to the dressing. Cut the chicken into thick slices and arrange over and around the salad ingredients. Drizzle half of the dressing over and serve the rest alongside.

CHICKEN DUMPLING SOUP

This is a combination of my Jewish mother-in-law's chicken soup and lemon spinach and lentil soups from Lebanese cuisine; light, refreshing and nourishing all in one. [SLB]

Preparation time 10 minutes

Cooking time 8–10 minutes

Serves 2

Season All ingredients available year-round

1 small garlic clove
Sea salt
2 skinless chicken breasts,
    maximum weight of 125 g each
1 tblsp corn flour
½ tsp ground cumin
1 egg
100 g vermicelli noodles
50 g baby leaf spinach or two handfuls
15 g fresh parsley
1 carrot
1 lemon, unwaxed or organic
600 ml chicken stock,
    homemade or store bought
A few granules chicken bouillon or stock
    cube (optional)
Freshly ground black pepper

Peel the garlic and place in a mortar, add a little salt and pulverise it to a paste with a pestle. Combine the garlic paste, chicken breasts corn flour, cumin, and the egg in a food processor. Pulse to bring the ingredients together into a coarse paste. Wet your hands with a little water and begin to shape the chicken mixture into small dumplings about the size of a 50p piece. Set the chicken balls on a dinner plate as you work your way through the mixture. They may stick slightly to the plate but don't worry, they will soon retain their rounded shape once in the broth.

Place a small saucepan filled with boiling water over a high flame. Again, using your hands, crush the noodles into small pieces and gently lower into the boiling water. Cook for 2 minutes and drain. Wash and dry the spinach and parsley. Grate the carrot and squeeze the lemons. Divide the noodles, raw spinach and grated carrot between each bowl.

Bring the stock to a simmer; taste and adjust the seasoning. If you haven't made your own stock you may want to add a few granules of chicken bouillon powder or a portion of a stock cube to the broth. Now gently lower the dumplings into the hot stock and lightly poach. The dumplings rise to the surface like gnocchi when they are cooked through, after about 5 minutes. If you would like to check to see if the dumplings are thoroughly cooked, remove one from the broth and divide in half. The dumpling should be an opaque white all the way through.

Ladle the poaching liquid and dumplings over the bowls of noodles and vegetables. Garnish with about a teaspoon of fresh lemon juice. Serve with fresh chopped parsley.

Cook's note The garlic in the chicken dumplings is lightly cooked, so therefore on the stronger side. If you are serving this to children you may want to leave it out.

CHICKEN WITH WHITE WINE, SAFFRON, PINE NUTS AND CURRANTS

I love this dish. It is not only simple to prepare but the combination of textures and flavours is immensely satisfying and comforting. The last minute garnish of parsley not only provides a splash of colour but lifts the entire dish by balancing its own raw fresh flavour with the sweet onion saffron sauce. [SLB]

Preparation time 15 minutes

Cooking time 45 minutes to an hour

Serves 4

Season All ingredients available year-round

1 medium chicken
1 tblsp plain flour
3 tblsp olive oil
2 large onions
6 garlic cloves
2 bay leaves
Sea salt
Freshly ground black pepper
600 ml white wine
1 pinch saffron threads (about 0·4 g)
75 g currants
60 g pine nuts
10 g fresh parsley

chicken

Joint the chicken and cut into eight pieces. For information on how to joint a chicken, see page 126. Dust with flour and set aside.

Heat half the olive oil in a large casserole dish and begin browning the chicken pieces on all sides. Take some time to do this as you don't want to overcrowd the pan – overcrowding steams the chicken rather than allowing it to brown and crisp. Remove from the dish and set aside and keep the oil inside.

Peel and remove the top and bottom from the onion. Slice into slivers. Peel and crush the garlic with a little salt into a paste with a pestle and mortar. Add the onion to the casserole dish and sauté in the leftover oil until lightly golden around the edges. Work up any browned bits of chicken which may be stuck to the bottom. Add the garlic and stir until fragrant, about 30 seconds. Return the chicken pieces to the casserole dish, arranging them snugly, skin side up. Wash the bay leaves and tuck under the chicken pieces. Season well with salt and pepper. Pour in the wine and disperse the saffron around the chicken, making sure that you submerge the spice in the liquid. Bring to a simmer.

Once simmering, lower the heat and cook for about 40–45 minutes. If you like, the casserole can be transferred to a moderate oven (180 °C / 350 °F / gas 4) for the duration of the cooking time. After 20 minutes, add the currants and pine nuts, sprinkling over the chicken. Some may stay on top and some may fall into the sauce, which is fine. Towards the end of the cooking time the wine may have evaporated a little. If necessary, add enough chicken stock or water to keep about 240 ml of liquid in the pot at all times.

Wash the parsley. Chop the fine stems and leaves, sprinkle over the chicken and serve.

ALL-IN-ONE SANDWICH

Picnics for me used to mean lots of heavy equipment: portable barbecue grills, coolers packed with fresh meats, bags full of garnishes. And, of course, these picnics had to be in the perfect spot, which inevitably meant lugging all of this kit around. But no more! Instead, I have created a sandwich especially for the occasion. Today, most café menus have their own version of a roast chicken sandwich. I've included a combination of fresh herbs, salty prosciutto, sweet red peppers and a succulent garlicky roast chicken. The emphasis in this recipe is not on the flavour combination but the convenience of preparation, transport and service. Let your own taste buds guide you. Below I've given instructions for roasting a chicken especially for this recipe. However, you will ideally be using this recipe when you already have a fridge full of leftover roast chicken meat. Quantities for the chicken are flexible, if you only have the meat from two legs try substituting roasted courgettes, aubergine or artichoke hearts.

   If you are anything like me and have a tendency to over-stuff your sandwiches there is no need to worry. Simply make your sandwich ahead of time and press the sandwich with something flat and heavy in the refrigerator – a few tins of tomatoes or jars of olives stacked on a plate should do the trick. As always, you can substitute store bought mayonnaise for the olive oil and egg yolks in the aioli if you wish. Fold the herbs, mustard and vinegar into the mayonnaise and continue with recipe as directed. [SLB]

Preparation time 30 minutes

Cooking time 1½ hours

Serves 6

Season This is ideal summer food, especially as the herbs called-for in the aioli will be at their most vibrant in aroma, colour and flavour.

1 head of garlic
300 ml extra virgin olive oil
3 sprigs thyme
1–1·5 kg chicken or leftover meat from a bird of a similar weight
Sea salt
Freshly ground black pepper
3 large red peppers
1 large bunch fresh herbs (any combination of parsley, chervil, sorrel, basil, mint)
2 medium eggs
1 tsp Dijon mustard
1 tblsp red wine vinegar
1 large wide baguette (long enough for a 6-person sandwich)
6 slices prosciutto

chicken

Preheat the oven to 180°C / 350°F / gas 4.

To roast the chicken

Halve the head of garlic and drizzle with olive oil. Stuff the garlic, along with the thyme, into the cavity of the chicken. Season the inside and outside of the bird with salt and pepper. Roast for 1½ hours. Once the bird is golden on top and the juices pierced in the leg run clear, the bird is done. Allow to cool while you prepare the remaining sandwich ingredients.

To make the other fillers

Increase the oven temperature to 200°C / 400°F / gas 6.

Place the red peppers on a baking tray and roast in the oven until the skin blackens. If you prefer, you can char the peppers under the grill or over a gas hob. Once the skin is blackened and begins to loosen, transfer to a clean bowl and cover with cling film. This will steam the peppers, which will help loosen the skin. Once cooled, peel off and discard as much blackened skin as you can. Cut open the peppers, remove the stem and de-seed.

Wash and blot dry the bunch of fresh herbs. Finely chop the leaves and fine stems of the herbs and combine with half of the olive oil. Separate the eggs. In a small bowl mix the yolks, mustard and vinegar until they are slightly thick. Season well with salt and pepper. Add the remaining olive oil in a slow steady stream – the slower the better. Continue with the herb oil, again in a slow steady stream. The mixture may loosen, but continue mixing until thick again. Check for seasoning and set aside in a cool place.

Using your fingers shred the dark and light meat from the chicken. Mix them together. Discard the skin if you wish, some people enjoy the added flavour and textural contrast in the sandwich. Make sure you don't let any small bones slip through your fingers. Remove the head of garlic from the chicken (if you have roasted a whole bird) and squeeze out the cloves into a small bowl. Mash with a fork and stir into the fresh herb aioli.

Slice the baguette in halve horizontally. Remove some of the soft centre and save for another use (this bit is ideal for making breadcrumbs). Spread the inside of the loaf with the herb aioli. Top with chunks of roasted red peppers, followed by shredded chicken, and then the prosciutto.

Place a large sheet of parchment paper on your counter top. The key to wrapping this sandwich is the parchment has to be wide enough to go around the circumference of the bread. If it is not, arrange overlapping sheets of parchment paper, perpendicular to the sandwich, on your counter top. Place the sandwich on the parchment. Wrap up the sandwich and twist the ends so it looks like you have a giant Christmas cracker. If you have placed your sandwich perpendicular to the parchment, once rolled, you may have to secure a few edges of parchment paper with tape. Using a good strong twine, tie the sandwich up at 8–10 cm intervals along the length of the sandwich.

To serve, slice the sandwich in between the strings, so each person is served a little parcel.

BUTTERFLIED LEMON CHICKEN WITH POLENTA AND ROASTED TOMATOES

Everybody has their own way of roasting chicken and this is mine. It is a cracking dish and I crave it at least once a week. Each bite is full of zesty lemon juice with a little kick of Dijon mustard, both of which help cut through the rich polenta and sweet tomatoes. In the summer months, take the chicken out onto the barbecue. Cook for 40 minutes in total, 20 minutes per side.

'Butterflying' or boning the bird before marinating and roasting it allows for easy serving. Wyndham House is a particularly helpful butcher. This is one of the key advantages to shopping at Borough — the butchers will bone or spatchcock almost all of their range, unlike most supermarkets. They are an extremely knowledgeable bunch and, if you don't need any butchering done, they will most certainly have some good cooking tips to share as well!

This technique (see page 126 for 'butterflying' instructions) lends itself to stuffing. The chicken can be spread with a cooked creamy spinach or mushroom duxelle (a mixture of mushrooms sautéed in butter with onions) before being rolled and then roasted. With a little practice you could be butterflying the Christmas turkey and rolling it with lightly spiced sausage and apricot stuffing. Delicious! [SLB]

Preparation time 15 minutes, plus 45 minutes marinating

Cooking time 35 minutes, plus 10 minutes for resting

Serves 4 as a main course

Season All ingredients available year-round

1·5 kg chicken, butterflied by your butcher or according to instructions on page 126
3 garlic cloves
Sea salt
20 g fresh thyme
15 g fresh parsley
2 small lemons
1 tsp Dijon mustard
Freshly ground black pepper
4 bay leaves
Extra virgin olive oil
300 g cherry tomatoes on the vine
125 g polenta or coarse cornmeal
60 g unsalted butter
100 g grated Parmesan

chicken

Preheat the oven to 200°C / 400°F / gas 6.

Carefully wipe the chicken clean with a few sheets of damp kitchen paper. Trim off any excess fat around the neck. Insert your fingers on top of the breast meat and, if possible, around the thigh to loosen the skin.

Peel and crush the garlic into a paste with a few pinches of salt using a pestle and mortar. Wash and finely chop the parsley. Remove the leaves from the sprigs of thyme and roughly chop with a sharp knife. Combine both of the herbs in a small bowl with the crushed garlic. Squeeze the lemons and add, along with the Dijon mustard, to loosen the mixture. Season well with freshly ground black pepper. Spread the marinade over the top and under the skin and on the underside of the bird. Allow to marinate for up to 45 minutes at a cool room temperature, or up to 4 hours in the refrigerator.

Wash the bay leaves, place them on the bottom of a roasting pan and lay the butterflied chicken on top, flesh-side down. Drizzle with olive oil. Roast in the preheated oven for 35 minutes.

Once cooked, allow the meat to rest, covered in foil, for 10 minutes. While it is doing so, keep the oven on and roast the cherry tomatoes (preferably still on the vine) on a baking tray for 8–10 minutes, or just until they start to burst.

Prepare the polenta while the tomatoes are roasting. Heat the 500 ml water in a 2-litre saucepan over medium heat. Bring up to a simmer. Gradually pour the polenta into the simmering water in a slow steady stream, stirring continuously so that lumps do not form on the bottom. Cook, stirring occasionally with a wooden spoon, for about 6 minutes. Add the butter and the grated cheese, along with a good seasoning of salt and pepper. The polenta can be prepared ahead of time, to soften the mixture before serving add a little additional water or milk and stir to combined.

Cut the chicken in half to split the two breasts. Then cut thick slices across the leg and breast and arrange on top of some polenta and garnish with the roasted cherry tomatoes. There should be some reduced chicken juices in the roasting pan. Spoon off any rendered chicken fat and pour some of the juice over the top of each portion before serving.

LABEL ANGLAIS CHICKEN WITH BASIL, ROASTED VEGETABLES AND GRUYÈRE POLENTA

I had planned to roast a whole Label Anglais Chicken with black truffles thinly sliced and stuffed under the skin (which is, by the way, one of the best ways to serve the gorgeous earthy fungus) but time got the best of me and I was hungry. So, I decided to break the chicken down and quickly grill the breasts for dinner, whilst saving the rest of the bird for other meals: the legs for a confit, the wings for a snack, the carcass to make a stock for a light chicken soup supper another day.

This quick dinner was one of those rare occasions when everything seems to work effortlessly together with bits and pieces of ingredients from the larder and refrigerator and was less about a specific recipe. I tend not to be a cook who plans ahead, and this meal certainly was proof enough for me that we should all trust our instincts more when we cook. Use this recipe as a 'mix & match' to design your own pantry concoction; change the vegetables and herbs according to what is in season and swap the earthy Gruyère for a salty hard Italian Parmesan, a strong English cheddar or even a young French goat's cheese.

Isle of Wight tomatoes (sold at Borough) are simply delicious and last summer I made a huge batch of tomato chutney with some marrow and plenty of apples. We couldn't wait for it to age, so the sweet spicy chutney helped us see off the last of the summer sunshine with this late summer meal. I finished off this meal with a peach raspberry crisp with a little ground cinnamon and a few left-over basil leaves – definitely a winner. [SLB]

Preparation time 15–20 minutes to cut up the chicken, 15 minutes to make the polenta, 20 minutes to clean and prepare the vegetables

Cooking time 30 minutes

Serves 2

Season You can find these ingredients year-round but the peppers and basil will be at their most flavoursome during the late summer months – July and August.

2 Label Anglais chicken breasts
2 carrots
1 yellow pepper
1 medium red onion
6 garlic cloves
4 sprigs fresh basil
50 ml extra virgin olive oil
400 ml water
100 g polenta
2 tblsp unsalted butter
2 tblsp Gruyère cheese, grated
Sea salt
Freshly ground black pepper

Tomato chutney for serving (see page 97)

Preheat the oven to 200 °C / 400 °F / gas 6.

Wash and roughly chop the sweet yellow pepper. Wash, peel, and roughly chop the carrots and red onion. Toss in the olive oil, (reserving 1 tblsp of the oil for the chicken breasts) along with the whole cloves of garlic still in their skins, a good pinch of salt and a generous grinding of black pepper. Rinse and roughly tear the basil leaves from the sprigs and fold them into the vegetables. Roast in the preheated oven for 30 minutes, or until they are charred around the edges and shrivelled slightly from the concentration of their flavours.

About half way through the vegetable cooking time, cook the chicken breasts. Label Anglais have an amazing marking of fat (especially around the wings) which particularly suits them to intense cooking methods like roasting. Begin by getting a grill pan extremely hot, without any oil in it. Rub the reserved olive oil into the skin of the chicken breast and place skin-side down in the hot pan. Cook for 5–6 minutes until the skin has taken up the grill markings and has crisped. Flip over and transfer to the oven with the vegetables and cook for an additional 10 minutes.

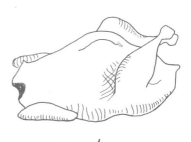

Chicken

Once the chicken is in the oven, bring 400 ml of water to a boil in a small saucepan. Grate the cheese. Once the water is boiling, slowly pour in the polenta, whisking continuously for about 5 minutes or until thickened. Season with salt and pepper. Add the unsalted butter and grated Gruyère cheese.

We topped our chicken breasts with a good dollop of sweet spicy tomato chutney. Occasions like these are what chutneys are made for – impromptu dinners with a few good ingredients. The combination of flavours, colours and textures made this a particularly satisfying meal – one I was keen to jot down and be able to recreate again and again.

CHICKEN RISOTTO WITH
AIR-DRIED HAM AND PEAS

Risottos are one of the easiest, most convenient and satisfying ways of using stock after you've served a Label Anglais chicken. The stock and the right kind of short-grained rice (arborio or carnaroli — I prefer the former) are essential, but given these, the only other item you may have to buy for this recipe is the ham. You don't need much, but you can use the rest for other dishes or it is delicious by itself.

If you can find fresh, young peas, then obviously they're the best choice; otherwise, use frozen ones. (Large old ones will be starchy rather than sweet and take very much longer to cook.) [SF]

Chicken

Preparation time About 5 minutes before you start cooking the rice.

Cooking time About 40 minutes

Serves One hungry person or two as a starter or light supper

Season All ingredients available year-round

450 ml chicken stock (see page 136), or 750 ml if you plan to cook a chicken breast
50–100 g leftover roast chicken, depending on whether there are one or two of you, or 1 skinned free-range chicken breast (if you're not using left over chicken)
Sea salt
3 large garlic cloves
2 slices Denhay Farms air-dried ham
2 tblsp olive oil
100 g arborio rice
15–20 g Parmesan cheese
20 leaves basil
15 g unsalted butter
Freshly ground black pepper
125 g fresh (podded) or frozen peas
1 tblsp double cream

Set 450 ml stock to heat in a small saucepan. If you plan to cook a chicken breast, put the breast into a second small pan with the remaining 300 ml stock and as much water to cover it as is necessary. Put a little salt into the saucepan with the chicken breast. Bring the pans just to the boil. Then, turn down the heat under both to a gentle simmer.

Peel the garlic cloves and finely slice two of them, keeping the other one aside. Dice the ham. Measure the oil into a wok or frying pan and set it over fairly high heat for a moment or two. Toss in the sliced garlic, turn down the heat to moderate, and as soon as the garlic shows signs of changing colour add the ham and rice. Cook, turning continuously for about two minutes, until all the grains of rice are coated with oil and starting to look translucent at the edges. Pour in 150 ml of the hot stock, bring it to the boil, and turn down the heat until it just simmers. Leave the rest of the stock simmering gently, as before. Turn the rice occasionally and when all the stock has been absorbed, add a little more. Repeat until all the stock is used, which should be in 35–40 minutes. By this time, the rice will be ready. If you run out of stock while it is still hard, add a little nearly boiling water.

While the rice simmers, finely grate the cheese. Wash and blot the basil dry. Tear the leaves from the stems, shred them with your fingers, and put them into a mortar with the remaining garlic clove and a little of the butter. Pound until the leaves are half pulverized. Put in the rest of the butter with a slight seasoning of salt and rather more pepper and continue pounding until you have a rough paste.

When the rice has been cooking for about 25 minutes, put on a pan of water for the peas. Start cooking fresh ones now: put them into the pan with a little salt, bring the water to a brisk boil, and cook them until they are tender. As frozen ones take only 2 minutes, don't start boiling them until the rice is almost ready.

If you're cooking a chicken breast, test it by sticking a knife into the thickest part: if no liquid emerges, it's ready. Drain it, leave it until it is cool enough to handle, and cut it into bite-sized slices. Alternatively, cut ready-cooked chicken into easy-to-eat slices.

When the rice has absorbed most of the stock, try it: it should be tender but still with a definite bite at the centre. As soon as it is cooked to your taste, stir in the chicken, peas, basil butter and cream. If the risotto is stiff rather than with plenty of sauce, add more stock if you have any or a little extra butter. Finally, very gently stir in about half the cheese. Sprinkle the rest on top. Serve immediately.

SMOKED DUCK TOASTS
WITH GINGERED RHUBARB

Perfect as a quick canapé but great as a tapas or even a salad starter. Smoked duck breasts keep exceptionally well and I usually toss one in my bag every time I am down at Borough. They are definitely a good thing to have on hand. Pink tender-stemmed forced rhubarb worked the best for this quick cooking compote. But don't be afraid to use outdoor grown, just remember to peel it. The easiest way to do this is to top and tail the rhubarb then hold the edge of a cut end in between your knife and your thumb. Pull down the length of the rhubarb stalk to remove the tough strings. [SLB]

Preparation time 15 minutes

Cooking time 15 minutes

Serves 6 as a starter, or makes 18 canapes

Season You should be able to find smoked duck year-round. For the rhubarb, opt for the sweeter forced variety from Yorkshire which is available from January through to early April.

1 large sourdough baguette
4 tblsp extra virgin olive oil
170g rhubarb stalks, about 4
3 cm piece fresh ginger
2 tblsp caster sugar
2 smoked duck breasts

Duck

Preheat oven to 230°C / 450°F / gas 8.

Cut 18 slices of the baguette on the diagonal. Pour olive oil into a small bowl and dip one side of each baguette slice into it and place the oiled-side up on a parchment-lined baking tray.

Place tray in a preheated oven and toast for 6–10 minutes or until nicely golden brown around the edges. Removed from oven and set aside to cool.

Reduce the oven temperature to 180°C / 350°F / gas 4.

Wash, top and tail the rhubarb and cut it into 0.5 cm slices. Place the slices in a baking dish. Peel and grate the ginger and rub it into the sugar. Sprinkle over the rhubarb and toss to coat. Bake the rhubarb for 10 minutes, until just soft.

Drain the rhubarb in a sieve set over a bowl to catch the juices, reserving the rhubarb. Measure 2 tsp of the rhubarb juices. Add and fold them into the cooked rhubarb. Discard the remaining cooking liquid or save for another use.

Remove any skin and fat from the duck breasts. Carve them into 18 slices, again on the diagonal, cutting across the grain.

Assemble the duck on top of the baguette toasts. Dot the gingered rhubarb compote on the top and serve warm.

Cook's note When rhubarb season is over try substituting 4 fresh figs. Cut into quarters and sprinkle with gingered sugar. Bake and allow to cool. Arrange caramelised figs on top of smoked duck and serve.

SEARED DUCK BREASTS WITH FRESH RASPBERRY VINAIGRETTE

Sweet tart fruits go extremely well with game, and raspberry vinegar is ideal with duck. Most raspberry vinegars you find nowadays are over-sweetened and artificially coloured. However if you make your own vinegars, you can experience the true joy of this natural partnership.

The olive oil you use is just as important as the raspberries in this recipe. Try to find one with a strong peppery edge, although not one that's bitter. Bedales at Borough has lots of oils to choose from and are most helpful in choosing one that is right for you. I've chosen Barbary ducks as they are farmed and slightly less gamy than wild ones in flavour. They also tend to be rather large, so have suggested only 2 breasts for 4 people. [SLB]

Preparation time 15 minutes

Cooking time 17–18 minutes,
   plus 10 minutes resting

Serves 4

Season As Barbary duck is farmed, you should be able to find it year-round. You'll find the sweetest, ripest English or Scottish raspberries for the vinaigrette from late July through early September.

---

200 g fresh raspberries
Sea salt
Freshly ground black pepper
4 tblsp extra virgin olive oil
2 large Barbary duck breasts,
   about 250 g–275 g in weight each
200 g spinach and watercress leaves

Preheat the oven to 180°C / 350°F / gas 4.

Crush the raspberries with a fork or in the bowl of a food processor and then push them through a sieve, extracting as much juice as possible. This amount of raspberries should yield about 4 tblsp of juice. Season with salt and a little pepper and stir to dissolve the salt.

Transfer the juice to a medium-sized bowl and while whisking constantly, slowly add the olive oil. The raspberries have a fair amount of natural sugars so it should quickly start to emulsify and thicken slightly. Check and adjust the seasoning. Depending on the sweetness of the fruit you may want to add about ½ tsp white wine vinegar. Try to make this on the day you wish to serve it as it looses it edge if it sits overnight.

Heat a large oven-proof frying pan over a medium-low flame. Trim any excess fat around the edges of the duck breasts and using a sharp knife make 3 to 4 slashes through the skin. Place skin-side down in the frying pan. Cook slowly, for about 10 minutes. This slow cooking will allow the fat to be released and the skin to become crisp. As the fat comes out of the skin, use a flat spoon to scoop it out of the pan (place the fat in a heat-proof dish, allow it to cool and discard).

After the 10 minutes have passed, flip the duck breasts and continue cooking in the preheated oven for another 7–8 minutes. Remove from the oven and allow a good 5 minutes more for resting, tenting the duck breasts with foil.

Wash and blot dry the spinach and watercress leaves and remove any large stems from the watercress. Pile them into the centre of 4 dinner plates. Slice the duck breasts on the diagonal into 5–6 thick slices. Arrange the slices over the leaves and spoon the raspberry dressing over the top.

For a more substantial main course, serve with steaming couscous with chopped fresh mint.

BRAISED GUINEA FOWL
WITH SAGE AND GARLIC

This is a variation on the classic recipe of braised chicken or pork loin in milk. The difference here is that I've chosen to add the milk at the end. In doing so, we loose the characteristic sweet milk curds but gain a lovely light creamy milk sauce to serve with chunks of juicy guinea fowl. I've used plain flour to slightly thicken and stabilise the milk sauce but have also used 2 tblsp of fresh sourdough breadcrumbs with equal success. [SLB]

Preparation time 25 minutes

Cooking time 1 hour 20 minutes

Serves 4

Season In season from September until February

1·6 kg guinea fowl
30 g unsalted butter, plus 1 tsp
1 tblsp extra virgin olive oil
1 unwaxed or organic lemon
4 sprigs fresh sage
1 head of garlic
100 ml white wine
1 tsp plain flour
200 ml full-fat milk

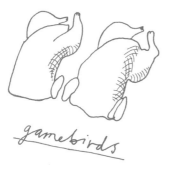

gamebirds

Preheat the oven to 170 °C / 325 °F / gas 3.

Wipe the guinea fowl with damp paper towels and pat dry. Heat the 30 g of butter and the olive oil in a large frying pan. Add the bird and brown on all sides. This should take about 10 minutes to achieve good colouring.

Transfer to a casserole which not only holds the bird but is deep enough for the lid to fit over it without touching the bird. Pare off a 7–8 cm strip of lemon zest and place, along with two sprigs of sage, into the cavity. Toss the remaining two sage sprigs into the dish. Slice off the head of the garlic and set it beside the bird. Pour over the white wine. Cover with the lid slightly ajar and place in a preheated oven.

Cook for half an hour. Then remove the dish from the oven and turn the bird over onto the other side. Cover, return to the oven and continue cooking for an additional half hour.

Transfer the guinea fowl to a plate, tent with foil and allow to rest in a warm place. Remove the sprigs of sage and garlic from the casserole. Pour off any liquid into a measuring jug and return the pot to the stove. Melt the remaining 1 tsp butter over a low flame. Sprinkle over the flour and work the mixture into a paste. Slowly, pour in the milk and any juices accumulated during cooking, and bring up to a simmer. Use the back of a wooden spoon to scrape the bottom of the casserole to incorporate any browned bits.

Carve the resting guinea fowl and spoon sauce over the top.

'Turkey heaven'
Temple Farm, Roydon, Essex

SPATCHCOCKED QUAIL WITH SWEET AND SOUR FIGS

The best thing about this recipe is that each component tastes absolutely wonderful on its own, but they taste even better together. The figs can be made well ahead of time and kept in the refrigerator or larder until needed. They are great to have on hand and are delicious with lamb, venison and most game birds.

Inspiration for the flavour combination comes from a book called A Thousand Days in Venice by Marlene de Blasi. It's a beautifully written book of food, love and travel, and one which can seduce almost anyone to cover their home in Damask drapery!

Quails are tiny birds, and I honestly can't be bothered picking over the little tiny bones once they are cooked. Wyndham House will open their packages of quail and de-bone them completely or they will kindly spatchcock the birds for you.

This dish is made even better with chicken liver pâté (see www.civicbooks.com). Smear a generous amount of pâté on a lightly toasted crostini and top with grilled marinated quail. If you do want to combine these recipes note that the pâté as well as the figs can be made up to 4 days in advance. [SLB]

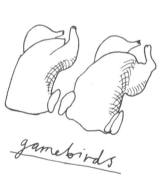

gamebirds

Preparation time 30 minutes marinating the quail

Cooking time 16 minutes to cook the quail, 10–15 minutes for the figs

Serves 2

Season Quail is in season year-round

2 de-boned, spatchcocked quail
1 garlic clove
½ tsp ground Chinese five spice
2 tblsp olive oil
1 tblsp orange juice (preferably freshly squeezed)
120 ml red wine vinegar
50 ml balsamic vinegar
90 g granulated sugar
2 bay leaves
1 stick of cassia bark (or a cinnamon stick)
8 fresh figs or 12 dried figs that have been soaked in hot tea for half an hour
Sea salt
Freshly ground black pepper

Special equipment
Skewers, either wooden soaked in water or metal

Begin by marinating the quail. Peel and crush the garlic with the Chinese five spice, some salt and black pepper with a pestle and mortar. If you can't find Chinese five spice use a pinch of cinnamon, ground star anise, ground cloves, Szechwan pepper (or black pepper) and a few fennel seeds. Transfer the spices and garlic to a large glass or ceramic bowl.

Pour in 1 tbsp of olive oil and the orange juice. Using your finger, rub the mixture into the spatchcocked quail, on both the skin side and the flesh side. The quail can be used straight away, but they benefit from at least half an hour of marinating. Using wooden skewers that have been soaked in water, slide two across the bird to keep it flat whilst cooking. Set aside until ready to cook.

For the figs, put the vinegars into a small sauce-pan and add the sugar, bay leaf and cassia bark (if using).

Cook's note The mix of vinegars is entirely up to you and what you have in your pantry. Keep the amounts the same but feel free to experiment with cider or even sherry vinegar.

Heat the mixture over a low flame until the sugar dissolves, then bring it up to a rolling boil. Turn the heat back down to low and simmer slowly for 5 minutes. Cut the figs in half and add them to the pan. Dried figs will need 10 minutes once added, fresh figs 15. If you are using dried figs and the liquid starts to look a little syrupy while the figs are still firm, add a tablespoon or two of water. Cover and continue cooking for another 5 minutes. Set aside to cool.

Preheat the oven to 180°C / 350°F / gas 4 and heat a small oven-proof frying pan over a medium-high flame. Drizzle 1 tblsp of olive oil over the quail and place, breast-side down into the preheated pan and cook for 3 minutes. Once the skin is nicely browned, flip and transfer the frying pan to the oven and cook for an additional 10 minutes.

To serve, remove the skewers from the quail and place on top of the pâté (if using) and drape 1 or 2 fig halves next to the quail with a little sticky fig syrup on the plate. Serve immediately.

QUAIL FARRO SALAD

Farro is a unique grain which forms the basis of this earthy salad and is a great foil for the richness of the quail. You may see it branded as either wheat berry or spelt grains. It has a similar appearance and nutritional profile to wheat but with 30% more protein. It may be tolerated by some wheat sensitive people, but those who are highly sensitive should proceed with caution. [SLB]

gamebirds

Preparation time 20 minutes, plus overnight marinating and soaking

Cooking time 35 minutes for the farro, plus 13–15 minutes for the quail

Serves 6 as a main course

Season Quail is in season year-round

2 rounded tblsp coriander seeds
1 tsp allspice berries
5 garlic cloves
2 tblsp runny honey
90 ml dry sherry
1 tblsp olive oil
3 sprigs fresh thyme
6 quail, boned and spatchcocked
200 g farro (spelt/wheat berry)
1 small butternut squash
30 g unsalted butter
4 shallots
Pinch dried chilli flakes
225 g fresh spinach
90 g Parmesan
100 g dried unsweetened cranberries
Sea salt
Freshly ground black pepper

Begin by preparing the farro first. Pour the grain into a medium-sized bowl, cover with plenty of cold water and leave to soak overnight at room temperature.

At this stage, you should also prepare the quail, which are best if left to marinate overnight. Crush the coriander seeds and the allspice berries with a pestle and mortar along with 3 peeled cloves of garlic. Place in a large glass or ceramic bowl with a good grinding of black pepper, the honey and sherry. Wash and remove the leaves from the thyme roughly chop with a sharp knife. Fold through the marinade. Add the quail and coat well. Cover and refrigerate for at least 2 hours – but preferably overnight.

After soaking the farro overnight, bring a large pan of water to a boil, add a pinch of salt. Drain the grains and add to the water and gently simmer for about 30 minutes or until the farro is soft but still retaining a bit of a bite. Drain and set aside.

Preheat the oven to 200°C / 400°F / gas 6.

While the farro is cooking, use a vegetable peeler to remove the tough skin from the squash. Cut in half, and scoop out the seeds and chop into a small dice. Toss in a little olive oil, season well and place on a non-stick baking tray. Roast in the preheated oven until tender and slightly tinged brown around the edges, about 15 minutes.

Reduce the oven temperature to 180°C / 350°F / gas 4.

Heat two large oven-proof frying pans over a medium-high heat. Take the quail out of the marinade and brown each breast of the quail – about 3 minutes on each side. Flip the quail over and transfer the frying pans to the oven to finish cooking for 10 minutes more.

While the quail are in the oven, finish the salad by melting the butter in a large frying pan over a low flame. Peel and thinly slice the shallots. Mince the remaining two garlic cloves and add, along with the shallots and chilli, to the butter in the frying pan. Cook for 3 minutes or until the shallots have begun to soften and caramelise around the edges. Rinse the spinach and allow to drain through a sieve. Have ready to fold through the salad along with some grated Parmesan. When the shallots have softened add the farro and toss to coat in the flavoured butter. Fold in the cleaned spinach, allowing it to wilt slightly, and finally gently add the roasted squash, Parmesan and the dried cranberries. Season with salt and pepper.

Spoon the warm salad on the plates and place the quail on top.

THE GINGER PIG

Tim Wilson *Grange Farm, Levisham, North Yorkshire*

Visiting Tim Wilson at Grange Farm is like taking a long step back in time. Levisham is a late seventeenth-century village, which I understand was built according to a plan laid out originally by William the Conqueror. All the houses are set back in a formal row on each side of the village green which was once cropped by sheep but is now kept impeccably mown. Each front door is approached by a long, straight stone path. There are no shops or signs of contemporary life apart from a few parked cars at the rear of the pub. At first it seems unreal, but if you poke around you realize that many of the houses are farmhouses, like Tim's, with yards and barns at the back.

At the time of our visit, the main part of Tim's house was virtually gutted, with neither windows nor flooring. A large barn was also being renovated. Tim promptly explained this: 'The trouble with employing farm workers is that you have to find something for them to do in bad weather. We're good employers and

pay them more than usual – but they have to multi-task.' The kitchen, however, was not only complete but remarkable for three stunning pieces of furniture: an eighteenth-century Welsh oak dresser, an enormous, intricately carved oak sideboard dating from 1660, and a very long, solid kitchen table where all the farm hands would once have taken their meals together.

Before accepting his fate as a farmer, Tim had been an antiques dealer specialising in oak furniture. He comes from a farming family but as a boy had rebelled, feeling that the last thing he wanted was to be tied by the needs of animals. As he already very well knew, 'Live animals have to come first. That rule is set in stone.' He tried various alternatives, favouring antiques because keeping a shop didn't seem to involve much work. However, antiques led to property and property, inevitably in this part of the world, led to farms.

He now owns four farms over 3,500 acres and has 2,000 sheep, over 1,000 pigs, and 400 cattle. Although not organic, the farms are almost self-sufficient: Tim will apply chemicals if necessary, but wheat, oats, and barley for animal feed and bedding are own-grown and the manure is used as fertilizer. Everything, he emphasizes, is interdependent. 'Dispense with barley and you dispense with bedding.'

The pigs include Gloucester Old Spots and ginger Tamworths (hence the name of his stand at Borough and the Marylebone shop). The cattle are Longhorns, who are distinguished by a white stripe going down their backs as far as their tails and 'bonnet' horns, which typically curl round their faces like bonnet-strings. The tips are kept trimmed with a butcher's saw. Like that of other traditional breeds, the meat is slow-growing. Tim doesn't market it until it is at least four years old (which meant that during the BSE restrictions, selling it was prohibited). All the cows have names: the eldest, who is eleven, is called Generous.

On the way back from admiring the cows, we met a party of very tame rams, or 'tups', as they are known in farming terms. They didn't run away at our approach or indeed take any notice of us at all. Some of them were limping. 'They're exhausted,' Tim explained. 'They've been with the ewes for two days.' We asked how many they were expected to serve in that time. 'About forty each,' he replied. That means an average of twenty a night. 'Well done, chaps,' murmured George (the photographer). The next morning, Tim introduced us to a group of junior bulls, pointing out one or two whom he thought promising. It seems that with

Left Tim Wilson, founder of 'The Ginger Pig'

Following pages English Longhorns, Grange Farm, Levisham, North Yorkshire

Above The Pickering Valley,
Levisham

Opposite *Sex machines —
the Texel cross tup's return*

bulls, as with human beings, everything depends on confidence. Without that, according to Tim, the cows would laugh at them. A little later he added, memorably, 'The thing about farming is that it's seventy per cent sex and thirty per cent violence.'

The animals are slaughtered at Nunnington, just a few miles away. That's the time above all others, Tim says, when they really need you. Interestingly, he thinks that taking a cow's calf away from her, as is the practice with milking herds, is more inhumane than slaughtering her for meat. When we asked him what his next plans were, he said that they might include founding a milking herd in which the calves were separated from their mothers at night but left with them during the day.

Borough is not only very profitable to him (his takings on a bad day are around £4,000) but was the cause of his founding his famous Marylebone shop. When he started selling at the Market, he tried to employ a part-time London butcher for his stand but couldn't find one: he opened the shop in order to provide full-time work, on the same principle as the conversion of his house. Today, the stand and the shop together have a staff of twenty-five. The charcuterie which is so prominently displayed is entirely the initiative of Paul Hughes, who used to be a chef at St John, near Smithfield, and is as passionate about the possibilities of pork as Tim is committed to his cows.

ROAST LOIN OF PORK
IN MULLED WINE

Here pork is richly flavoured with cardamom, juniper berries and currant jelly. Ask the butcher to cut the chine bone from the meat but not completely off. Then tie the chine bone back on to the roast. This will allow the bone to flavour the roast but still make cutting through each rib easier when serving. [SLB]

Preparation time 20 minutes,
  plus minimum 12 hours marinating

Cooking time 1 hour 25–30 minutes

Serves 8

Season All ingredients available year-round.

12 whole cardamom pods
12 juniper berries
½ tsp whole black peppercorns
3 cloves
1 tsp sea salt
Half an orange
Loin of pork on the bone with 8 to 10 ribs,
  2·75–3·0 kg or 2 x 1·3–1·5 kg
600 ml red wine,
  divided into 120 ml and 480 ml
180 ml apple juice
120 ml brandy
1 cinnamon stick
3 bay leaves
2 tblsp red currant jelly

Using the side of your knife, crush the cardamom pods and remove the tiny black seeds. Crush these seeds with a pestle and mortar with the juniper, black peppercorns, cloves and salt into a coarse powder. Set aside.

Place the pork in a glass or ceramic baking dish. Rub the orange over the entire pork roast. Drizzle the 120 mls of wine over the meat. Sprinkle the spice blend over the meat and massage the spices into the meat. Cover with cling film and refrigerate at least 12 hours or overnight.

Remove the pork from the refrigerator an hour before cooking. Preheat oven to 180°C / 350°F / gas 4.

Take the pork from the marinade and pat it dry with paper towels. Place it in a roasting pan. Rub olive oil into the skin and sprinkle with ½ tsp sea salt. Transfer to the preheated oven.

After 15 minutes, add the wine, apple juice, brandy, and cinnamon stick. Wash and add the bay leaves. Make sure the pork skin is about 6cm away from the heat element.

Roast uncovered 1 hour and 15 minutes, basting often with the pan juices. After an hour and 10 minutes, turn the oven temperature to grill to crisp up the skin if it isn't crisp already. Before removing the pork from the oven, insert a meat thermometer into thickest part. It should register 66°C / 150°F. If not, cook a bit longer – until the meat reaches this temperature.

Transfer the pork to a platter, tent with foil and allow to rest for 20 minutes. Strain the pan juices into a large glass measuring cup. Spoon any fat off the top. Pour pan juices into a small saucepan. Add the jelly 1 tblsp at a time, tasting as you go. Simmer until the sauce lightly coats a spoon, 6–8 minutes. Season to taste with salt and pepper.

Carve the pork and spoon over the sauce. Serve with a creamy mash.

Tamworths at Grange Farm

MERGUEZ SAUSAGES WITH HOMEMADE FLATBREADS AND SMOKED AUBERGINE

You can purchase tortillas or even proper unleavened bread these days but once you have tried these homemade flatbreads I am confident you won't go back to the bought sort. Merguez sausages are spiced lamb sausages which instantly add a little pizzazz to any meal. If the flatbreads prove to be too much, try the Merguez cooked with the smoked aubergine on a bed of rocket or spinach leaves for a lighter supper. [SLB]

Preparation time 1 hour

Cooking time 20 minutes

Serves 6

Season You can buy beautiful Italian-grown violet pearl aubergines (the voluptuous rounded ones with the slightly white tint to their flesh) in May. Or, opt for deep purple home-grown varieties in July, August and September.

2 large aubergines
1 garlic clove
Sea salt
1 lemon
3 tblsp tahini
1 tsp cumin seeds
1 tblsp olive oil
Freshly ground black pepper
225 g plain flour
120 ml boiling water
3 tblsp sesame oil
1 red onion
1 red pepper
12 small Merguez sausages
Rocket for serving (optional)

Preheat the oven to 200 °C / 400 °F / gas 6.

Brown the aubergines on all sides, either directly on a gas hob or under the grill. Transfer to a baking tray and continue cooking them in the preheated oven until they start to collapse, about 30 minutes. Once soft, remove from the oven, slice in half and place in a sieve. Allow the darkened juices to drain through the sieve and discard. Leave them to cool. Scrape the flesh from the skins into a medium sized bowl and mash them allowing some chunky bits to remain. Set aside.

Keep the oven on and reduce the temperature to 180 °C / 350 °F / gas 4.

Peel and crush the garlic clove in a mortar with a bit of salt. Squeeze the lemon. Mix the garlic in a small bowl with the lemon juice and tahini. Toast the cumin seeds and add to the lemon-tahini mix. Stir the mashed aubergine through the dressing and bring together with a good splash of olive oil. Season with salt and pepper.

For the flatbreads, measure the flour into a bowl and slowly mix in the boiling water with a fork. when cool enough to handle, work the dough for several minutes until it holds together, and then knead on a lightly floured board until smooth and satiny (4–5 minutes). Wrap it in cling film and let it rest at room temperature for 30 minutes.

Roll the dough into a 30 cm long log and cut it into 12 equal pieces. Keep the dough covered with a tea towel as you prepare each piece. Roll each piece into a ball and then flatten it slightly. Brush sesame oil on one side and cover the sesame coated side with another round. Press the two rounds together. Place the double round on a lightly floured board and roll out, from centre to edges, until 20 cm in diameter (don't worry if the rounds are not perfect). Turn frequently, dusting the board lightly with flour as needed to keep the dough loose on the surface. Repeat the procedure until you have 3 sandwiched flat breads (ie 6 of the 12 pieces); then cook before making more. Heat a frying pan over medium flame. Place one sandwiched flatbread onto the pan without adding any oil. Cook until slightly toasted and flecked with brown spots on one side. Flip over and cook the other side. Remove from the heat, allow to cool for a few minutes before seperating the sandwiched pieces of bread. Stack on top of one another and continue cooking the remaining breads. Whilst the flatbreads are cooking begin to prepare the remaining pieces of dough as before.

Heat another large frying pan over medium heat with a drop of oil. Wash and slice the red pepper; peel and slice the red onions. Stir-fry together until slightly tinged brown around the edges. Add the Merguez sausages and brown them all over. Transfer to the preheated oven and continue cooking for about 15 minutes.

Wash and blot dry the rocket if you are using it. To assemble each wrap, place a flatbread in front of you with the soft side facing up. Divide the onion and red pepper mixture between the flatbreads leaving a small space in the end of the bread closest to you. Cut the Merguez sausages in half and place both halves on top of the onions and peppers in each bread. Dollop on some smoked aubergine. Top with a few leaves of rocket for an added crunch if you want before folding the base of the bread a third of the way over the filling and rolling from side to side. That way when you lift the bread roll no filling will escape from the bottom!

Sausages & sausage meat

LENTIL AND CHORIZO SALAD WITH SHERRY VINAIGRETTE

This is a barbecue staple in our house. It is zesty, full-flavoured and actually quite substantial. You could easily have it as a meal in itself, certainly a lunch. It is also a great way to introduce lentils to someone who doesn't think they like them. Chorizo is a sure-fire winning addition when it comes to tempting people to try something. [SLB]

Preparation time 15 minutes

Cooking time 30 minutes

Serves 8 as part of a barbecue spread

Season Green beans are at their best in July and August, as are the cherry tomatoes and fresh English spinach.

300g Puy lentils
250g chorizo
200g green beans
1 garlic clove
Sea salt
3 tblsp sherry vinegar
1 tsp Dijon mustard
6 tblsp olive oil
1 bunch spring onions
30g fresh parsley
200g cherry tomatoes
225g baby spinach
200g feta cheese

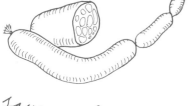

Sausages & sausage meat

Begin by putting the lentils into a medium-sized saucepan. Cover with 2·5cm of water. Bring to a simmer and cook gently for about 20–25 minutes. Puy lentils should retain most of their shape during cooking and a bit of a bite. Strain off any remaining water.

While the lentils are cooking, peel the skin from the chorizo and slice it thinly. Place it in a frying pan over a low heat to render out some of the fat. Once the chorizo takes on a slightly tinged golden crust, remove with a slotted spoon and drain off the fat into a small bowl.

Bring a large pan of water to a boil and remove the stalk end from the green beans, leaving the thin thread top. Blanch the beans in boiling water, cooking for about 2 minutes. Drain them and rinse under cold running water. Set aside.

Peel and crush the garlic in a mortar with a little salt. Place in a small bowl, along with the sherry vinegar and Dijon mustard. In a slow steady stream, add the olive oil to emulsify the dressing. Once the lentils are cooked, drizzle over the vinaigrette and toss to coat.

Bring the salad together by washing the remaining salad ingredients apart from the feta. Peel and finely chop the spring onions and chop the leaves and the fine stems of the parsley. Slice the tomatoes and pick through the spinach leaves removing any that may be damaged. Combine all the veggies and crispy chorizo with the lentils and taste for seasoning. Garnish the salad by crumbling the fresh feta over the top.

HONEY MISO SAUSAGE NOODLE SOUP

Miso is a fermented soybean paste usually mixed with brown rice or barley. Buy the unpasteurised form and take care not to boil the miso once added as you will loose all the fantastic nutritional benefits it contains. This recipe is a weekly occurrence on our household supper menu; it is fast, flavourful and nourishes both the mind and body.

Honey miso sausages are the perfect balance of sweet and salty. All I've added are a few subtle spices and some fresh green vegetables to add a crisp edge. The mature-flavoured paste creates a great flavour base for all sorts of additions: black cabbage and baby bok choy, seared slivers of duck breast or roast pork belly, shaved coconut instead of noodles. The recipe is for two but can be reduced or doubled without any trouble. [SLB]

Preparation time 15 minutes

Cooking time 15 minutes

Serves 2

Season All ingredients available year-round

---

2 honey miso pork sausages
114 g egg noodles
600 ml chicken stock,
    homemade or store bought
3 star anise
1 rounded tsp coriander seeds
Pinch red chilli flakes
4 tblsp soy sauce
3 tblsp mirin
2 tsp sesame oil
2 tblsp spicy miso paste
50 g fresh spinach (about 2 handfuls)
1 red jalapeno chilli
4 spring onions
Bean sprouts (optional)
6 sprigs fresh coriander
Sea salt
Freshly ground black pepper

Preheat the oven to 180°C / 350°F / gas 4.

Slice the sausages in half lengthwise. Place them on a baking sheet and into the preheated oven and cook for 20 minutes. The sausages will release a lot of their fat, brown and curl slightly when cooked.

While the sausages are cooking, bring a medium-sized pan of water to a boil. Cook the egg noodles according to the pack's instructions – mine usually take about 5 minutes. Cook them *al dente* as you want them to finish cooking in your individual soup bowls. Drain and set aside.

Pour the chicken stock into another medium-sized pan and bring to a simmer. Crush the coriander seeds with a rolling pin or pestle and mortar and add to the stock along with the star anise and chilli flakes. Simmer the stock mixture for at least 10 minutes. In a small bowl combine the soy sauce, mirin, sesame oil and miso paste, mixing thoroughly to remove any lumps. Spoon into the spiced chicken stock and bring to a slow simmer once again (but don't allow the soup to boil).

Wash and dry the spinach and place it in the bottom of your serving bowls. Wash and slice the chilli in half, de-seed and remove as much of the white rib membranes as you can. Cut it into extremely thin strips. If chillies are too hot for you, you can either cut them into strips and soak them in water or leave them out entirely, but they do add a nice kick. Wash and thinly slice the whole of the spring onion. Rinse and pick over the bean sprouts, removing any damaged ones. Wash the coriander, blot or shake it dry and pick the leaves from the stems. Have all garnishes ready.

Once the sausages are cooked, divide the noodles between the bowls, top with strips of honey miso sausage and ladle over the hot broth. Scatter over the combination of garnishes and serve.

7-HOUR ROAST LEG OF LAMB WITH WHITE BEANS AND KALE

This recipe is a classic way of preparing lamb and will fill your kitchen with the most fantastic aroma. The mature lamb flavour is tempered by a lightly acidic white wine and aromatic fresh herbs. The use of bacon in this recipe came about through long conversations with Sarah Freeman about the use of prosciutto in slow cooking. Sarah was experimenting with a pro-sciutto-anchovy paste smeared over a boned leg of boar. The idea of insulating the meat whilst lightly curing, tenderising and flavouring the meat with a prepared salted product during cooking stuck with me. The unsmoked bacon in this recipe adds richness to the sauce, protects the flesh whilst cooking, and is delicious served alongside the tender lamb. The white beans and kale are a must in my book but crushed potatoes with oven-roasted vine tomatoes are fantastic too. [SLB]

Preparation time 20–25 minutes

Cooking time 7 hours

Serves 5

Season Lamb is in season from May until December

---

4 large garlic cloves
4 anchovy fillets
4 sprigs rosemary
2 kg leg mature lamb (hogget) or mutton
Sea salt
Freshly ground black pepper
1 tblsp olive oil
200 g unsmoked bacon either back or streaky, preferably Denhay
750 ml white wine, preferably Sauvignon Blanc
4 sprigs fresh thyme
1 sprig fresh parsley
2 sticks celery, preferably from the leafy heart
3 bay leaves
White beans with kale (recipe follows)

The important thing about this recipe is the pot. You need an ovenproof dish with a tight-fitting lid that will hold everything fairly snugly – it is ideal to have a 5cm gap all around the lamb. An oval cast-iron pot is perfect.

Preheat the oven to 130°C / 250°F / gas ½. Peel the garlic and slice, along with the anchovy fillets, so you have 12 slivers of each. Wash the rosemary and set aside. Make 12 x 2·5cm deep incisions all over the lamb. Stuff a piece of anchovy, garlic and a broken sprig of rosemary into each incision.

Season the lamb all over with sea salt and black pepper. Heat the oil in the pot, then lay the bacon slices in the bottom and lightly brown on both sides. Transfer the bacon to a plate and set aside while you brown the leg in the remaining oil and fat. Take a good 10 minutes to do this properly.

Transfer the lamb to the plate with the bacon. If there is a lot of fat in the pan, more than 3 tbsp, use a large spoon to remove and discard. Add a splash of the wine and use the back of a spoon to work any brown bits into the wine. Then, line the base of the casserole with the browned bacon slices and lay the lamb on top. Wash the fresh herbs and celery and tuck them around the lamb along with the bay leaves. Pour over the rest of the wine. Cover the top of the pot with aluminium foil and a tight-fitting lid.

Place the casserole on a baking tray and into the preheated oven. Cook for 7 hours. The meat will be so tender that it easily falls off the bone and it will smell fantastic.

As the lamb cooks for its final hour, prepare the white beans (recipe below).

Cook's note Both the lamb and the white beans can be prepared well ahead of time. Add the kale or cabbage to the beans just before serving.

BRAISED WHITE BEANS WITH KALE OR BLACK CABBAGE

Preparation time 10 minutes

Cooking time 1 hour 5 minutes

Serves 5

Season Kale and black cabbage can be found in the winter months – from November until late February

1 tblsp olive oil,
    plus extra for drizzling over final dish
6 to 8 garlic cloves
1 large onion
1 jar El Navaricco farmhouse beans
    (sold at Bedales in Borough)
440 g tin of chopped tomatoes
    or tomato passata
480 ml chicken stock
3 sprigs fresh thyme
3 sprigs fresh rosemary
225 g fresh kale or black cabbage
15 g fresh parsley to serve
Sea salt
Freshly ground black pepper

Peel and crush the garlic with a little salt in a pestle and mortar. Peel and finely chop the onion and place, along with the crushed garlic, in a large saucepan. Drizzle over the oil and sauté for 4–5 minutes until soft and translucent – avoid colouring. Drain the beans and rinse under cold running water. Add the beans to the pan along with the tomatoes and stock. Wash the sprigs of fresh thyme and rosemary. Submerge the herbs into the bean tomato mixture. Simmer for 45 minutes or until the liquid has reduced into a chunky bean sauce. Rinse the kale or black cabbage and remove any tough large stalks. Roughly chop the kale or stack the leaves of black cabbage and thinly slice; fold into the beans cooking for an additional 15 minutes. Check seasoning and finish with a drizzle of olive oil and fresh chopped parsley.

A Swaledale

SLOW ROASTED PORK LEG WITH GARLIC AND FENNEL SEEDS

Absolutely sensational! This is a flavour match made in heaven. The pork legs (usually either Gloucester Old Spot or Wiltshire Horn) have been hung before coming to market. This technique keeps their customers coming back for more as it makes it easier for the home cook to achieve a crisp crackling crust with tender flesh. You can use either pork shoulder or leg for this recipe. But remember the shoulders are a work-horse muscle and will have a slightly stronger flavour. [SLB]

Preparation time	15 minutes
Cooking time	6–7 hours
Serves	8
Season	All ingredients available year-round

3 kg leg of pork, bone in,
    skin scored by the butcher
5 garlic cloves
1 rounded tblsp fennel seeds
1 level tsp red chilli flakes
½ tsp freshly ground black pepper
3 tblsp extra virgin olive oil
5 tsp sea salt
475 ml white wine

Gloucester Old Spot and litter

When you get home after purchasing your pork leg, remove all packaging and place the pork on a rimmed plate and refrigerate, uncovered to allow the skin to dry. When ready to roast, remove the meat from the refrigerator an hour before cooking, to allow the meat to come to a cool room temperature.

Preheat the oven to 220°C / 425°F / gas 7.

Peel the garlic cloves and place them in a mortar along with the fennel seeds, red chilli flakes and 1 tsp sea salt and black pepper. Work into a paste as best you can. Using your fingers, cup the garlic fennel paste and rub over the fleshy sides of the leg, really working the paste into the meat.

Transfer the pork leg to a roasting pan. Try to fit the leg into a pan which will leave a 5 cm border around the meat – this will reduce the chance of a quick evaporation of the wine and lessen the chance of burning around the base of the meat and pan. Brush the top of the meat with olive oil and sprinkle the remaining sea salt over the skin only. Transfer the roasting pan to the oven and cook for 30 minutes.

After an hour, remove the pork from the oven and reduce the temperature to 150°C / 300°F / gas 2. Make sure the roasting pan is secure either on the hob or on a suitable sized trivet. Spoon off any fat which may have accumulated in the pan. Using a metal spatula flip the pork so that the skin side is down. It is best to always flip meat away from you so you don't get any spray of hot meat juices or fat on you. Return the roast to the oven and continue cooking for 5–6 more hours at the lower temperature.

After 5 hours have passed, remove the pork from the oven. Increase the heat to 220°C / 425°F / gas 7. Again, secure the roasting pan either on the hob or on a suitable sized trivet and flip the meat over (away from you). Pour in the wine and return the pork to the oven for 45 minutes longer. Baste the meat every 10 minutes or so with the wine and pan juices.

Test by inserting a fork and giving it a little poke. The meat should be quite juicy and pull apart easily. If not, continue cooking the meat for up to 30 minutes longer. Allow to rest for 20 minutes before cutting and serving.

Serve with oven roasted tomato chutney (see page 97) or homemade barbecue sauce.

Cook's note I believe the above method is the easiest way to produce a tender juicy roast with crisp crackling. Yet, I have cooked the roast at a lower temperature (100°C / 200°F / gas ¼) than the above 150°C / 300°F / gas 2 for an additional hour with equal success. It is a very flexible recipe both in terms of cooking time as well as flavour. Try substituting cider for wine and roasting on a bed of leeks with a few sage leaves tucked in around the meat.

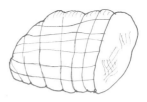

Pork

PORK KEBABS WITH PINEAPPLE SAGE AND HONEY ORANGE DRESSING

Served as part of a barbecue or for a quick weeknight dinner, kebabs are easy to cook, and easy to serve. Pineapple sage can be purchased at most garden centres and grows wildly if left alone in most gardens. 'Herbs from Heaven' at Borough sells small plants which sit perfectly on a windowsill or nestle comfortably in a garden bed. This variety of sage truly does taste of pineapple. So if you don't have any on hand, alternate the pork cubes with chunks of fresh pineapple and three leaves of ordinary fresh sage. [SLB]

Preparation time 10 minutes, plus 20 minutes marinating and an additional 30 minutes soaking time for the skewers

Cooking time 10 minutes, plus 5 minutes to rest

Serves 3 as a main course

Season Pineapple sage is a half hardy perennial and is at its best in summer with beautiful red flowers

450–500 g pork fillet
Small bunch pineapple sage
  (enough for 15 g leaves)
1 quarter of a pineapple (if using)
  plus 3 ordinary sage leaves
1 large orange
1 tblsp clear runny honey
Sea salt
Freshly ground black pepper

Special equipment
3 wooden or metal skewers

Preheat the oven grill or prepare the barbecue. If using gas grill, preheat to a hot setting, then reduce the heat to medium.

Cut the pork fillet into 2·5 cm square cubes. If you are using pineapple, cut the pineapple into similar sizes. Pull off and wash the sage leaves. Place in a glass bowl. Squeeze the orange. Mix together up to 120 ml of the juice with the honey in a small bowl before pouring over the meat (and pineapple, if using). Season with salt and pepper and allow to marinate for at least 20 minutes.

If you are using wooden skewers, soak in water for 30 minutes. Thread the pork and pineapple sage leaves (or, alternate the pineapple cubes and sage with the pork if this is what you're using) onto the skewers, alternating as you go. Place the kebabs on a barbecue or under the grill and cook for 10 minutes, turning occasionally. Using a brush, drizzle over any remaining marinade whilst cooking.

Serve with some grilled sweet potatoes tossed with some watercress leaves on the side.

Cook's note For variation, chop 15 g fresh oregano and mix with juice from half an orange, 1 tblsp tahini, ½ tblsp honey and 1 tsp of toasted cumin seeds. Marinate and grill as above.

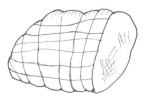

Pork

ROAST PORK LOIN
WITH DARK BEER

Having three young children never seemed to deter my parents from having friends around for supper or to play bridge. Without fail my mum would make sausage rolls or 'pigs in a blanket' (as she would call them) with a honey mustard dipping sauce. And again, without fail I would always sneak a sip of my father's beer! Together the flavours have left a lasting impression. Here is my interpretation of my own childhood favourite combination! [SLB]

Preparation time 15 minutes,
    plus minimum 8 hours marinating

Cooking time 25 minutes per pound,
    plus 15 minutes resting

Serves 6

Season All ingredients available year-round

1 large onion
1 tblsp olive oil
4 tblsp Dijon mustard
4 tblsp runny honey
1 pint dark beer, preferably German but I
    have also made this with Guinness
1·6 kg boneless pork loin (skin removed)
Sea salt
Freshly ground black pepper
2 tblsp vegetable oil
1 tblsp softened unsalted butter
1 tblsp plain flour

Begin by peeling and finely dicing the onion. Combine the onion with the olive oil in a small saucepan over a low flame. Cover and sweat the onion for 5 minutes. Remove from the heat and add the mustard and honey, stirring to combine. Slowly pour in the beer. At this stage, the mixture should be cool: if it is not, set it aside for 20 minutes before continuing.

Place the pork in a glass or ceramic baking dish and pour over the marinade. Cover and refrigerate for 6–8 hours, but preferably overnight turning occasionally.

Before cooking, remove the pork from the refrigerator and allow it to reach a cool room temperature before cooking, about 45 minutes.

Preheat oven to 190°C / 375°F / gas 5.

Transfer the marinade to a saucepan and bring it to the boil. Simmer for 3 minutes and turn off the heat. Pat the pork dry with paper towels and season with salt and pepper. Heat the vegetable oil in a frying pan over a moderately high heat until hot but not smoking and brown the pork on all sides. Transfer the pork to a roasting pan, and place into the centre of the preheated oven. Baste frequently with the boiled marinade until a meat thermometer registers 66°C / 150°F – for slightly pink meat this should take 1 hour to 1 hour 15 minutes.

Transfer the pork to a cutting board, reserving the juices in the roasting pan, and let it rest, covered loosely with foil, for about 15 minutes. Remember that during this time the internal temperature will increase by at least 5 degrees. While the pork is resting, combine the unsalted butter and flour together in a small bowl. Skim and discard fat from the pan and add any remaining marinade. Deglaze the roasting pan by stirring over moderately high heat, scraping up brown bits. Bring just to the boil and add the butter mixture, whisking until the sauce is smooth (apart from the onion) and thickened.

Slice the pork, divide between plates, spoon over some sauce and serve with buttery mashed potatoes and a salad.

PORK STIR FRY WITH SHITAKE MUSHROOMS AND CABBAGE, WITH CORIANDER PANCAKES

30 minutes is a generous preparation time. It usually takes me about 15–20 minutes to get everything together. So, the faster you chop the quicker you will be at putting this dish together. I've suggested using pork tenderloin or fillet for this recipe but in a pinch I have used a good quality minced pork with equal success (which can reduce the preparation time even further) to give a 'popcorn pork' effect to the recipe which you often find in Chinese restaurants. If you are going to use mince, make sure you keep an eye on the fat when cooking the meat. Spoon off any residual fat left in the pan before adding the vegetables back to the wok and tossing with the sauce. The pancakes are a fun way to dress up a stir fry for a special occasion but they are obviously not an integral part of the dish. For weeknight stir frys, simply serve over steamed rice or wrap in store bought flatbreads. [SLB]

Preparation time 30 minutes

Cooking time 15 minutes

Serves 4

Season Savoy cabbages love the cold weather. November, December and January are the best months to buy them.

4 tblsp soy sauce
2 tblsp Chinese cooking wine
1 tsp sugar
1 tblsp sesame oil
2 tsp cornflour
Freshly ground black pepper
Sea salt
2 medium eggs
125 g plain flour
250 ml full-fat milk
3 tblsp fresh coriander
3 tblsp sunflower oil
225 g pork tenderloin
5 cm piece ginger
8 spring onions
2 carrots
1 savoy cabbage (quarter only needed)
125 g mushrooms, preferably shitake or chestnut

Place the soy sauce, cooking wine, sugar and sesame oil in a small bowl. Mix the cornflour in a little cup with 1 tblsp of cold water. Add to the soy sauce mixture. Season with a little black pepper and sea salt. Set aside until ready to use.

Before you cook the stir-fried pork, make the pancakes. Place the flour in a large mixing bowl and form a well in the centre. Crack the eggs and pour the milk into the centre of the well. Begin to mix, breaking up the eggs and gradually incorporating the flour around the bowl until you have a fairly smooth batter. Wash, dry and finely chop the fresh coriander leaves and fine stems only. Add the herb to the batter and whisk to combine. Place a frying pan over a medium-high heat. Drizzle with a little oil and swirl to coat the bottom of the frying pan. Ladle or pour in about 2 tblsp of batter, swirling the frying pan to coat the bottom evenly. When you can start to lift the pancake after the edges have become slightly crispy, carefully slide a palette knife or spatula under the pancake and flip over. Cook for a further minute and remove from the pan. Continue with the remaining batter, adding another drizzle of oil as needed.

Cut the pork into thin matchsticks about 3mm by 12mm thick. Peel the ginger and carrots and slice into thin slivers. Cut the green onion into thirds and then slice lengthwise into thin strips. Take one quarter of the cabbage, wash it and remove the bitter core. Slice it into 3mm slices. Remove any stems from the mushrooms, wash and squeeze dry the caps and slice them finely.

Heat 1 tblsp of oil in a large wok or frying pan over high heat. Add the ginger, green onion, cabbage, carrots and mushrooms; cook, stirring constantly, until the vegetables are wilted but still crisp. Transfer the cooked vegetables to a small bowl. Wipe the wok clean. Add another tblsp of oil to the wok and heat gently. You want it hot but not smoking. Lower in the pork strips and stir fry for about 3 minutes. Put the vegetables back to the pan and pour over the soy sauce mixture. Toss the pork constantly in the hot pan for another 2 minutes.

Serve the pork and vegetables wrapped up in the warm pancakes.

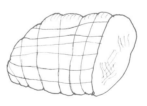

Pork

'The Ginger Pig' and piglets

BAKED SCOTCH EGGS

Walking into The Ginger Pig for the first time I was in awe of their vast array of sausages. They seem to have something to suit every palate.

These scotch eggs are quite large so you may want to cut them in half. For a great variation devil the egg yolks by scooping out the yolk, mashing it with some grainy mustard and mayonnaise, spooning the mixture back into the halved scotch egg.

Ginger Pig does make its own version of delicious Scotch eggs. The below recipe is a variation on my mother's baked Scotch eggs. Along with the All-in-One Chicken Sandwich (see page 148), these eggs are perfect food for travelling. Most Autumn weekends for our family centred around going to watch my father's alma mater play football. Those weekends wouldn't have been the same without my mum's Scotch eggs.

Herbes de Provence is a mix of aromatic plants, usually dried. These herbs are native to the Provence region of France and the blend traditionally consists of rosemary, marjoram, basil, bay leaf and thyme. Lavender is the secret ingredient lending a degree of authentic southern French flair to a recipe. [SLB]

Preparation time 7–8 minutes to boil the eggs

Cooking time 30 minutes, plus 5 minutes resting

Serves 6

Season All ingredients available year-round

7 medium eggs
4–5 sprigs fresh parsley
About 600 g Toulouse sausage meat
1 tsp Herbes de Provence
A pinch of freshly ground nutmeg
Sea Salt
Freshly ground black pepper
1 small brown onion
2 garlic cloves
1 tblsp plain flour
170 g fresh breadcrumbs
Dijon mustard and pickles for serving

Preheat your oven to 175 °C/ 340 °F/ gas 4.

Fill a large saucepan with water and place over a high heat. Bring to a simmer and using a large spoon gently lower the eggs into the hot water. Allow the water to come to a low boil and cook the eggs for 7 minutes. Drain, rinse in cold water and peel.

While the eggs are cooking, wash, blot dry and finely chop 1 tblsp of parsley. Combine the sausage meat, remaining egg, parsley, Herbes de Provence and a good grating of nutmeg. Season with sea salt and freshly ground black pepper. Peel and finely dice the onion. Peel the garlic and work into a paste with a little salt in a mortar. Add to the sausage and mix thoroughly.

Divide the sausage meat into 6 portions and shape into thin patties. Dust each peeled egg with flour and using your hands, mould each patty around each flour-dusted egg. Then roll the sausage-coated egg in breadcrumbs and place in a shallow baking dish. Bake for 25–30 minutes in a preheated oven until the sausage meat and breadcrumbs are nicely browned.

Allow to rest for 5–10 minutes before serving or let cool to room temperature. Serve with Dijon mustard and pickles.

GAMSTON WOOD OSTRICHES

Sue & Jim Farr *Retford, Nottinghamshire*

Sue and Jim Farr's farm is next to Gamston Wood, which is only a few miles from Sherwood Forest. Classified as a Site of Special Scientific Interest, the area is best known for the picturesque black and white striped White Admiral butterfly. It's also a site of historic note, since it was mentioned in the Domesday Book and was used by the parishioners of Gamston village as a source of free firewood (which was not quite such a welcome arrangement as it sounds because it is quite a long walk to the village).

Their backdrop of ancient English woodland makes the ostriches seem all the more exotic. They're native to Africa and, as this might suggest, adapted to life in the desert. In the wild, much of their need for water is satisfied by plants and, according to Sue, they eat considerably less than one might expect. Similarly, they can endure very high temperatures. Like other poultry, their fat is concentrated under the skin, which serves as insulation. They also have relatively few feathers and in hot weather will aerate themselves by lifting their wings. Their feathers, or plumes, were nearly the cause of their destruction, since they were once so fashionable that ostriches were hunted to near extinction.

Right Eggs in the hatchery.
Opposite Jim Farr with ostrich chick as it hatches.

BOROUGH MARKET COOKBOOK **Meat**

When you see them, however, the first thing to strike you is their size. With their long legs and sinuous necks, which they twist as improbably as the flamingoes used as croquet mallets in *Alice in Wonderland*, the adults are seven to eight feet tall and can draw themselves up to nine feet if they feel aggressive. Although their legs don't look strong, they can run at speeds of up to forty miles per hour and carry a load as heavy as a jockey: hence, like horses, they have been saddled and raced. On the other hand, their wings are little more than vestigial, which means that they can't fly.

Inevitably, one of the first questions I asked the Farrs was, 'Why ostriches?' Basically, the answer is that Jim loves birds and has kept one sort or another since he was at primary school. The specific idea of ostriches, however, came from his mother, who happened to be reading an article about them at around the time when he bought the farm.

He started his career as an engineer; Sue meanwhile worked in the dispensary at Boots but spent her spare time studying the business patterns in neighbouring towns. This showed her that Retford had no delicatessen. When the recession of the 1980s

Mature ostriches
by Gamston Wood

led Jim to suspect that he might be made redundant, she decided to leave Boots and open one (she is a wonderful cook and had always been more interested in food than medicine). Their original plan had been that Jim would join her if he lost his job: in the event, by the time this happened she was running it so successfully that she didn't need him. He, therefore, started a health-food shop on the other side of the road. Eventually, the two shops were amalgamated – which before long meant that again he wasn't needed. At this point 'Jobless Jim' bought their present farm, which was in a very run-down state, 'a dump, in fact', and renovated it himself.

At present, they keep 100–120 ostriches over nine acres, and own about another 200 who are looked after elsewhere. As no ready-made feed was available, they had to develop their own; to start with, they made mistakes, but they have now perfected a set of five pellets suitable for the different stages of an ostrich's life, ie chicks, growing birds, those being 'finished', birds being brought into peak condition for breeding, and mothers. The feed is eighty-three per cent organic (not all the ingredients can be obtained in organic form) and is based on wheat, barley, and lucerne. They also run the only licensed ostrich slaughterhouse in Britain again necessarily, since ostriches are too big to be handled in those for other kinds of poultry. The ostriches at Gamston, therefore, don't have to travel at all. They are blindfolded and immediately stunned with electric tongs applied to the brain, which is about as humane as you can get.

Sue and Jim made a positive decision to stay small rather than expanding and wholesaling, partly because of the fluctuations of the international wholesale market. Farms in South Africa, New Zealand, and elsewhere rear ostriches for skins (rather than feathers) and slaughter very large numbers all at the same time. This temporarily lowers the price of the meat, which is also not of the same quality as Sue and Jim's.

The Farrs have various other retail outlets, including a few restaurants, but Borough is an important part of their sales strategy. Sue says, 'I never like the thought of the drive, but when I get there I just love it.' Besides the meat, which has the density of beef and a distinctive, albeit delicate flavour, they sell ostrich eggs, blown egg-shells, which have a ceramic quality and can be decorated or used for lamps, and feathers – but not skins, which have to be sent abroad because of the lack of tanneries in the UK.

OSTRICH STEW
WITH MUSHROOMS
AND LEMON ZEST

One of the reasons for buying ostrich is that it is remarkably low in fat and cholesterol. It's also full of flavour, which is interesting in that our perception of flavour is supposed to be heightened by the presence of fat: marbling in red meat is looked on as desirable. (Venison is another low-fat meat with a distinctive flavour, but in this case the taste is developed by hanging, which doesn't apply in the case of ostrich.)

In case anyone is seriously worried about cholesterol, I should say here that, to bring out the sweetness of the meat, I have seared it with a little butter. I haven't used much (only 15g), but if you want to omit it, you can replace it with an extra tablespoonful of olive oil.

The lemon zest, instead of being removed before serving, is diced and left with the other ingredients in the stew. It ends up relatively soft, almost as if it was caramelised, and is delicious.

Please bear in mind that I am a slow (as well as Slow Food) cook: hopefully, your preparation time will be somewhat shorter than mine.

Have the bacon thick-cut as this is easier than thin-cut to dice. [SF]

Preparation time 35 minutes

Cooking time 10 minutes for frying,
    plus 2½ hours in the oven

Serves 4

Season All ingredients available year-round

100g (1 small) onion
6 cloves garlic
125g smoked back bacon,
    preferably thick-cut
1 unwaxed or organic lemon (zest only)
225g mixed Portobello and chestnut
    mushrooms
450g ostrich steak
Sea salt
Freshly ground black pepper
25g plain white flour
15g unsalted butter
3 tblsp olive oil
600ml dry white wine, *eg* a Chardonnay
¾ tsp yellow mustard seed
Good-sized sprig of rosemary

ostrich

Peel and finely chop the onion. Peel the garlic but leave the cloves whole. Cut off the bacon rind and snip the bacon into 0·5 cm by 1·25 cm strips (use scissors). Wash the lemon, pare off half the zest, and cut the zest into strips about the same size as for the bacon. Trim the mushroom stalks and peel the mushrooms; wash and squeeze as much moisture as you can from open ones and leave them to drain on kitchen paper. Chop the steak into 2 cm squares. Lay it on a plate, season it moderately with salt and pepper, and shake the flour over it, turning each piece so that it is lightly coated on all sides. Transfer it to a clean plate, shaking it slightly so that any surplus flour falls off or is left behind.

Set the oven to 180 °C / 350 °F / gas 4.

Put the butter and 1 tblsp of the oil in a large, preferably non-stick frying pan over moderate heat and wait for a moment or two, until the butter has melted and the oil is hot but not smoking. Add the meat, or as much of it as will fit in the pan in a single layer: if necessary, fry it in two batches. Sear it lightly all over and return it to the plate.

Pour half the wine into a measuring jug. Wash and dry the frying-pan and put in the remaining 2 tblsp of olive oil. Set it over medium heat and add the onion and bacon. Fry for 4 minutes or until the onion is soft, turning constantly. Add the mustard seeds and turn. Add the mushrooms, garlic, and lemon peel and continue to fry, turning continuously, until the mushrooms start to shrink (probably after about 2 minutes). At this stage, the pan will be very dry. Rather than adding more oil, moisten it with a couple of tablespoons of wine from the mug. Fry for another minute or so; then remove the pan from the heat.

Arrange half the meat in the bottom of a medium-sized casserole with a tight-fitting lid, preferably deep and narrow rather than shallow and wide (if it is wide, the juices from the stew will evaporate more quickly). Next, put in half the bacon and mushroom mixture. Repeat, finishing with the mixture, and pour in the rest of the jug of wine. Rinse and add the rosemary, cover, and bake for an hour. Take the casserole out of the oven and stir it gently: by this time, the mushrooms will have absorbed the wine and the stew will be dry. Pour in the rest of the wine and cook for another 1½ hours.

Serve with mashed or baby new potatoes.

OSTRICH PLUM AND PORT CASSEROLE

This is two recipes combined. Firstly, in Moroccan cooking, beef is sometimes paired with prunes. And, if you go into Chinese restaurants, you may see steak served with a plum sauce. Here, I have combined the technique of one cuisine with the flavour combination of another. The ostrich is given a Provençal flavour note with a bouquet garni, nutmeg and port. Make sure your plums are on the tart side. Try one before cooking: if sweet, use a fruity, full-flavoured Grenache-based red wine instead of port. [SLB]

Preparation time 15 minutes

Cooking time 15 minutes to brown the meat, plus 2 hours in the oven

Serves 3

Season Due to alternating mating seasons, you can buy ostrich year-round

25 g butter
1 tblsp extra virgin olive oil
450 g ostrich steak
2 tsp plain flour
1 onion
2 garlic cloves
Sea salt
Freshly ground black pepper
150 ml port
2 tsp balsamic vinegar
2 tsp soy sauce
1 bouquet garni (4 sprigs thyme, 2 sprigs parsley, 2 bay leaves)
300 g fresh plums
Freshly grated nutmeg

Heat the butter and oil in a large casserole over a low flame. Cut the ostrich steak into large cubes and toss to coat in the flour. Gently lower the meat down into the hot pan. Brown on all sides and remove.

Preheat the oven to 150 °C / 300 °F / gas 2.

Peel and finely dice the onion. Peel and crush the garlic with a little salt in a pestle and mortar and place both aromatics into the hot pan; cover and sweat for 5 minutes. Once the onion and garlic have softened, pour in the port, along with the balsamic vinegar and soy sauce. Bring the mixture up to a rolling simmer. Add the bouquet garni and gently lower the meat into the hot broth. Season well with salt and pepper.

Wash and stone all the plums and cut them into quarters. Scatter them around the meat and give a good grating of nutmeg before covering the casserole with a layer of parchment paper and a tight fitting lid.

Transfer the casserole to the preheated oven and cook for 2 hours, after which time the meat should be pull-apart tender. The juices should be slightly thickened from the flour, but plums can vary in their juice content. If you have a particularly thin sauce, lift the meat out from the sauce and bring the cooking liquid up to a boil. Reduce the liquid until it has a nice viscosity before spooning over the meat and serving.

Opposite Heads in the Sky

CORIANDER CRUSTED OSTRICH FILLET WITH CABRALES CHEESE

Cabrales is a strong Spanish blue cheese, which helps to cut through the weighty flavour of the ostrich. Brindisa at Borough sells an amazing selection of Spanish cheeses, including Cabrales, and I'm sure they would be happy to find you a wine to match this gutsy dish. Cabrales is usually served young, and thus has a high acidity. The pairing with the cracked coriander seeds works extremely well and provides a mature depth of flavour to the young cheese. Considering this is a variation on the classic combination of steak and stilton, a good strong creamy stilton would work equally as well. [SLB]

Preparation time 5 minutes

Cooking time 17 minutes, plus 5 minutes resting

Serves 4

Season Alternating mating seasons mean that you can buy ostrich year-round

---

500 g ostrich fillet
3 tblsp olive oil
1 tblsp coriander seeds
1 tsp black peppercorns
1 level tsp sea salt
200 g Cabrales cheese

Preheat oven to 200 °C / 400 °F / gas 6.

Rub the ostrich fillet with olive oil and set aside. Crush the coriander seeds, black peppercorns and sea salt together with a pestle and mortar. Rub this mixture into the ostrich.

Heat a frying pan over a medium-high flame for a minute before putting the ostrich into the pan. Brown on all sides for 2–3 minutes. Then transfer to the preheated oven. Cook for 15 minutes for rare, 18 minutes for medium, longer for well done.

Remove the fillet from the oven. Allow it to rest for 5 minutes. Slice the fillet into 8 slices and arrange on warm plates. Crumble Cabrales over each portion and serve with a salad.

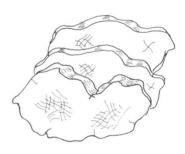

ostrich

OSTRICH 'OYSTER' MINUTE STEAKS

Everyone who carves the Christmas turkey knows where and how deliciously tender the 'oyster' is. This sweetest morsel on any bird is located at the top of the thigh, where it is attached to the backbone of the bird. It's an extremely under-used muscle, about the size of a fifty pence piece, full of flavoursome and juicy dark meat. Now, imagine this tiny pocketful of gorgeousness on a huge ostrich. Fantastic! Oyster muscles on ostriches are about the size of a medium-small chicken breast and they are a generous 2·5cm in thickness.

Ostrich has an extremely soft texture with the flavour of a game bird. We found a simple marinade and flash grill on a hot barbecue brings out the best in this bird. It is extremely low in fat (lower that roast chicken) and lower in cholesterol than beef, pork, game birds, duck, venison and chicken, making it a gem in terms of healthy, well-rounded eating.

If you can't find oysters, a 225g fillet or tenderloin of ostrich would work equally well. Also try stuffing the oyster with sautéed mushrooms with a wrapping in Sillfield Farm's wild boar prosciutto. Sear on both sides and finish in a hot oven for 12 minutes. [SLB]

Preparation time 15 minutes, plus at least 1 hour for marinating

Cooking time 2–3 minutes

Serves 2

Season Due to alternating mating seasons, you can buy ostrich year-round

2 ostrich oysters
60ml red wine
1 tblsp Worcestershire sauce
1 tblsp balsamic vinegar
Sea salt
Freshly ground black pepper
2 tsp olive oil

Lay the oyster down flat on your work surface. You should have one end which comes to more or less a point with the other end being slightly rounded – like a chicken breast. Hold your knife parallel to the work surface. At the rounded end, carefully slice along the middle of the oyster towards the pointed end to open it up like a book. Cut out any large pieces of sinuous white fibre and discard. Repeat the preparation technique with the remaining oyster.

Sandwich the opened oysters in between two pieces of parchment paper. Using a rolling pin gently bash the oysters into an even thickness, 1 cm thick. Usually you just have to hit the meat 3 or 4 times on the rounded end to even it out. Transfer to a shallow baking dish and cover with wine, Worcestershire sauce, balsamic vinegar and a good seasoning of salt and pepper. Cover and refrigerate for at least an hour (or up to 24 hours).

Preheat a griddle or frying pan until it is very hot. Remove the oysters from the marinade and drizzle with olive oil. Place the slices on the hot pan. Cook for about 1–1½ minutes, flip and cook for another minute or a little longer if you like it more well-done.

Have a salad ready on the plates for serving as you want to serve the steaks straight from the pan. Rocket, watercress or even lightly dressed mustard greens with lemon juice go well with the full-flavoured ostrich meat.

OSTRICH STIR FRY

A sophisticated stir fry for a fuller-flavoured meat. Orange juice and dry sherry add depth of flavour whilst enrobing each piece of ostrich meat in the aromatic sauce. The elegant fiery heat of dried red chilli flakes balances the more astringent heat of fresh ginger while the added vegetables provide a varying mix of textures and colours. In the end producing a very satisfying stir fry indeed! [SLB]

Preparation time 25 minutes

Cooking time 6–7 minutes

Serves 4

Season Due to alternating mating seasons, you can buy ostrich year-round

1 garlic clove
Sea salt
Freshly ground black pepper
2·5 cm piece ginger
½ tsp dried red chilli flakes
4 spring onions
100 g mange tout
115 g mushrooms, preferably wild
1 red pepper
50 g bean sprouts, for garnish
2 tblsp sesame seeds
½ tsp cornflour
2 tblsp soy sauce
2 tblsp dry sherry
2 tblsp fresh orange juice
350 g ostrich mince
2 tblsp extra virgin olive oil
Basmati rice for serving

Wash, prepare and measure all the ingredients before you begin cooking. Peel and crush the garlic with some salt in a mortar into a paste. Peel and slice the ginger into thin matchsticks. Chop off the root end of the green onion, peel off the outer layer and finely slice on the diagonal, using the whole onion. Slice the mange tout and mushrooms into slivers. Remove the core and deseed the red pepper and as with the mange tout and mushrooms, cut into thin slivers. Have the bean sprouts out and ready to use as a garnish.

Place a small frying pan or a wok over a low flame. Lightly toast the sesame seeds, but keep an eye on them, once they start colouring they can burn fast. Set aside in a cool place or they will continue to toast.

In a small bowl dissolve the cornflour in 1 tsp of cold water. Pour the soy sauce, sherry and orange juice into the same bowl and set aside. If you are serving the stir fry over Basmati rice, bring a small saucepan filled with water to a boil over a medium-high flame. Place Basmati rice in a sieve and rinse thoroughly in plenty of cold water. Season the boiling water with salt and add the rice. Cook for 10 minutes or according to the manufacturer's instructions. Drain and set aside.

Heat a wok or a large frying pan over a medium-high flame. Add 1 tblsp of olive oil and heat until hot but not smoking. Add the ostrich mince and stir continuously, moving around the hot pan for 3 minutes. Empty the meat into a bowl.

Add the remaining olive oil to the wok and again heat until hot. Add the garlic, ginger and chilli flakes and cook for 30 seconds or until they become fragrant. Add all the vegetables at once. Toss in the aromatic oil until they wilt but are still crisp, no longer than 3 minutes.

Add the ostrich back to the wok and toss with the vegetables. Pour in the soy sauce mixture and toss to coat. Serve immediately with Basmati rice.

Sue Farr,
Gamston butchery

FARMHOUSE DIRECT

Jackie & David Kitson *Long Ghyll Farm, Bleasdale, Lancashire*

The first time I tried to visit Jackie and David Kitson we didn't make it because of a hold-up on the motorway. The next time, their van broke down, so that although we reached the farm as arranged, nobody was there. The visit wasn't wasted, however, since it enabled us to see how delightful the countryside around Long Ghyll is, with lush fields and woods set against the slightly forbidding silhouette of Beacon Fell behind the house. The farm is on the southern edge of the Forest of Bowland, which is famous for its beauty. On the one hand is the Lake District across Morecambe Bay and on the other the area around Preston, traditionally known as the dairying region of the North West.

The visit was also an illustration of the realities of farming – as was that of George Nicholson (the book's photographer) a few weeks later, although in a very different way. In Jackie and David's absence, I made friends with a group of Highland cattle in a barn:

The Highland Cattle nursery

subsequently, I was unhappy to learn that they were there because they were destined for slaughter. As for George, he too had a transport problem, since Jackie had a puncture on the way to meeting him at the station. Instead of waiting, he took a taxi and arrived before her. Seeing the Highland cattle, he set out to photograph them and slipped – not on a mere cowpat but on and into a ditch of what can politely be described as liquid manure. Jackie returned to find him standing trouserless, in his shirt-tails, having had to abandon his clogged, stinking trousers. He had to borrow a pair of David's jeans for the rest of the day.

The Kitsons have had to battle hard to make the farm pay. Unlike some, they didn't inherit it: David started out as a forester, while Jackie was a saddler (and also a very keen and successful horsewoman). However, David had always longed for a farm and one day simply decided to buy one. Long Ghyll was irresistible but, as they soon found, uneconomically small. They tried buying a second farm and running the two in tandem, but this proved impracticable; then they looked for a bigger one but could find nowhere as attractive as Long Ghyll. Finally, some land adjoining their own came up for sale, which solved the problem.

Apart from the land issue, their farming career has been shaped by BSE and foot-and-mouth. Before BSE, they had never thought of selling meat: David reared Highland cattle (he had no sheep or pigs in those days) and sold them on as livestock. After BSE, livestock prices collapsed and they were forced to move over to meat instead. At this stage, the quantities were relatively small and Jackie continued working as a saddler. After foot-and-mouth, however, it became very clear that they would have to put every ounce of their combined energies into their meat business in order to survive. Rather than wholesaling, they concentrated on selling at fairs (as they still do), with the enormous amount of work that this entails. Typically, they set out in the evening, arrive at the venue probably at midnight, and spend until around 3am setting up their stall. Then at 6am they have to start laying out the stock. Nevertheless, David says that he loves it: lots of their friends go, and he enjoys the buzz. However, apart from Christmas, fairs don't take place in the winter: Borough, where they have sold for the past four years, has meant that they have an income all the year round. Now the new market at the Arndale Centre in Manchester, which will be open daily, promises a second year-round outlet and indeed seems likely to usher in a new, more stable and prosperous phase of their lives.

At present, the Kitsons have 300 sheep and a herd of 150 Highland cattle, which is one of the largest in the country. They also own a sizeable herd of Gloucester Old Spot pigs, who are not kept at Long Ghyll for the same reason as Amanda Streatfeild stopped keeping pigs at Denhay: rich soil and mud. 'They'd turn the ground into liquid in no time,' says David. Instead, they are reared on a farm with drier land in Yorkshire. In addition, the family owns nine horses and two show ponies. Since having a daughter, who is also a keen horsewoman, Jackie has resumed her own riding career and David himself enjoys eventing and hunting (nowadays with a drag, which he feels is ridiculous).

Their animals are killed at a small family slaughterhouse only forty minutes' drive away. They sell mutton as well as lamb, and now that the ban following BSE has been lifted, they can offer three to four-year-old beef: according to David, the flavour isn't fully developed until the cattle are aged at least three. Currently, Borough accounts for about twenty per cent of their sales. A notable point about their pork is that rather than being sold fresh, as is usual, it is hung for ten days. 'I don't know why no-one else 'hangs pork,' says David. 'It improves the cracking because it dries the skin.'

Opposite *Highland cattle, Long Ghyll Farm, near Preston*

Right *Sheep carcass, Borough Market stand*

QUICKLY COOKED LAMBS' KIDNEY WITH RED-WINE SAUCE AND RICE

People tend to forget that animals don't consist only of fillets, sirloins, or in the case of sheep, legs: there are also the less popular cuts such as shin and shoulder, plus offal. I've made a point of giving recipes for shin and shoulder: now it's the turn of offal. As David Kitson of Farmhouse Direct says, every lamb has two kidneys.

This is a quick, simple dish which works excellently for just one person: you can easily scale up the quantities for more. The exact amount of rice and whether you use three or four kidneys is a matter of appetite.

As the fresher the kidneys the better, you should cook them on the same day as you buy them.

If you haven't any stock, I suggest using brown rice, which has a good deal more flavour than white; the nutty texture also suits the lambs' kidneys especially well. [SF]

Preparation time about 10 minutes

Cooking time 25 or 30 minutes for the rice, depending on whether it is brown or white, plus 10–15 minutes while it rests. The kidneys can be cooked while it rests.

Serves 1

Season Kidneys are available throughout the year, but autumn is the best time for mushrooms

---

125 g brown or white Basmati rice
225 ml meat or vegetable stock
125 g mushrooms, which could be mixed,
    eg chestnut and oyster mushrooms
    and/or chanterelles
2 garlic cloves
3 or 4 very fresh lambs' kidneys
Sea salt
Freshly ground black pepper
1 tblsp olive oil
Generous ½ tsp Dijon mustard
Generous ½ glass full-bodied red wine
    (eg Cabernet Sauvignon or Shiraz)
    plus a little extra if necessary
1–2 tblsp double cream

Start by cooking the rice. Rinse it under the cold tap until the water runs clear and put it into a saucepan with a lid. Add the stock or the same amount of water. If you're using water or the stock is unseasoned, add just a few flakes of salt (stock made from cubes tends to be salty). Bring the water to the boil, reduce the heat to a slow simmer, cover, and leave to simmer for 20 minutes. Check that there is still moisture in the pan: if too dry, the rice will stick to the bottom. Add a little water if necessary and continue simmering (still covered) for 5 minutes if the rice is white, 10 minutes if it is brown. Turn off the heat and allow to rest (still covered) while you cook the kidneys. You will find that it is perfectly separate-grained and dry: if the rice at the bottom of the pan has stuck slightly and formed a golden crust, don't worry: to some cooks, the crust is the best part.

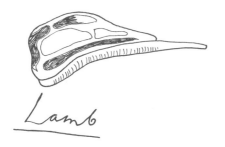

Lamb

Carefully clean the mushrooms by blotting the earth off. Trim the ends of the stalks, and cut them into moderately thin slices (say 1 cm or a bit more). Peel and slice the garlic. Wash and peel the kidneys. Slice them to about the same thickness as the mushrooms, cutting round the hard cores (which should be thrown away). Season them lightly with salt and generously with pepper.

Measure the oil into a wok or frying pan and set it over fairly high heat. Add the garlic and cook for a moment or two. Turn down the heat to moderately low and add the mushrooms. Sprinkle them with a very little salt and slightly more pepper and fry gently, turning constantly, for 5–7 minutes. Add and stir in the mustard. Splash in the wine, raise the heat to fairly high, and cook about half of it away. Add the kidneys and stir-fry, still over fairly high heat, for 2–3 minutes or until they are grey rather than red on all sides. If there isn't much liquid left in the pan, pour in a little more wine. Lower the heat, let the sauce bubble gently for another minute or so, and stir in the cream. Serve on top of the rice.

Bleasdale, Lancashire

SHEPHERD'S PIE

These days, people generally cook what they are in the mood for, or what they feel their body requires at the moment – be it vegetables, beans, fish or meat. Sometimes, though, you just crave something comforting and familiar. My husband William has been extremely helpful and supportive in tasting and helping to test recipes for this book. He's a fantastic cook in his own right. One day, after going to the market, I returned home find to him rustling about in the kitchen. He was making a shepherd's pie. I thought it only appropriate to give him the credit he so rightfully deserves. He will undoubtedly look at this recipe with a quizzical eye thinking that it is not his own. But it is at its heart, although I have made some alterations which I hope he will approve of. So here is our collaboration in the kitchen!

Think ahead when cooking neck or leg of lamb as shepherd's pie can easily be made with left over roasted or braised meat. Follow the recipe below but skip the browning step, halve the amount of flour, and add it before the wine and stock. Cook only for 10 minutes to allow the flavours to mingle and reduce before transferring the lamb mixture to a baking dish. [SLB]

Preparation time 25–30 minutes to prepare the lamb excluding the potato

Cooking time 10–30 minutes, plus an additional 30 minutes in the oven

Serves 4

Season Lamb is in season from May until December

450g (or equal weight leftover lamb neck fillet or leg)
Sea salt
Freshly ground black pepper
1 tblsp plain flour
1 tblsp extra virgin olive oil
4 small onions
4 carrots (or a mixture of celeriac, parsnips, turnip and carrot)
3 garlic cloves
4 sprigs of fresh thyme
½ tsp cinnamon
¼ tsp allspice
1 tblsp tomato purée
2 bay leaves
300ml red wine
300ml chicken stock, homemade or store bought lamb stock
900g potatoes
50g unsalted butter, softened, plus 1 additional tsp for the baking dish
85g pecorino Romano cheese (optional)

Lamb

Preheat the oven to 180°C / 350°F / gas 4.

Season the lamb with salt and pepper. Dust with flour and toss to coat. Then heat the oil in a large casserole dish and brown the meat. Make sure that you do not overcrowd the pot or the meat will steam rather than brown. When nicely browned, transfer the lamb to a plate using a slotted spoon, and continue with the remaining meat.

Peel and cut the onion into 6 pieces through the root. Peel the carrots and cut them into thick slices on the diagonal. Gently fry the onions and carrots in the fat left in the casserole dish. If you have a lot of browned meat stuck to the bottom, cover and turn the heat down to low; the steam released from the onions and carrots will help to 'deglaze' the bottom of the casserole dish.

While the vegetables are softening, peel and crush 2 of the cloves of garlic into a paste with a little salt in a pestle and mortar. Wash the thyme and remove the leaves. Add them to the garlic and gently bruise the leaves to release their flavour.

Once the vegetables are softened, after about 7–10 minutes, add the garlic mixture, cinnamon, allspice and the tomato purée. Fry for 30 seconds or until it fills your kitchen with it's aroma and then gradually pour in the red wine and stock. (If you are using leftover lamb neck fillet or leg, add to the pot now, along with ½ tblsp plain flour.) Bring the mixture to a boil and allow the liquid to reduce by half. Return the meat to the casserole and tuck in the bay leaves and season well with salt and pepper. Cook for 30 minutes.

Meanwhile, prepare the potatoes. Peel and place in a medium-sized saucepan covered with water. Bring to a boil and cook until a knife can be inserted into them easily. Drain and put them back into the pan. Turn on a low flame and crush the potatoes with a masher. Allow the potatoes to release steam (and thus, moisture) for about a minute before adding the butter. Season with salt and pepper. If using cheese, finely grate and fold it into the potatoes. The potatoes may look slightly dry but the body of the potatoes will absorb moisture from the lamb steaming below, whilst the top will crisp up nicely.

Rub the inside of a high-sided 23 cm round or 18 cm square baking dish with 1 clove of garlic and a knob of butter. Transfer the lamb mixture to the prepared pan. Dot the potatoes all over the top of the lamb and smooth out with a fork or back of a spoon. Place in the preheated oven and cook for 30 minutes or until the top is tinged golden brown.

SHORT RIBS BRAISED IN DARK ALE WITH MAPLE SYRUP

With the hustle and bustle of a busy market and heavy bags starting to tear into your hands it is easy to miss something special. I nearly did just that a few months back. Briskly heading for the archway out of the market I caught a glimpse of something out of the corner of my eye, Highland Flat Ribs. Farmhouse Direct short ribs are the ultimate in comfort foods. They sell them fairly regularly. If not available, this recipe works equally well with shin of beef or oxtails. Short ribs and oxtails make a more gelatinous, clear sauce which is stunningly sweet, meaty and delicate all at the same time.

Short ribs come in two different cuts, English-style and flanken-style. Farmhouse Direct has the English-style short ribs which are best described as being a meaty, long rib, usually about 12 cm long. The flanken style or 3-bone centre cut is a sawed off end cut of the ribs from the upper chest which results in three small rib pieces held together by perfectly marbled meat and connective tissue. It is these two aspects of both styles of shortribs which particularly suit them to long and extremely slow braising. They do have a fair amount of fat, especially the highland beef, which is why it is necessary to brown and render off a portion of the fat before cooking.

As with most braised dishes, this recipe is best made the day before but you must remove the ribs at the end of cooking. This will allow you to skim off most of any remaining fat from the sauce with ease before reheating and serving. [SLB]

Serves 6

Preparation time 1 hour

Cooking time About 3½ hours including braising time

Season All ingredients available year-round

1·8 kg/about 6 small short ribs
15 g fresh thyme
1 rounded tblsp black peppercorns
2 tsp sea salt, plus a little more for seasoning
2 tblsp extra-virgin olive oil
1 carrot
1 parsnip
2 large brown onions
600 ml ale or dark beer
800 ml chicken stock, homemade or store bought, or water
3 large sprigs rosemary
2 bay leaves
2 tbsp maple syrup
Freshly ground black pepper

Beef

Before cooking, trim any excess fat from the short ribs. Begin by washing and removing the leaves from the thyme sprigs and roughly chopping them on your work surface. Crack the peppercorns with a pestle and mortar to give you a fairly level tablespoon when crushed. Using your hands rub the black pepper, sea salt and chopped thyme all over the meat. At this stage the meat can be left in the refrigerator to allow the flavours to penetrate, or be cooked straight away. If you are going to leave the meat in the refrigerator, make sure that you remove it a good 30 minutes to an hour before cooking so that it can come up to a cool room temperature.

Preheat the oven to 150°C / 300°F / gas 2.

Pour the olive oil into a large heavy-bottomed casserole that can hold the ribs in a single layer. Brown the ribs in batches in the hot oil. This should take about 4 minutes per side or rib. Give yourself a sufficient amount of time to do this. It is time consuming but essential when cooking short ribs as you will remove a lot of the fat and add depth of flavour to the finished dish through caramelising and browning the exterior of each rib. Transfer to a platter when browned and continue browning the remaining ribs. Pour off most of the fat from the casserole, leaving about a tablespoon behind. Wash and peel the carrot and parsnip and peel off the papery skin from the onions. Finely dice the root vegetables, along with the onions and add to the casserole. Reduce the heat to medium-low, cover and cook for 3 minutes. After which time, remove the lid and with a wooden spoon scrape any browned bits stuck to the bottom of the pot. Pour in the ale or beer, and stock and bring the mixture to a boil. Once hot, reduce the heat to a simmer and put the ribs back in the casserole. Pour in any juices which may have collected on the platter from the ribs. Rinse the rosemary and tuck into the casserole along with the bay leaves.

Cover with a piece of parchment paper followed by a tight fitting lid. Transfer the casserole to a preheated oven and cook for 3 hours. After about ten minutes, check to see if the stock and ale are boiling too fiercely. If so, turn the temperature down by 10–15 degrees celsius. After three hours the meat should be fork tender. Using a spatula, gently lift the ribs from the pot. Allow the mixture to cool. At this stage it is best to refrigerate the cooking liquid so the fat will rise to the surface and solidify. But you can just tilt the pan with the cooking liquid to one side and skim the fat from the cooled cooking liquid and, if the broth seems a little thin, bring it up to the boil and reduce slightly to thicken it. Check for seasoning.

When ready to eat, preheat the grill to its highest setting. Drizzle the maple syrup over the top of the ribs. Don't worry if you don't completely coat each one. Slide the ribs under the grill and cook until sizzling and slightly browned, about 4 minutes. Ladle the cooking liquid into shallow wide bowls and top with a short rib. Mashed potatoes with horseradish are a must for this dish and a tall glass of the ale or beer you cooked with wouldn't go amiss either.

WHISKEY ESPRESSO MARINATED STEAK WITH CHIMICHURRI SAUCE

The use of black coffee in this dish is inspired by Argentinean barbecues. Here I've combined their traditions with my own by mixing coffee with a more American style barbecue sauce. Whiskey combined with maple syrup adds a malted-oaky sweetness whilst soy brings the whole marinade together. The steak is great on it's own but all the better with the authentic chimichurri, another export from South America. The zesty herbs add a necessary freshness that lifts the entire meal. [SLB]

Preparation time 25 minutes, plus optional marinating

Cooking time 8 minutes, plus 5 minutes resting time

Serves 4 as a main course

Season All ingredients available year-round

4 x125 g–150 g rib eye steaks, about 2·5 cm thick
4 cloves garlic
4 tblsp whiskey
4 tblsp maple syrup or honey
2 tblsp soy sauce
2 tblsp strong, freshly brewed coffee
1 tblsp sherry vinegar
15 g fresh parsley
10 g fresh coriander
½ tsp dried chilli flakes
¼ tsp smoked paprika
½ tsp ground cumin
120 ml olive oil
60 ml red wine vinegar
Sea salt
Freshly ground black pepper

Place the steaks in a glass or ceramic baking dish. Peel and crush two of the garlic cloves with a little salt in a mortar. Combine with the whiskey, honey, soy sauce, coffee, and sherry vinegar. Mix thoroughly and pour over the steaks. The steaks can be cooked straight away, but they do benefit from marinating anywhere up to 24 hours.

To make the chimichurri sauce, wash and finely chop the leaves and small stems of both the fresh parsley and coriander. Peel the remaining two garlic cloves and crush with a pinch of salt in a mortar until you have a fine paste.

In a small frying pan, gently dry toast the chilli flakes, smoked paprika and cumin. Combine the dried spices with the garlic and fresh herbs in a small bowl. Pour over the red wine vinegar and olive oil and taste for seasoning. Season with salt and pepper to taste. Set aside.

Place a medium frying pan (preferably with ridges) over medium-to-high heat for 1 minute. Remove two steaks from the marinade. Drizzle a drop of olive oil onto each steak. Place, oil side down, in the hot pan and cook for 4 minutes. Flip the steaks, reducing the heat, and cook for another 4 minutes for medium, or cook less or longer according to how rare or well done you like your steak. Allow the steaks to rest for 5 minutes before serving.

As the steaks rest, place the remaining coffee/ soy sauce marinade in a saucepan and bring to a boil. Simmer until the sauce is thickened, about 5 minutes. Create a base of salad greens on a large plate. Thinly slice the steak and arrange on top of the lettuce. Glaze with the reduced marinade and serve chimichurri alongside.

CORIANDER AND FENNEL CRUSTED SIRLOIN SALAD WITH HOISIN VINAIGRETTE

This substantial salad makes a great weeknight supper. These days more and more people are avoiding late night carbohydrates and are thus keeping suppers light. Vinaigrettes are an easy way to add a lot of flavour without much work. Hoisin sauce is sweet and spicy with a predominantly tomato base. It keeps well in the refrigerator once opened. [SLB]

Preparation time 20 minutes

Cooking time 10 minutes, plus an additional
     8–10 minutes resting time

Serves 3

Season All ingredients available year-round

5 cm piece fresh ginger
1 garlic clove
Sea salt
Freshly ground black pepper
4 tblsp hoisin sauce
4 tblsp white wine vinegar
4 tblsp water
2 tblsp olive oil
1 tblsp soy sauce
2 tsp Dijon mustard
1 rounded tsp black peppercorns
2 tsp coriander seeds
2 tsp fennel seeds
1 x 450 g top-sirloin steak (about 2·5 cm thick)
Olive oil for rubbing on the steak
200 g mixed bitter leaves
     (such as watercress, frisee and rocket)

Begin by making the vinaigrette. Peel the ginger and clove of garlic. Finely grate the ginger: you want to make sure that you don't have any fibrous bits in the finished dressing. Crush the garlic and work into a paste with a pinch of salt in a mortar. Transfer both ingredients to a small bowl. Whisk together with the hoisin sauce, white wine vinegar, water, olive oil, soy sauce and mustard to make the vinaigrette. Add salt and pepper to taste.

Using a pestle and mortar, grind peppercorns, coriander and fennel seeds to medium-fine powder. Lightly rub oil onto the steak and sprinkle each side with salt, pepper and spice mix.

Preheat a ridged frying pan for a minute or two. Place the steak in the hot pan and cook for 5 minutes per side for medium. Using tongs, transfer the steak to foil-lined cutting board. Tent the foil to keep the steak warm and allow to rest for 8–10 minutes.

Meanwhile, wash and dry the salad greens thoroughly and scatter around each plate to create a base for the meat. Cut the steak cross-wise into thin slices. Arrange into ribbons over the each plate, drizzle with some vinaigrette and serve.

Beef

FURNESS FISH, POULTRY & GAME

(See page 238 for the trader interview)

Les Salisbury (Jnr)
and fallow deer

ROASTED GROUSE WITH APPLES, BACON AND CALVADOS

The opening of the grouse season is known as the 'Glorious Twelfth'. Typically, the Red Grouse is found in Britain and is a subspecies of the Willow Grouse found in Europe, North America and Asia. Levels are maintained through carefully managed breeding and burning of the heather on the moors where grouse nest. Early September sometimes sees the best shooting, as the birds are more mature and fly strongly and the bloom is off the heather, which makes collection easier.

Grouse weigh anywhere from 450g to 2·5kg. Whatever size you end up with, 450g in weight is usually enough for 1 person. [SLB]

Preparation time 10 minutes

Cooking time 40 minutes

Serves 4

Season Grouse season begins on 12 August and ends late November / early December.

1 large unwaxed or organic lemon
50g unsalted butter
Sea salt
Freshly ground black pepper
4 small grouse (450g in weight each)
2 apples (Braeburn, Granny Smith or Bramley all work well)
6 slices of smoked streaky bacon
3 tblsp Calvados (you can substitute with Cognac if you prefer)

Preheat the oven to 200°C / 400°F / gas 6.

Squeeze the lemon. Mix together the unsalted butter, 2 tblsp of the lemon juice and a good seasoning of sea salt and black pepper in a small bowl. If the butter is cold and hard, chop it into small pieces and work it until it softens. Rub the mix on the outside and inside of each bird.

Quarter the apples and place 1–2 pieces inside each of the birds' cavities. Cut 2 slices of the bacon into 8 pieces. Tuck a small piece of bacon between the leg and breast on each bird. Then, cut the remaining 4 slices of bacon in half and wrap over the breasts.

Wrap each bird securely in foil and place on a baking tray fitted with a roasting rack. Turn the birds so they are breast-side down. Cook in a preheated oven for 25 minutes. Birds larger than 450g may need a little longer, but no more than 35 minutes.

Flip the birds over so they are breast-side up. Cut open the foil parcels and sprinkle Calvados or Cognac over the top of each bird. Return to the oven and cook for another 5 minutes. The bacon will take on a little colour and juices from the thigh should be lightly pink when pricked. Cooking them in foil will ensure they come out of the oven deliciously juicy, perfect on their own or served with a cranberry relish or caramelised onion jam.

If you are lucky enough to get the livers still intact upon purchase, fry them in a little butter and mash them during the final 5 minutes of cooking. Serve this on some crusty bread drizzled with some Cognac flavoured roasting juice alongside the roasted grouse.

ROAST PHEASANT STUFFED WITH APPLE AND WET WALNUTS

My advice on cooking pheasants is to roast them in the autumn and pot-roast them after the New Year. This is because they were probably hatched the previous spring and, although young and tender in October, will become progressively older and tougher as time goes by. They're technically wild, but (like deer) managed: estates buy them as young birds, before their feathers have grown, and feed them in pens until they fly away into the surrounding woods or farmland. In the nineteenth century, enormous resentment was caused by landowners who fed their pheasants with hard-boiled eggs when many of the people in the country nearby were too poor to be able to afford eggs for themselves.

Traditionally, pheasants were hung until they acquired a strong gamy flavour. It is now impossible to buy them in this state because, according to EU law, all birds have to be chilled within six hours of being killed. If you want them high, you will have to shoot them yourself. Les Salisbury's are hung for a week, which gives them a distinctive but not strong flavour. You may like to add a stuffing: this is a particularly good idea if there are four of you, since it makes the pheasant go further.

Wet walnuts have a subtler, fresher, earthier taste than ordinary ones. Unfortunately, they're also more difficult to crush: however, I think the result is well worth the extra effort. If they're not available, the new season's nuts in their shells will taste fresher than the packaged version.

Whether stuffed or not, I suggest serving a roast pheasant with bread sauce (see page 135) and crisp, oven-roasted chips which can be cooked at the same time. Other traditional accompaniments to an unstuffed bird are rolls of bacon and redcurrant jelly. [SF]

Preparation time 1 hour

Cooking time 45–70 minutes including 10 minutes resting time

Serves 2 people, or 4 at a pinch if the phesant is large (cock birds are larger than hens)

Season Season for the pheasant, from mid October until Christmas; for wet walnuts, October

---

2 garlic cloves
5 wet walnuts, or 40g shelled weight (if you use ordinary walnuts, you will probably need 7)
1 small or ½ medium onion
40g (1½ rashers) smoked back bacon
1 medium Cox apple (to provide 75g when peeled and cored)
2–3 tblsp (about) olive oil
1 organic and/or unwaxed lemon
½ tblsp cider or other brandy
400–450g or (for 4) 800–900g floury potatoes
1 pheasant (ask for its weight when buying)
Sea salt
Freshly ground black pepper
1 wide or 2 narrow rashers streaky bacon to cover the breast
Bread sauce, for serving (see page 135)
About 150ml spicy red wine (eg a Shiraz blend)
Redcurrant jelly, about 1tblsp (optional)

Peel the garlic cloves and crush them in a mortar. Crack and crush the nuts into pieces about the size of coarse breadcrumbs. Peel and finely chop the onion. Cut the rind off the 40g back bacon and dice it finely (use scissors). Peel and dice the apple.

Put 1 tblsp of oil into a wok or small frying pan and fry the onion and bacon over medium heat for 5 minutes or until they are soft and just on the point of changing colour; turn constantly. Add the apple and fry for about another two minutes, turning continuously. Add the nuts and garlic and fry for another minute or so, still turning constantly. Remove the pan from the heat. Wash and dry the lemon and grate in about half the zest. Stir in the brandy.

Set the oven to 220°C / 425°F / gas 7.

Scrub or peel the potatoes and cut them into slices 75mm thick. Spread a thin film of oil over the bottom of a baking dish large enough to take them in a single layer. Roll both sides of each slice in the oil and season them modestly with salt and pepper.

Weigh (if you didn't find out the weight upon purchase) the pheasant and wipe it thoroughly all over with damp kitchen paper making sure you remove any blood stains. Stuff it: for this, I suggest using a teaspoon. If the pheasant is only 900g, you may have about a teaspoonful of stuffing left over.

Set the stuffed bird in a roasting dish, rub it with oil and season with a little salt and plenty of coarsely ground pepper. Lay the slices of streaky bacon over the breast to keep it moist and put the pheasant into the oven. Roast for 18–20 minutes per 450g. Unless it weighed much more than 1kg, put the potatoes into the oven at the same time; if it is larger, put them in 5–10 minutes later. Remove the bacon to allow the breast to brown about 15 minutes before it is due to be ready. Look at the potatoes at the same time: if they are browning too fast, take them out for a few minutes (different varieties take slightly different times to cook).

After 35 minutes for a 900g bird, stick a skewer into the thickest part of the breast: when no pink liquid spurts out, it is ready. Turn off the oven and leave it to rest for 10 minutes. While it rests, you can attend to whatever vegetables you're planning to serve and finish the bread sauce.

When dishing up the pheasant, keep the roasting-pan to hand. Make the gravy while someone else carves. Pour the wine into the pan and stir energetically with a rubber spatula to scrape up all the juices and any bits of stuffing which may have escaped. Transfer the juices and wine to a small saucepan and set them over high heat for three minutes or until they are reduced to 3–4 tablespoons. Taste the gravy (cautiously, because it will be very hot): if it seems sharp, stir in just a very little redcurrant jelly. While it reduces, put the potatoes into a serving-dish. Serve both the gravy and potatoes at once.

POT ROASTED PHEASANT WITH CREAM AND ALMONDS

This is one of the most delicious ways I know of cooking a pheasant whatever the time of year. The cream and almonds offset its slightly gamy flavour, coriander seeds add warmth, and lemon peel gives it freshness and fragrance.

I suggest using an organic onion only because you want a strong one, with plenty of bite (the sort that makes you cry, I'm afraid).

The perfect accompaniments to the stew are Brussels sprouts and small baked potatoes with which to mop up the gravy: put them in the oven 20 minutes after the pheasant. [SF]

gamebirds

Preparation time 25–30 minutes (but I'm slow: I'm pretty sure that others would be quicker)

Cooking time 12–15 minutes to sear the pheasant and fry its accompaniments, 1 hour 20 minutes to roast it and 10 minutes' resting time

Season October to the end of January

Serves 2–4: a pheasant weighing 1 kg will be enough for 4 provided that you're not too hungry and don't expect second helpings

1 largish leek
1 onion, preferably organic, weighing about 150 g (you need 125 g prepared weight)
1 carrot
6 cloves of garlic
125 g lean smoked back bacon, preferably thick-cut
1 small unwaxed or organic lemon (zest only)
1 pheasant weighing 1 kg
Sea salt
Freshly ground black pepper
1 tblsp olive oil, plus more if necessary
300 ml or a little more dry white wine
1½ tsp coriander seeds
½ tsp black peppercorns
150 ml double cream
50 g whole almonds

Trim the bottom and green top of the leek, peel off the outer layer and chop it into slices about 1cm thick. Then wash it and leave it to dry on kitchen paper (if you wash it before slicing, you may not remove any mud or grit between the layers). Peel and finely slice the onion. Peel the carrot and cloves of garlic: slice the carrot but leave the cloves of garlic whole. Using scissors, snip the rind plus any large pieces of fat from the bacon and cut it into narrow sticks. Wash and dry the lemon and pare off half the zest in three or four long strips. Cut each piece of zest diagonally into sticks about the same size as the bacon.

Set the oven to 190°C / 375°F / gas 5.

Untruss the pheasant and remove any bacon tied to its breast with which it may have been sold. Wipe it with damp kitchen paper and season it lightly with salt, uncrushed if you wish, and a little more generously with black pepper. Choose a deep casserole which fits it neatly but leaves a little space round the edges for the vegetables, and place it conveniently to hand near the hob. Put 1 tblsp of oil into a wok or frying pan over fairly high heat and sear the bird all over, spooning the hot oil over the parts which don't touch the pan. Transfer it to the casserole. If the feet stick up too much for the lid to close properly, you must either cut them off or force them down. Pour the oil in the pan into a mug (don't throw it away) and replace it with about 2 tablespoonsful of the wine. Set the pan momentarily over the heat and scrape up any pieces of salt and other remains with a spatula or spoon. Add them with the warm wine to the pheasant in the casserole.

Wipe the pan, make up the oil in the mug to 1 tablespoonful and add it to the pan with the bacon and onion. Fry over fairly high heat for 5–7 minutes or until the onion has softened; turn constantly. Add the coriander and peppercorns and turn; add the garlic and turn. Finally, add the leek, carrot, and lemon zest. Turn continuously until the leek starts to wilt, which will probably be in about 2 minutes. The pan will be very dry: rather than add more oil, which may mean that there will be globules of it in the finished sauce, add another couple of tablespoons of the wine. (It is similarly to avoid an oily sauce that I suggest using lean bacon.) Turn the contents of the pan into the casserole, pour in the rest of the wine, and cook, covered, for 1 hour 5 minutes.

After 1 hour 5 minutes, take the casserole out of the oven and lift the pheasant on to a plate with as much of the bacon and vegetables as you can. Pour the liquor in the casserole into a small saucepan through a sieve to catch the spices and the rest of the vegetables. Measure the liquor in the pan. There will probably be 150 ml: if there is more, set the pan over high heat and reduce it to that amount; if less, add a little extra wine. Stir in the cream.

Turn up the oven to 200°C / 400°F / gas 6.

Put the pheasant back into the casserole, breast-side up, with all its accompaniments including the contents of the sieve. When it has been out of the oven for 10 minutes, pour the cream and wine mixture over it and put it back into the oven, uncovered, to brown. Test it after 15 minutes by sticking a skewer into the thickest part of the breast. If the juice runs clear, it is ready: if pink (which is very unlikely), cook it for another few minutes.

When the pheasant has been returned to the oven for 5 minutes, spread out the almonds in an ovenware dish and put them into the oven with it to crisp. Shake them over the pheasant, sizzling hot, just before serving.

WARM WOOD PIGEON AND
BLACK PUDDING SALAD
WITH MIGAS

The idea for this salad came from one of my favourite restaurants in London, Moro on Exmouth Market. Occasionally, they serve a spicy rich black pudding with laboriously peeled fresh broad beans served on top of crisp bread as a starter.

Here I've added a lightly marinated wood pigeon to that magical combination of black pudding and crispy bread. Our recipe gives a nod to the Middle East with the addition of 'migas' – the most delicious crouton you will ever eat.

Wood pigeons are available throughout the year, which is a quite a good thing really, as I truly enjoyed chasing crumbly bits of black pudding and chunks of wood pigeon around my plate and wouldn't want to wait until next season to do it again! [SLB]

Preparation time 15 minutes,
    plus minimum 6 hours marinating

Cooking time 30 minutes

Serves 4

Season Wood pigeons available year-round

2 garlic cloves
4 wood pigeon breasts
2 tblsp olive oil
1 tblsp runny honey
¼ tsp allspice
¼ tsp ground cinnamon
Sea salt
Freshly ground black pepper
200 g day-old bread, sourdough preferably
90 ml milk
1 tblsp olive oil
100 g black pudding
2 bunches watercress
1 tblsp pomegranate molasses
1 tblsp balsamic vinegar
2 tblsp extra virgin olive oil
50 g walnuts

Begin by making the marinade. Peel and crush the garlic and work into a paste with a bit of salt in a mortar. Place the garlic paste into a bowl large enough to accommodate all four of the wood pigeon breasts comfortably. Pour over the olive oil, honey, allspice, and cinnamon. Add the breasts and season with pepper and toss to coat. Cover with cling film and leave to marinate for 6 hours or overnight in the refrigerator.

Preheat the oven to 200°C / 400°F / gas 6.

Remove the crusts from the bread and cut up into bite-sized chunks. Place in a small bowl and pour over the milk. Allow the bread to absorb all of the milk. Don't worry if it hasn't coated all the pieces evenly. The milk will moisten the inside of the bread so that it can retain a soft texture during cooking. The end result will be like that of a roast potato.

Heat the olive oil in a frying pan over a medium flame. Slice the black pudding into 6mm–10mm slices and gently lower into the preheated frying pan. Add the soaked bread cubes as well. Gently turn the bread over in the olive oil and any fat which may have come from the black pudding. Transfer the frying pan to the oven and continue cooking in the oven until the bread and the pudding crisp, about 5–7 minutes. Once cooked, set aside in a warm place while you cook the wood pigeon.

The wood pigeon doesn't take long to cook, so ensure that you have your watercress washed and salad dressing ready. Distribute the watercress evenly amongst four plates. Whisk together the pomegranate molasses, balsamic vinegar and olive oil and season well with salt and pepper. Set aside.

Remove the wood pigeon from the marinade. Heat another frying pan over medium-high flame. Gently lower the wood pigeon into the hot pan and cook for no more than 2 minutes a side. Transfer from the pan to a warm plate and allow to rest for 4 minutes; cover with foil to retain the heat.

Divide the warm black pudding and croutons amongst the plates. Using a sharp knife cut each wood pigeon breast into 4 slices and fan out over the top of the salad. Crush the walnuts and crumble over the top of each wood pigeon. Drizzle over the dressing and serve immediately.

gamebirds

SOY WOOD PIGEON SALAD
WITH PORK BELLY LARDONS

When I was a line cook, my old local haunt served a delicious chicken liver salad with fennel. It's a meal to satisfy the hungriest of stomachs. This is my version of their truly special dish. Chicken liver is a hard one to press on most people so I've substituted something I like better: wood pigeon. The dark flesh and fine texture is reminiscent of chicken liver but with a wonderful earthy flavour. Sweet mirin and soy sauce work together to temper the gamy bird, whilst the fennel and frisee balance the overall taste and texture with liquorice and bitter flavour notes. [SLB]

Preparation time 12–15 minutes

Cooking time 9–10 minutes

Serves 4 as a main course

Season Wood pigeons available year-round

200 g smoked pork belly lardons (or pancetta)
4 plump wood pigeon breasts, skinned
2 tblsp extra virgin olive oil
1 garlic clove
2 sprigs fresh thyme
1 medium bulb fennel
1 tblsp rice wine vinegar
2 tblsp mirin or Chinese cooking wine
3 tblsp soy sauce
200 g frisee lettuce
Sea salt
Freshly ground black pepper

Place a large frying pan over medium heat. Add the olive oil and fry the lardons until crisp and lightly browned around the edges. Using a slotted spoon, transfer them to a warm plate. Check the level of oil/rendered fat in the frying pan: you want about 1 tblsp. If there is more, spoon off the surplus into a ramekin to solidify and discard later (into the rubbish, not down the sink).

Remove the outer layer of the fennel and slice the bulb into quarters. Using the tip of your knife, cut out part of the fennel heart, leaving only the thin portion that will hold the fennel leaves in place. Slice the fennel as thinly as possible, lengthwise through the core. Add to the frying pan and sauté until slightly browned around the edges.

Peel and crush the garlic with some salt with a pestle and mortar. Wash and remove the leaves from the thyme stems; bruise a little by rubbing them between your fingers. Add the thyme, along with the garlic, to the frying pan with the fennel. Cook for 30 seconds to sauté and release their flavour.

If there is enough room in the pan, push the fennel to the sides and place the pigeon breasts into the hot pan. Sprinkle with a little salt and pepper. The breasts don't take long, 2 minutes on each side should be perfect. Remove the pigeon and fennel from the pan and place on the plate with the lardons. Cover and allow to rest whilst you make the sauce.

Add the rice wine vinegar and mirin to the pan. Using a wooden spoon, work any bits stuck to the bottom of the pan into the liquid. Reduce the wine and vinegar down to about 1 tblsp. Add the soy sauce and again reduce until slightly thickened. Remove from the heat and set aside.

Slice the breasts on the diagonal into three or four thick slices each. Wash and dry the frisee thoroughly and pile the leaves onto four plates. Arrange the fennel and pork belly lardons on top, along with the wood pigeon. Spoon over the pan juices, season with a little salt and freshly ground black pepper and serve.

Field fare – pheasant and rabbit

To joint a rabbit

First, lay a rabbit on its back. Spread the chest cavity open and look to see if the kidneys and liver are still visible. Give them a gentle tug or use a sharp knife to remove them and discard. Pull out one of the large hind legs to expose the spot where the leg is connected to the backbone. Using a sharp knife, separate the leg from the body by cutting around the top of the leg meat leaving as little meat as possible on the carcass. Cut down through the joint just below the hip-bone, where the leg bone meets the backbone. As you remove the leg, you will leave a long 'tail' of the backbone connected to the body. Repeat with the second leg and set aside.

Next, pull one of the front legs to extend it and locate where the shoulder meets the rib cage. With your knife, separate the front leg from the body by cutting between the muscle and the ribcage. Repeat with the other front leg and set aside.

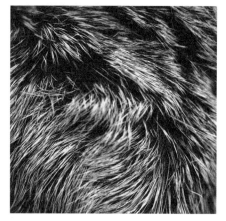

With the rabbit still on its back, belly side up, you should now be able to see the meaty centre portion of the rabbit called the saddle. Using a sharp heavy knife, carve out this centre portion with one cut above the hip and the other below the ribs. Trim off and discard the belly flaps which hang from the saddle. This centre piece will usually be about 7·5–10 cm in length with a piece of the backbone in the middle.

BRANDIED RABBIT
IN MUSTARD SAUCE

This is a rarity for me. I tend to shy away from the cream-mustard-wine trilogy but sometimes what is most familiar can be the most comforting and definitely stands pride of place in any cooking repertoire. I've used this recipe with guinea fowl and Cornish game hens as well. Rabbit, to me, almost seems a happy medium on the flavour spectrum with both a sweet flesh and a full flavour. Rabbit can vary in strength of flavour with wild rabbits being strong and farmed rabbits more mild. It is (generally) the farmed rabbits that many people refer to as 'tasting like chicken'. But I encourage you to try this recipe with all of the above animals as this combination is a classic magical one with simple elegant flavours. [SLB]

Preparation time 30 minutes,
plus a minimum of 4 hours to marinate

Cooking time 45 minutes to 1 hour

Serves 4

Season Rabbit is at its best from July to November.

1 rabbit (weighing about 1·8 kg),
cut into 4 pieces
2 garlic cloves
4 sprigs fresh thyme
4 tblsp brandy
100 g streaky bacon
15 g unsalted butter
1 medium onion
6–8 whole cloves
3 sprigs parsley
1 bay leaf
120 ml white wine, preferably Sauvignon
Blanc
4 tblsp double cream
1½ tblsp coarse-grained Dijon mustard
Sea salt
Freshly ground black pepper

Trim the rabbit of any fat and place in a dish for marinating. (For information on how to cut up a rabbit please turn to page 222) Season the rabbit pieces with salt and pepper. Peel and crush the garlic with the side of your knife to release its natural oil. Wash and remove the leaves from 3 sprigs of the thyme and roughly chop. Sprinkle the thyme and crushed garlic over the top of the rabbit and drizzle with the brandy. Cover with cling film and marinate overnight in the refrigerator or for at least 4 hours.

Dice the bacon into 1 cm slivers. Heat the butter in large deep braising pan or casserole dish until bubbly. Add the bacon and cook until it is brown and some fat has rendered out. Using a slotted spoon, transfer the bacon to a small plate.

Gently lower the rabbit pieces into the buttery bacon drippings and sauté all sides until browned. Peel and cut the onion into four pieces and press the whole cloves into onion quarters. Once the rabbit is browned on all sides add the onion to the braising pan or casserole dish in between the meat pieces. Tuck the parsley, remaining thyme sprig and bay leaf in the pot alongside the rabbit. Pour the wine and any remaining marinade juices over the meat and cover. Bring the mixture up to a low simmer and cook for about 45 minutes to an hour or until the meat is cooked through and tender either on your stove top or in a preheated moderate oven.

Remove the rabbit pieces from the casserole or pan and keep warm. Discard the clove studded onion quarters and herbs. Increase the heat to medium-high and add the cream and mustard. Bubble to thicken slightly; correct the seasoning. Return the meat to the pan and coat on all sides with sauce. Serve hot.

BRAISED RABBIT MUSHROOM AND ROASTED GARLIC RAGU

Don't be intimidated by the long list of ingredients or the labourious preparation time. The sauce can be made without the addition of cream well ahead of time and frozen. In our house we tend to make about three times the recipe and freeze in a 2-portion, pint-sized yoghurt pot ready for weeknight dinners. Shredding the meat at the end of cooking is probably the most difficult aspect of this recipe yet gives the sauce the thickened meaty 'ragu' appearance we are familiar with. But in all honesty, after the lengthy cooking time the meat just falls off the bone. This tomato-less ragu is my tribute to an old restaurant that is sadly no longer called Michela's who built a undeniably good reputation for producing delectable Italian food with 'no red sauce'. [SLB]

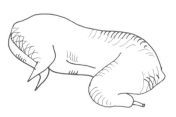

Rabbit

Preparation time 45 minutes

Cooking time 1 hour 15 minutes

Serves 4

Season Rabbit is at its best from July to November.

3 tblsp olive oil
1 rabbit (weighing about 1·8kg),
    cut into 4 pieces
150g pancetta or unsmoked streaky bacon
250g fresh brown chestnut mushrooms
125g dried porcini mushrooms
120ml boiling water/mushroom hydrating
    liquid
1 large onion
2 small heads garlic, plus 2 large garlic cloves
60ml white wine vinegar
120ml dry white wine
480ml chicken stock,
    homemade or store bought
1 sprig rosemary
3 sprigs thyme
2 sprigs sage
Splash of double cream (optional)
340g parpadelle pasta
15g fresh parsley for serving
Sea salt
Freshly ground black pepper

Preheat oven to 170°C / 325°F / gas 3.

Cut fresh chestnut mushrooms into 10mm thick slices. Bring 240ml of water to a boil and pour over the dried porcini mushrooms. Set aside for 30 minutes whilst you brown off the rabbit.

Season the rabbit with salt and pepper. (For information on how to cut up a rabbit see page 222). In a large, heavy-bottomed, ovenproof casserole dish heat the oil over moderately high heat until hot but not smoking and brown the rabbit on all sides. Give yourself a good 10–15 minutes to do this thoroughly. Transfer the rabbit to a plate.

Chop the pancetta into 1cm cubes and in the same casserole dish sauté the pancetta until golden. Peel the onion and chop into a small dice. Peel 2 garlic cloves and work into a paste with a little salt in a mortar. Sauté the onions and garlic with the pancetta until the onion starts to turn golden brown.

Pour over vinegar and white wine and using the back of a wooden spoon scrape up any brown bits which may have stuck to the bottom of the dish. Simmer onion mixture until liquid is evaporated, about 5 minutes. Then, add the stock and half of the porcini mushroom hydrating liquid. Tuck in the washed sprigs of fresh herbs. Bring the mixture to a simmer and season with salt and pepper.

Stir in the fresh mushrooms, re-hydrated porcini and the browned rabbit. Covered the pot with a tight-fitting lid and braise in the oven for 1 hour.

Once the casserole is in the oven, cut the tops off each head of garlic. Place them on a square of foil, drizzle with a little olive oil and seal. Cook in the oven alongside the casserole to cook for an hour.

Once cooked, remove the casserole and garlic from the oven. Transfer the rabbit to a plate and allow to cool slightly. Open the garlic parcel, avoiding the steam, and squeeze the softened cloves into the casserole discarding skins. Mash the garlic with a fork and stir into the juices at the bottom of the pan. Using 2 forks shred the rabbit meat, discarding bones, and stir it into sauce. Pour in double cream (if using) and bring to a simmer. Check seasoning. The sauce may be made 1 day ahead: allow to cool before refrigerating.

Bring a large pot of water to a boil. Cook the pasta according to the manufacturer's instructions for al dente. Wash and chop the leaves and fine stems of the parsley. Tip the pasta into a pot, preferably the one in which it was cooked as it will still be warm, and toss with sauce and chopped parsley. Serve in warmed bowls.

Fish

General notes on fish

Fish and shellfish

Not long ago, in letters of a size usually reserved for matters of major national importance (as indeed this is), the headline on the front page of *The Times* proclaimed 'The end of cod'. The article began,

> A complete ban on cod fishing is the only way to prevent the species from dying out in the North Sea, scientists said last night.
>
> The much-trumpeted European rescue plan for cod is failing, the official committee of European experts will tell governments on Friday. Stocks of cod – Britain's favourite fish – are still so depleted in the seas around the UK that there should be a complete ban on catching the fish throughout next year....
>
> The main problem is that, although cod catches have been cut to 26,500 tonnes a year, more than twice that amount is being caught in bycatches by fishermen chasing other species such as haddock, whiting, hake and plaice. Fishermen accidentally caught about 50,000 tonnes of cod last year, and have to throw the dead fish back in the sea because it is classed as an illegal catch.
>
> The bycatches are difficult to avoid because cod are bigger than other fish and no method has been devised to catch the other fish without scooping up cod in the process.[1]

The article didn't comment on supplies of other fish, but a subsequent BBC news item quoted a prediction that, if commercial fishing continues at its present level, fish stocks will collapse completely within fifty years.[2]

Is this surprising? If you consider the situation in context, the really surprising thing is that stocks have held out for as long as they have. Agriculture has been practised since prehistory: why not aquaculture too? In fact, the need for aqua-management and the conservation of stocks was recognised by the EU over thirty years ago, when the Common Fisheries Policy was formulated. Yet only last summer I heard a fishmonger declare, 'There are plenty of fish in the sea!' He spoke in tones of complete conviction. I don't know if he would still say the same today, but the problem is certainly acknowledged by the two general fishmongers in the Market, Graham Applebee and Les Salisbury of Furness Fish, Poultry and Game.

As *The Times* makes clear, the main reasons for the lack of fish, apart from the underlying force of demand, are trawling-nets and bycatches, which make the quota system meaningless. The nets are much larger than they used to be: sometimes, enormous ones are slung across the sea between a pair of trawlers. For the last five years, fishermen have been encouraged to use nets with larger meshes to reduce the size of bycatches, but the effect has clearly not been significant. Not only fish are caught but other creatures, including turtles, which themselves are severely threatened. The fish thrown back, although unwanted by the fishermen, would have served as food for other species, so that their death has a knock-on effect. The nets used for catching flat-fish such as plaice or for large-scale scallop- and oyster-gathering further deplete the marine food-supply by ploughing up the sea-bed (see page 269).

Scientists express optimism about the ability of stocks to recover if their recommendations are followed. However, even if they are, farmed supplies will become increasingly important as demand grows in the future. Some people may be surprised to know that already about a fifth of the fish eaten world-wide is farmed: most of it is accounted for by prawns, mussels, rainbow trout, and salmon, but cod farming has been practised on a small scale for some years and experiments are being carried out with haddock.

There are concerns about salt-water farming especially because of the mobility of the sea, which means that it is virtually impossible to recapture escaped fish or contain disease. It is feared that in the case of Scottish salmon, escaped farmed fish may cause wild stock to degenerate. Worse is the potential threat of genetically modified salmon, which has already been produced in Canada.

There is also a problem with feed. According to the Marine Conservation Society, it takes 5kg of wild fish to feed 1kg of farmed fish. Most of the fish feed used is produced in South America, thus adding to food miles. The usual high-protein sub-stitute for animal food, soya, will not answer on its own because it doesn't provide all the amino acids needed by species such as salmon. Another drawback is taste: the captive versions of salmon and sea-bass, like intensively reared animals, never achieves the same flavour and texture as the free-swimming (or free-range) equivalents. Nevertheless, if farms are responsibly managed and the fish are given plenty of space, the results can be good, indeed even very good.

These are the facts. The question of how customers can help is easily answered. Graham Applebee feels that solutions have to come from fisheries management, since by the time the fish are caught, the damage is done – which is true. However, if the demand for cod wasn't there, the incentive to catch it wouldn't be there either. Therefore, don't ask for it: instead, choose the less popular sorts of fish such as bream, gurnard, and herring.[3] To give you ideas about how to cook them, Sarah Leahey-Benjamin has created a remarkable collection of adventurous, delicious recipes composed almost entirely of sustainable species. As yet, so far as I know, no one else has produced anything like it. Or, if you want to stay with the kind of fish you know, try Applebee's farmed salmon from Loch Duart, which is quoted by the Marine Conservation Society as an example of how fish farming should be carried out. Scottish National Heritage has pronounced it '"sustainable and conservation friendly"'[4] and Rick Stein praises the fish as the nearest to the wild version that he has tasted.

1 *The Times*, 18 October 2006, pp. 1–2

2 BBC Radio 4 News, 2 November 2006

3 For a list of fish with their stock status, see Bernadette Clarke,
   Good fish guide, Marine Conservation Society 2002

4 *Good fish guide*, p. 131

*Opposite A work of art –
Furness fish stall*

Fish recipes

APPLEBEE'S FISH

Fish stock 295
Crabcakes with summer herb aioli 296
Summer herb aioli 297
Grilled fish parcels with sweet and sour dipping sauce 298
Sea bream baked with capers and olives 300
Salmon fillets with lemon and parsley butter 301
Paella magnifica 302
Fish curry 304
Penne with lemon crab, peas and prosciutto 306
Scottish langoustines with roasted garlic aioli 307
Oven roasted wild trout with cherry tomatoes 308
Weeknight linguine with prawns, chilli basil and cherry tomatoes 309
Herb crusted halibut with fennel and orange salad 310
Razor clam, chorizo and tomato stir fry 312

BROWN & FORREST

Tortiglioni with smoked eel and celeriac 318
Smoked eel pearl barley risotto with watercress 320
Smoked salmon and fresh goat cheese pizza with dill 322
Smoked trout and pear salad with horseradish cream 323
Kipper salad, whiskey sauce with crème fraîche and Dijon mustard 324
Smoked eels with celeriac apple sage rosti and remoulade sauce 325
Smoked eel potato croquettes with caramelised pear sauce 326

FISH PREPARATION

Fishmongers can scale, gut and fillet fish for you but it is a good skill to have and fairly simple to do. The best part about preparing your own fish is that you end up with a 'fish frame' and head which make excellent fish soups and stocks. Purchasing and filleting your own fish also allows couples, singles or small families to eat larger fish over several meals.

Preparing mussels

Using a stiff brush, scrub mussels well under running water, scraping the shells with a knife to remove any barnacles. To remove the beard, tug towards the pointed end of the shell. Mussels are usually sold fresh in the shell. However, some may not be alive on purchase and need to be discarded. Most shells should be closed, but if left undisturbed they may open. Gently tap or squeeze any open shells, if they shut, keep them, but if they remain open throw them away. Some mussels may be line-grown or cultivated, in which case usually you don't have to worry too much about any grit inside their shells. It is always a good idea to soak them in plenty of cold, salted water for about 30 minutes which will force the fish to expel any grit it may be hiding. If you have room in your refrigerator, keep the mussels chilled during this process.

Opening (shucking) oysters

Oyster knives are a good thing to invest in if you like oysters. They are small, stout blades that won't flex or snap. They are easy to use, generally have finger-guards, and help you to open oysters without too much effort. They usually cost £18–20. To open the oysters with or without them, start by scrubbing the shells gently under running water to remove any sand and grit. Place the oysters, flat side up, on a board and press on the end opposite the hinge (usually the more rounded end) using a cloth to protect your hand or, ideally, a chain glove. Insert the tip of an oyster knife or a small, firm-bladed knife next to the hinge and push firmly against the hinge to prise the shells apart, sliding the knife against the inside of the top shell to sever the muscle holding the shells together. Discard the top shell. Using the knife, loosen the oyster meat from the bottom shell. Check thoroughly to see if there are any fragments of the shell or bits of large grit under the oyster on the bottom shell.

Opening scallops

Place a scallop on a cutting board with the flat shell up. Insert the point of a strong paring knife between the shells and run it across the underside of the top shell to sever the internal muscle. Pull the shells apart. Slide your knife under the scallop to release it from the bottom. Lift out the scallop and pull off any traces of stomach leaving only the white scallop flesh with the coral attached. Remove any dark membrane adhering to the scallop flesh plus remnants of muscle tissue which attaches the scallop to the shell. Rinse well and drain. Wash and dry the bottom shell to use as a receptacle for cooking and serving the scallops.

Clam and cockle preparation

Place live clams and cockles in a bucket of cold salted water for 30–60 minutes. The soak will allow any sand and débris to be expelled. Lift out the fish, rinse and cook immediately. If only the flesh is required, open the shellfish as for opening mussels rinse and then remove flesh.

Squid preparation

Pull off the head and attached tentacles: the gut should also come away from the body (hood). Discard the gut and pull out the quill-shaped bone from the hood cavity. Cut off the section of head containing the eyes and beak, and throw it away. You will be left with tentacles joined together with a section of the head and the hood. Pull off the thin purple skin to expose the white body. The skin may be rubbed off the tentacles, if you wish: use a cloth dipped in salt to do this. Rinse well and drain. If you are planning to stuff the squid, leave the body intact with the flaps attached. If the recipe calls for rings of squid,

gently pull off the flaps and slice the hood into rings. Or, if you require strips of squid, simply slice the hood and flaps into strips. Chop the tentacles or leave them intact as required: intact tentacles from small squid make a good garnish as they curl up into rosettes during cooking. If you have particularly large squid you may want to tenderise them. Do this by cutting half a lemon into 6mm slices (for about 680g squid). Place the squid and lemon slices in a bowl, cover with milk and refrigerate for 3 to 6 hours. If you want to tenderise them overnight or for longer than 6 hours, leave out the lemon slices.

Razor clam preparation

Razor clams can be pretty sandy. Therefore, it is a good idea to soak them in plenty of salted water, or preferably sea water, for a good hour before cooking. Then, rinse them thoroughly with plenty of cold water before cooking. Prepare them in this way and the entire contents of the razor clam can be eaten. Some people remove the innards of clams, by steaming, removing from the shell and then slicing them along their length to discard the darkened sack. This is the only part of the bivalve which may contain sand. The 'foot' or digger, which helps the clam move through the sand, is viewed by some as a delicacy and can be eaten raw.

Picking crab meat

All you need are a mallet, a blunt knife and plenty of newspaper to cover your table. Begin by removing the front claws. Put them aside for now. Pull off the rest of the legs. You might get lucky and find some crab meat pulls out from the body with them. Flip the crab over and pull up the 'apron', the flap on the backside of the crab, and break it off. You can now easily pull the hard shell off the top of the crab to open it up. Working with the bottom side of the crab, scrape out and discard anything that does not look appealing to you such as the yellow 'mustard' (the hepato pancreas) and the 'devil's fingers' (the lungs). You are now down into the main part of the crab. Simply grasp it in both hands and break it in half to expose the sweet crab meat (if you are not feeling strong, this is where the mallet comes in handy). The crab meat can be hidden in all the cracks and crevices of the crab. The dull knife will help you reach these parts, whilst a mallet will help you crack the claws open as there is plenty of meat in there as well.

Butterflying and filleting sardines & mackerel

Have your fishmonger gut the fish and remove the head for you. Trim the fins with a sharp knife. Hold on to the tail end and de-scale the fish with a butter knife by brushing the knife away from you towards the head. It is best to do this outside or over a sink as the scales tend to go everywhere. Using a sharp knife, continue the cut made from gutting all the way to the tail on both sides of the belly, only just breaking the skin. Turn the fish over, so that the skin side is up and gently press on the backbone of the fish. You will hear the meat pull away from the bone. Flip the fish over and using your fingers remove the backbone by pulling from the head end towards the tail. The larger pin bones may come out with the backbone. Run your fingers down the length of the fish and remove any pin bones that remain. Unlike salmon bones, mackerel and pilchard bones are easy to grab with the fingers, but tweezers or pliers make for lighter work. Each fish will take a few minutes, so this is something to be done well in advance. To make two fillets, cut down the centre of your butterflied fish.

Skinning fish

Place the fish on a plastic cutting board, skin side down. Starting at the tail end, grasp the very end of the fillet with your left hand (if you are right handed). Holding a serrated knife in your right hand, place it on the fish tail next to your left hand at a 30 degree angle to the cutting board with the blade facing away from your left hand. Gently move the knife backwards and forwards in a sawing motion whilst holding the tail end taught. Keep the knife blade on the skin as you do so. Continue down the length of the fish until all the skin is removed.

Skinning flat fish

To skin a flat fish such as megrim sole, place the fish on a cutting board with the tail towards you. Grasp the tail with your left hand (if you are right handed) and holding a sharp knife in your right, make a small cut just behind the tail in between the skin and the flesh. Brush this small cut with strokes from the tail towards the head. This will help to lift the skin from the flesh. When you have a piece you can hold on to, pull the skin towards the head. Once you are about a third of the way up the fish, move your left hand, placing your palm of your left hand directly on the fish flesh. Continue pulling the skin towards the head with your right hand until it pulls over the head. Flip the fish over and repeat on the other side.

Filleting flat fish

Cut off the fins using a pair of sharp kitchen scissors. Cut off the head from just behind the gills by making a diagonal cut. Using a sharp knife, make a slit along the backbone from the head end to the tail down the centre. Starting from the central cut, slide the knife under the flesh and as close to the bone as possible. Allow the bones to guide the knife. Making long, continuous stokes, gently lifting the fillet as you cut. Each knife stroke should be smooth and shallow. It is better to make more long knife strokes rather than fewer deep cuts. Continue in this way until you can see the remains of where the fins were attached. Cut down from the head to the tail along this line to separate the fillet from the bone carcass. Remove the other fillet on the first side. Turn the fish over and repeat on the other side till you have four fillets.

Filleting round fish

Cut off the fins using a pair of sharp kitchen scissors. Using a sharp knife, make an incision just behind the head and cut through the flesh along the top side of the backbone, running the knife across the length of the backbone (in long continuous strokes). Use the bones as your guide as you cut across the backbones. You will eventually reach the 'rib cage' bones, at which point you may have to arch the knife up slightly. Flat fish bones from large fish are fairly strong so don't be afraid to apply a little pressure. Keep lifting the fillet from the bone as you make your long-flowing strokes down the length of the fish until you can release the whole fillet. Cut the fillet at the head end and at the tail. Turn the fish over and repeat on the other side. Identify any 'pin bones' by running your finger along the fillets from head to tail. They can then be removed with standard tweezers.

Gutting large sprats

Small sprats are usually eaten whole. However, if your fishmonger only happens to have large ones you can easily clean and fillet them. Place the fish on the work surface with the belly towards you and the head facing towards the left. Place your knife directly behind the head and cut through the backbone. In one swift action arch the tip of the knife to the left and away from the fish towards you in order to remove the head and innards at the same time. If you prefer to leave the head on, just run a little knife through the belly and sweep out the innards before cooking.

Extra tips

The most vital tool for filleting fish is a sharp (and preferably flexible) knife. The flexibility in a knife allows you to cut very close to the bone using long strokes, which minimise waste and help create much neater fillets. You will also need a pair of tweezers for pulling out bones and kitchen scissors for cutting off fins and tails.

Freezing fish

Fish can be frozen whole or portioned, provided it has not been previously frozen.

Freezing fillets (or steaks) is the easiest method and uses freezer space well. Keep the skin on fish that is to be frozen and rinse the fish in salted water before wrapping in several layers of clingfilm. Improper care can affect the texture of the fish. Place in small, labelled, airtight bags in the coldest part of the freezer.

FURNESS FISH, POULTRY & GAME

Les Salisbury *Ulverston, Cumbria*

Les Salisbury junior manages the stand in the market; the stock is supplied by his father, Les (Leslie) senior, who is currently based at Ulverston, on the coast of Morecambe Bay (although he will soon be moving to larger, smarter premises at Flookburgh, a few miles further east). The Salisburys have been fishermen for at least five generations. As a little boy, Les senior used to go shrimping with his great-grandfather, who made him walk ahead of his horse to test the sand. In those days, the shrimp-catchers attached their nets to horse-drawn carts. I'm told that the horses loved their trips to the beach even though they sometimes had to paddle in water up to their stomachs. On a busy day at low tide, the beach would be dotted with horses and carts, marking the channels of water in which the shrimps were trapped. Once, according to local tradition, as many as seventy-six were counted. As this suggests, the supply of shrimps at that time was plentiful: now, probably because the bay is slowly silting up and the channels of water are becoming shallower, it has dwindled to the point where there are only a dozen fishermen left. Needless to say, horses and carts have long since been replaced by tractors, which can go faster and in deeper water. I saw Les's, with several others, parked on the shingle just above the tide-line: they all looked fairly rusty, but that's inevitable, given their continuous exposure to salt.

Morecambe Bay, looking out over the Irish Sea towards the Isle of Man, is not only a shrimping-ground but a natural harbour for fishing-boats bound for seas as far north as Iceland. Except for The Wash off Norfolk, it is the biggest bay in England: standing on the sands just west of Ulverston, you can scarcely see as far as the other side. The beach is given character, not by cliffs or dunes but the fact that trees grow right down to the sea, as on the west coast of Ireland, so that you could sit at the top of the beach without needing a sunshade (or, come to that, an umbrella. This is England!) The flat seabed means that the tide goes out an exceptionally long way, which is dangerous for anyone not knowing the coast because it comes in with astonishing speed. There are also currents which pose a threat even to very strong swimmers: hence the tragedy of the drowned cockle-pickers a few years ago. Far more dramatically than with the shrimps, however, the cockles have now completely disappeared. In this instance, no one can suggest why: perhaps it was due to over-fishing but, as Les junior points out, fish change habitat for subtle reasons. I used to fish for mackerel off the coast of Wales: some years you could catch more fish in three minutes than you could eat whereas at other times not a single one was to be seen in a month.

Furness is particularly well known for Morecambe Bay potted shrimps, but also sells the huge variety of other fish landed in the bay. In the interests of sustainability, Les never stocks young fish (which, for example, cuts out the small haddock used for smokies). In fact, however, as its name suggests, Furness was started to sell not only fish but poultry, and also game, which still forms an important part of its business. It comes from estates in Lancashire and the Lake District, where Les discovered that gamekeepers couldn't find a market for their pheasants and, instead of selling, were reduced to burying them. During the summer, fish is to the fore, but game takes precedence in the autumn.

The shrimps to be potted are shelled, cleaned, and boiled as soon as they are brought up from the shore (which is less than five minutes' drive from Les's present workshop). They are potted in butter from Garstang, which is on the other side of the bay, and lightly flavoured with spices, including mace. Local people eat them on toast generously buttered with the spicy shrimp butter; they are also very good on brown or rye bread such as Matt Jones's from Flour Power, accompanied by cherry tomatoes and rocket or watercress. Alternatively, you can serve them on pasta.

Like Herdwick mutton and Colchester native oysters, shrimps from Morecambe Bay are boarded on the Slow Food Ark of Taste.

Les Salisbury
aboard his shrimper

SESAME MORECAMBE BAY SHRIMP TOASTS

This quick and easy starter or canapé recipe is always good to have up your sleeve. From start to finish, you can have these ready in 20 minutes flat — not bad, after a long day. Remember when spreading the prawn paste over the bread to press the mixture firmly into the bread so that it stays on while cooking. [SLB]

Preparation time 10–15 minutes

Cooking time 5–6 minutes

Serves 4–5

Season Morecambe Bay shrimps are in
    season from August Bank holiday until
    Christmas

---

1 medium egg
225 g Morecambe Bay shrimps
    (both raw or cooked shrimps are suitable)
1 rounded tsp cornflour
1 tsp Mirin, plus 1 tblsp for the dipping sauce
    (a dry sherry will work as well)
Sea salt
Freshly ground black pepper
8–10 slices of a Parisienne (also known as
    'French stick') from Flour Power
1 tblsp sesame seeds
2 small garlic cloves
2 tblsp soy sauce
1 tblsp sesame oil
3 tsp rice wine vinegar
1 spring onion
Pinch of chilli flakes
Sunflower oil for frying

Begin by separating the egg and peeling the shrimps if necessary. Place the egg white only (save the egg yolk for another use), shrimps, cornflour, 1 tsp of mirin and seasoning of salt and pepper into a food processor and blend until smooth. Spread the shrimp paste over the bread slices and sprinkle sesame seeds over the top. Press the seeds into the paste to secure.

Make the dipping sauce before you fry the toasts. Peel and mince the garlic and transfer to a small bowl. It is okay if you don't mince the garlic too finely. I quite like having a few little chunks of milky white garlic floating around in the sauce. The occasional garlicky bite gives a pleasing kick to the sauce. Pour in the soy sauce, 1 tblsp of mirin, along with the sesame oil and rice wine vinegar. Peel off the outer layer of the spring onion and chop into fine slices on the angle using both the white and green parts. Add the spring onion to the soy sauce mixture, along with the chilli flakes and stir well to combine.

Heat some sunflower oil in a large frying pan. You want about 1 cm of oil to cover the bottom of the frying pan. Heat the oil to 170°C / 325°F: use a thermometer to test the heat if you have one. Otherwise, gently lower in a small piece of bread to test the temperature. If the oil bubbles up rapidly around the piece of bread rather than soaking into the bread, the oil is ready to cook. Gently lower in the toasts, prawn-side down, and cook until the edges of the bread turns golden brown. Flip and continue to fry until golden all over. Remove from the oil and drain slightly on a plate lined with kitchen paper. Keep warm while you fry the remaining toasts. Transfer to a platter and serve with the dipping sauce on the side.

Opposite *Preparing the nets
for the trawl*

Page 243 *Grading the
shrimp catch*

POTTED SHRIMPS

Potted shrimps and Morecambe Bay in Lancashire have long been associated with one another. There are two types of shrimps: grey and brown. When cooked the grey shrimps turn pink, while cooked brown shrimps turn a darker brown. Supposedly, the brown ones are the best, but that is coming from the people of Morecambe Bay, Ulverston and Flookburgh, where brown shrimps are caught. I have been told that brown shrimps also soak up more of the melted butter than pink shrimps which may sway ones opinion in one way or another. You may have to order raw shrimps ahead of time from your fishmonger. However, pre-cooked shrimps work equally well in this recipe. Simply toss the pre-cooked shrimps with the cooled shallot mixture, citrus zest and juice and finish with the clarified butter. [SLB]

Preparation time 20 minutes, plus 4 hours chilling

Cooking time 5 minutes

Serves 4

Season Morecambe Bay brown shrimps are in season from August Bank holiday until Christmas

4 shallots
2 garlic cloves
Sea salt
300g unsalted butter, divided
¼ tsp freshly ground nutmeg
¼ tsp ground mace
Small pinch cayenne
1 tsp olive oil
Freshly ground black pepper
300g brown shrimps peeled
1 lemon
1 unwaxed or organic orange
15g fresh chives or basil (optional)

Peel the shallots and cut it into very fine dice. Peel and crush the garlic. Work it into a paste with a little salt in a mortar. Warm a large frying pan over a low flame. Cook the shallots and garlic in 50g of the butter. Add the nutmeg, mace and cayenne and cook the shallots and garlic until softened and slightly translucent without colouring. Set aside to cool.

Place 200g of butter in a heat-proof dish and into a low oven, about 38°C / 100°F / gas ⅛ and heat gently to separate out the milky impurities. The milk fat will settle to the bottom. Once the butter is melted, remove it from the oven, pour the clear yellow liquid into a small glass. Discard the white milky solids. Heat olive oil and remaining butter in a frying pan over a medium-high heat. Season the shrimps well with plenty of salt and pepper and cook in the hot oil until they turn a darker brown. Cook only until the colour changes, about 1–2 minutes. Spoon the shrimps into a large bowl. Fold in the cooled shallot-garlic mixture. Squeeze the lemon and add the juice. Wash the orange, grate in half the zest. The combination of citrus fruit gives a well balanced sweet/tart flavour and also goes particularly well with mace and nutmeg. Wash and blot the chives and basil if you are using them, chop them finely and fold them into the shrimps. Chives complement the shallot, whilst basil adds a pleasant astringency to the richness of the butter. They are by no means traditional, but delicious nonetheless.

Transfer shrimps to a serving vessel or individual ramekins and pack in tightly. Pour the clarified butter over the shrimp mixture and stir well to disperse the butter and coat the shrimps. Some butter will be floating on top of the shrimps, which is what you want. This thin layer will act as a preservative. Chill well for a minimum of 4 hours. It is best served 'spreading' consistency so allow a good hour of sitting at room temperature before eating. Serve on granary or sourdough bread.

MACKEREL WITH PUY LENTILS, ORANGES, WATERCRESS AND CORIANDER SEED DRESSING

This recipe packs a punch in the nutrition department. I've lightened up the traditional cream sauce with a yoghurt base yet kept the classical accompaniments of cracked coriander and grainy mustard. Feel free to use 120ml of double cream instead of the yogurt. If you do this, add the juice from a half of lemon to give it a tart edge. [SLB]

Preparation time 10 minutes, plus 30 minutes
marinating

Cooking time 20–30 minutes

Serves 2

Season Mackerel is in season from June until
October

2 mackerel
3 sprigs thyme
1 garlic clove
Sea salt
6 tblsp extra virgin olive oil
100g puy lentils
2 oranges
1 small bunch watercress
1 tblsp coriander seeds
2 tsp Dijon or grainy mustard
120g Greek yoghurt
½ lemon or enough for 1 tblsp lemon juice

Begin by filleting the mackerel. I found this easiest by butterflying the fish and removing any stray pin bones as described on page 236. Cut each butterflied fish in half to split into the fillets.

Wash and remove the leaves from the thyme sprigs. Run your knife over the top to roughly chop and slightly bruise the leaves. Peel and crush the garlic with a little salt in a mortar and work into a paste. Combine the crushed garlic, thyme and 4 tblsp of the olive oil in a small bowl.

Coat the mackerel in the garlic, thyme, and olive oil mixture. Arrange the mackerel in one layer in a glass or ceramic dish. Cover with cling film and refrigerate for 30 minutes.

While the fish is marinating, place the lentils in a small saucepan, cover with twice their volume of water and bring up to a rolling boil. Reduce the heat and simmer for 20–30 minutes, until the water is absorbed and the lentils are tender.

Peel and remove pith from the oranges and cut them into segments. Set aside. Then, remove the large stems from the watercress and discard. Wash the watercress thoroughly and blot dry with kitchen towels.

In another small saucepan lightly toast the coriander seeds until fragrant, about 30 seconds to 1 minute. Transfer to a mortar and grind the seeds into a coarse powder. Decant the seeds into a small bowl and add the Dijon or grainy mustard, remaining olive oil and yoghurt. Squeeze the lemon and fold in 1 tblsp of juice. Set aside until ready to serve. The fish can be marinated and the dressing made well ahead of time.

Preheat the grill to its highest setting.

Arrange the mackerel fillets on a baking tray, with the skin side up. Place under the preheated oven and cook for 7–9 minutes, after which time the mackerel skin should crisp and brown while the flesh stays juicy.

To serve, toss the lentils with half the watercress leaves. Spoon onto plates and arrange more watercress and orange segments over the top. Place the grilled mackerel alongside the lentils with a dollop of yoghurt mustard sauce.

CHARGRILLED CORNISH SARDINES WITH GREEK SALAD

Chargrilling is an intense form of cookery which imparts a lovely smoky flavour. The crisp, briny, herb salad cuts through the rich oily fish. Fennel is not a traditional flavour for Greek salads, but the quick 'pickling' of the fennel adds a fresh, sharp crunch to this dish. [SLB]

Preparation time 15 minutes to fillet the fish and 15–20 minutes to make the salad

Cooking time 6–10 minutes

Serves 4 as a starter

Season Cornish sardines are in season from late May until early September

8 whole small sardines
1 fennel bulb
1 large lemon
200 ml extra virgin olive oil, divided
250 g block of feta cheese
200 g fresh rocket
Handful of good quality black olives, preferably Kalamata
½ large cucumber, thinly sliced
4 ripe tomatoes

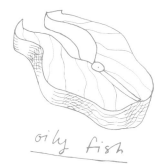

oily fish

Preheat your barbecue.

While your barbecue is preheating butterfly the fish as described on page 236. I've chosen to grill the fish in the butterflied form compared to cutting them in half into fillets. When opened up like a book, the fish is easier to flip on a barbecue.

To make the salad remove any bruised outer leaves of the fennel and rinse thoroughly under cold running water. Quarter the bulb and remove the innermost part of the core with the tip of your knife. Thinly slice each quarter of the fennel and place in a small bowl. Try to cut through the remaining part of the core. This will hold a few of the fennel leaves together and make for a cleaner presentation. Squeeze the lemons and add the juice to the bowl, together with 160ml olive oil to give it a quick pickle. Break the feta into large chunks and add to the fennel. Toss to coat and set aside. Wash and dry the rocket and place in a separate large bowl. Remove the stones from the olives, if necessary, by crushing each one on a work surface and peeling off the olive flesh. Halve the cucumber and remove the seeds by running a small spoon down the centre. Thinly slice. Cut the tomatoes into 8 segments each and combine with the rocket, cucumber and olives. Season well with sea salt and freshly ground black pepper.

Use the remaining 40ml olive oil to drizzle over the fish on both the skin and flesh side. Place the sardines on a hot grill, skin side down for 4 minutes. Flip and cook for an additional 2 minutes. Arrange the rocket salad into a mound on each of the 4 plates. Then top with two hot sardines (1 if they are big). Garnish with fennel and the feta mixture. Spoon the lemony dressing you used to pickle the fennel over the top and serve straight away.

BARBECUED SPRATS
WITH COBNUT SAUCE

Cobnuts* are one of the few nuts grown here in Britain. They are members of the hazelnut family and when grown in the United Kingdom they are mostly referred to as Kentish Cobs, although there are other varieties grown around Britain such as Lambert's Filberts. Cobnuts are sold fresh, unlike most other nuts, which is one reason why their season is so short (from late August until late October). Early in the season the nuts have a green husk and the nut meat is rather wet inside. Nuts harvested late in the season have a brown-tinged husk with a stronger flavour. Stored nuts can be kept until Christmas in a cool dry place.

The flavour of cobnuts is almost a cross between a hazelnut and an almond. They do lack the lovely perfume of a hazelnut, but they have the rich buttery texture more characteristic of the seasonal marcona almonds. My use of cobnuts here in this recipe is a slight variation on a Spanish classic, ajo blanco. Usually, this tapas soup is traditionally thickened with sourdough breadcrumbs and served with sweet grapes. I've kept it on the thin side by omitting the bread and substituting parsley for the grapes as a finish. Even if you do love garlic, try to keep to one clove as you want the delicate sweetness of the cobnuts to come through.

Sprats are at their best from September through November which perfectly coincides with the cobnut season, a natural pairing in the eyes of Mother Nature. Sprats are small marine fish (Clupea sprattus) of the northeast Atlantic waters. They are mostly eaten fresh but can be smoked or preserved for later use. [SLB]

*Cobnuts are on the Slow Food Ark of Taste.

Preparation time 10–15 minutes, plus 30 minutes soaking time for the skewers

Cooking time 5–6 minutes

Serves 4

Season Sprats are in season from September through to Christmas

16–20 sprats,
   depending on how hungry you are
Olive oil for grilling
200g cobnuts, shelled weight
   (about 400g in the shell)
1 clove garlic
200ml extra virgin olive oil
1–3 tsp aged sherry vinegar
Sea salt
Freshly ground black pepper
4 leafy sprigs fresh parsley

Special equipment
Wooden skewers, soaked in water for
   30 minutes before cooking.

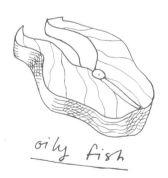

oily fish

Prepare the sprats as described on page 237.

Preheat the barbecue to a medium-hot setting or if you are using charcoal preheat the coals until they develop a nice coating of grey ash.

To secure the sprats on the skewers, thread through the belly side straight to the backbone right behind the head. Push the sprat up to the top of the skewer and continue pushing more sprats onto the skewer but keep a few inches at the bottom for you to grab hold of the skewer when on the barbecue. If your sprats are large you may want to secure the tail end with a skewer in the same manor which will make for easier flipping whilst cooking. Drizzle over a little olive oil and rub into the skin. Place the fish skewers onto the hot barbecue and cook for 3 minutes. Flip over and cook for another 2 minutes.

To serve, pile the sprats high on a plate with the sauce on the side. Finely chop the leaves and fine stems of the parsley and sprinkle over the top of the sauce and serve. I like to serve these sprats as finger food. The fish are perfect for dipping, just make sure to provide plenty of napkins – they will undoubtedly be needed at the end of the meal.

Cook's note Although the sweet flesh of the sprats is most certainly enhanced from a charcoal barbecue, they can be cooked under a grill in the oven. To cook the sprats indoors, preheat your oven grill to its highest setting. Place on a non-stick baking tray and drizzle with oil. Cook for 4 minutes in total, flipping the sprats halfway through.

POTTED SMOKED MACKEREL

This is a very quick, easy and elegant way to serve smoked mackerel. It's delicious spread on toast as canapés, or potted in ramekins and served as a first course. I've chosen red onions, coriander and lime to flavour the mackerel. But spontaneity and improvisation in the kitchen is the key to successful cooking. If coriander isn't for you, try substituting 2–3 spring onions, a few sprigs of dill and fresh lemon juice to sample another favourite combination of mine. [SLB]

Preparation time 25 minutes

Cooking time 20 minutes to clarify the butter

Serves 6

Season Mackerel is in season from June until
    October

285g smoked mackerel
300g unsalted butter, softened
    (including 220g to clarify)
½ small red onion
1 small garlic clove, peeled
15g fresh coriander
1 lime
Sea salt
Freshly ground black pepper

Remove the skin from the mackerel and run your fingers along the flesh to check for any hidden pin bones.

Use two forks to flake the mackerel in to smallish pieces. Place 40g butter into a small saucepan. Peel and finely chop the red onion. Peel and crush the garlic into a paste with a little salt in a mortar. Add the chopped red onion and garlic to the butter. Cook gently for 2 minutes, without letting them colour. The trick here is to let the heat of the butter alone cook the onion and garlic. This gentle cooking of the onion will help to retain a little texture whilst eliminating the bitter raw onion flavour. Combine another 40g butter with the mackerel in a bowl and blend with a fork to form a coarse paste. Add the softened onion and garlic to the mackerel and stir to combine. Wash the coriander and blot dry with kitchen paper. Finely chop the leaves and thin stems. Fold into the mackerel. Squeeze the lime and pour over the juice. Season with sea salt and pepper. Spoon the mackerel into small ramekins and smooth the tops.

Place the remaining butter in a heat-proof cup and into a low oven, about 38°C / 100°F / gas ¼. Heat gently until the butter melts and the milk curds separate to form a thick white layer on the bottom. Remove from the oven, and using a spoon, ladle 2–3 tblsp of the clear, golden butter over the top of each ramekin. Allow the butter to cool and harden at room temperature.

Cover and store in the refrigerator for up to one week.

ROLL MOP CORNISH SARDINES

Filleting or butterflying small fish is not as laborious as people think. Often, when purchasing a whole fish rather than fillets I've found I end up with a fresher product, and having all the bones and heads left over for fish stock is an added bonus. These freshly pickled sardines are great eaten straight out of the jar or with a salad. The term 'roll mop' comes from the technique used in putting them together. The fish is rolled around a dill pickle and secured with a toothpick. [SLB]

Preparation time 30 minutes to fillet the fish

Cooking time 30 minutes to make the mixture, cool and assemble

Serves 4 as a starter

Season Cornish sardines are in season from late May until early September

---

125 ml cider vinegar
150 g caster sugar
10 sardines
1 tsp black peppercorns
1 tsp white peppercorns
50 g sea salt
40 g dill
1 red onion
2 red jalapeno chillies
3 dill pickles

Special equipment
Toothpicks

Have the fishmonger gut the fish for you. Begin by filleting the sardines, see page 236.

Next, bring 150 ml water, plus the vinegar and the sugar to the boil. Cook just until the sugar has dissolved. Allow to cool. Season the sardine fillets with sea salt. Crush the black and white peppercorns in a mortar and sprinkle over the fillets. Wash the dill, remove the fronds from the sprigs and chop them finely. Peel and finely dice the red onion. Halve the chillies, remove their seeds and finely mince. Combine the dill, onion and chilli together in a small bowl and sprinkle the spice mixture over the fillets. Cut the dill pickles into 20 pieces, and, starting with the head, roll each fillet around a piece of pickle. Secure with a toothpick and place the rolls into a bowl, tray or glass jar in which they fit snugly. Repeat with the remaining fish fillets. Sprinkle over any remaining dill, onion and chilli then pour over the cooled vinegar mixture.

Refrigerate for at least 24 hours before serving. Serve with crisp leaves and warm bread.

oily fish

POLENTA-CRUSTED GOUJONS OF MEGRIM SOLE WITH WATERCRESS SALSA VERDE

This is a simple, gorgeous way to cook sole. It's quick and perfect for a summer evening when you want sharp tastes and crisp textures. All you need is a lovely full-bodied glass of rosé to go with it. [SLB]

Preparation time 20–30 minutes,

Cooking time 6–7 minutes

Serves 4

Season Avoid eating megrim during its spawning season, between January and April

500g megrim sole fillets, without skin
1 medium egg
100g flour
Sea salt
Freshly ground black pepper
100g polenta
2 tblsp olive oil for frying
100g watercress
4 spring onions
2 tblsp white wine
2 tblsp white wine vinegar
1 rounded tsp Dijon mustard
120ml extra virgin olive oil
Pinch caster sugar

Cut the sole into 3cm wide strips. Crack the egg into a small bowl and lightly beat to break up the egg yolk. Spread the flour over a large plate and season with a little salt and pepper. Spread the dry polenta over another plate. Dip the strips first into the seasoned flour, then egg and then into the polenta. Arrange on a plate, cover with cling film and place in the refrigerator until ready to cook, allowing the polenta to be softened by the egg which makes for a crispier crust.

Make the sauce. Wash the watercress and remove the leaves from the thick stems. Peel and finely chop the spring onions and place them in the bowl of a food processor with the white wine, white wine vinegar, Dijon mustard and watercress. Pulse a few times to break up the herbs. Add the oil in a steady stream. Season with a pinch of sugar, salt and pepper.

In a shallow frying pan, heat 2 tblsp of olive oil. Once hot, fry the goujons until they are golden brown, about 3 minutes per side adding more oil as needed. Serve with a green salad and the sauce along side.

Cook's note For a lower-fat alternative, dip the fish in buttermilk instead of egg. Dredge in polenta. Refrigerate for at least half an hour before cooking to allow the moisture from the buttermilk to soak through the polenta. Bake on a foil-lined baking trays for 10 minutes in an oven preheated to 200°C / 400°F / gas 6. Serve with the watercress salsa verde.

Opposite Morecambe Bay

GURNARD WITH FLATBREADS AND AVOCADO SALSA

Gurnard has almost iridescent red and white scales and is a great substitute for red mullet or snapper, although it has a much more delicate flavour. Its head is disproportionately large, similar to that of monkfish, and the price will reflect this. So what you end up with is a delicious, versatile fish that is very inexpensive. But make sure you ask your fishmonger for the head, as it makes a fantastic fish stock (see page 295).

Inspiration for this dish comes from the Barrio district of San Francisco, where fish taco stands are on every street corner. Crisp fresh fish is quickly fried and then wrapped in a soft flatbread or a corn tortilla. For me it is the ultimate fast food. Avocados add a richness and creamy texture that matches perfectly the mild gurnard taste. [SLB]

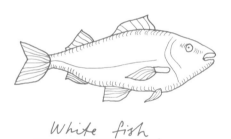

White fish

Preparation time 15 minutes

Cooking time 10–14 minutes

Serves 4

Season Gurnard spawn during the summer months (June, July and August), so avoid it during that time and enjoy it from September until May

AVOCADO SALSA

1 red onion
1 red jalapeno chilli, or to taste
1 lime
2 tblsp extra virgin olive oil
2 ripe avocados
150g cherry tomatoes (optional)
15g fresh coriander (a small handful)

1 tblsp olive oil
Sea salt
Freshly ground black pepper
4 gurnard fillets, with skin (200g each)
4 flatbreads for wrapping
    (a larger pita bread torn in half or
    Middle Eastern lavash bread works well)
4–8 leaves of Little Gem lettuce

Prepare the avocado salsa before you begin cooking the fish. Peel and finely dice the red onion. If you are not a raw onion fan, you can leave it out or try boiling the kettle and pouring the hot water over it through a sieve. This will remove a lot of the bitterness but still retain the crunch of a raw onion. Wash, deseed and finely chop the jalapeno chilli. Juice the lime. Combine the onion and chilli with the lime juice and olive oil. Cut the avocados in half length-ways and twist to open. Place the stone-side of the avocados on the counter. Tap the knife blade into the stones, and twist to remove. Keep the stones. Slide a large flat spoon in between the skin and the flesh of each avocado half. Loosen on all sides and lift out the flesh. Crush the avocados and add to the onion-chilli mixture. Wash and roughly chop the coriander leaves; finely chop any thin tender stems then fold through the salsa. Wash and quarter the cherry tomatoes and toss them into the avocado, seeds and all. Season with sea salt and black pepper. Top with your stone and cover with cling film. The stone will help to keep the salad from discolouring.

Preheat your oven to 200°C / 400°F / gas 6. Place an oven-proof frying pan over a medium high heat. Rub a little olive oil onto both sides of the fish and season with salt and pepper. Place the fish in the hot pan skin side down. Cook for 3 minutes or until the skin is starting to brown and crisp. Carefully, flip the fish over transfer to the oven and continue to cook for 7–10 minutes depending on the thickness. The fish should look opaque and flake easily.

While the fish is cooking wash the lettuce and prepare your flatbreads. Open up the pitas or cut a 25 cm square of lavash. Place one or two pieces of lettuce towards the edge furthest away from you and top with 1–2 tblsp of the crushed avocado mix. Place the fish on top and lift the side of bread closest to you to fold over the base of the fish. Then roll the fish up (side-to-side) into a log shape. The flatbreads are great with a tall glass of Sierra Nevada Pale Ale.

PAN-FRIED SQUID
WITH HARISSA

This is delicious served as tapas or equally good as a starter. If you can't find a good quality harissa, either make your own (see recipe following). Store covered with a drizzle of olive oil in the refrigerator for up to 2 weeks. [SLB]

Preparation time 30 minutes

Cooking time 5 minutes

Serves 6–8 people as a tapas, 4 as a starter

Season Squid is in season from September until November

550–600 g squid
2 tblsp olive oil
Sea salt
Freshly ground black pepper

HUMMUS

2 garlic cloves
½ tsp salt
1 lemon (enough for 2 tblsp juice)
200 g dried chickpeas,
    or 1 x 440 g can chickpeas
5 tblsp well-stirred tahini
2 tblsp extra virgin olive oil
up to 4 tblsp water
Freshly ground black pepper
15 g fresh parsley

VINAIGRETTE

1 clove garlic
½ tsp cumin seeds
½ tsp sea salt
½ lemon
1 tblsp harissa paste (store bought or
    homemade according to the recipe below)
1 tsp honey
½ tsp black pepper
3 tbsp extra virgin olive oil

Begin by preparing and tenderising the squid (see page 235) and slice it into rings.

Next make the hummus which, along with the vinaigrette, can be made ahead of time. On a cutting board, mince the garlic to a paste with the salt. Squeeze the lemons and measure out 2 tblsp juice and set aside. Purée the chickpeas in a food processor with the garlic paste, lemon juice, tahini, olive oil and up to 4 tbsp water, scraping down the sides, until the hummus is smooth. Season well with black pepper and salt. Transfer to a shallow serving dish. Wash the parsley and finely chop the leaves and set aside in a small bowl until ready to serve.

Prepare the vinaigrette by peeling the garlic and crushing the cloves with the cumin seeds in a mortar with the sea salt. Squeeze the half lemon and add to the mortar, along with the harissa paste, honey and water, stir well to combine. Season with black pepper and slowly drizzle in the olive oil. Set aside until ready to use.

Wash and chop the parsley. Preheat a ridged frying pan for a minute over a high flame. Toss the prepared squid in olive oil and season with salt and pepper. Place the squid in the preheated pan and cook for 1–2 minutes. The squid will curl and take up a little colour. Once it is visibly firm, remove from the pan and spoon onto the hummus. Sprinkle with the chopped parsley. Serve with harissa vinaigrette alongside for dipping or drizzling.

Cook's note This recipe is great as part of a barbecue. Cut the squid into slightly large pieces and make sure you have a fine-meshed grill rack, so the pieces won't fall through onto the coals.

HARISSA PASTE

Harissa is a fiery spice paste and is delicious when served with most grilled meats. It jazzes up casseroles and tagines for those who like a bit of heat. Below I've suggested a few ways to add a smoky element to the harissa, with the guajillo chillies being the most mild. Guajillos are leathery, dark, red-brown chillies and have a thick skin which necessitates a 25–30 soaking time before puréeing. Treat them like dried spices, if they have been in your cupboard for a while dry toast them in an empty frying pan before soaking and proceed as below.

Preparation time 20 minutes

Cooking time a few minutes to toast the dried spices and soak the guajillo chillies if using

Serves 6

Season Fresh jalapeno peppers are available year-round but are at their best in August

100 g long red jalapeno chillies
4 garlic cloves
1 tsp caraway seeds
1 tsp coriander seeds
1 tsp cumin seeds
1 tblsp tomato purée
1 tsp red wine vinegar
Up to 2 tblsp extra virgin olive oil
Sea salt
Freshly ground black pepper

Ingredients to add an optional 'smoky' flavour:
1 tsp medium to hot smoked paprika
1 tsp chipotle chilli in adobo
55 g dried guajillo chillies, soaked in warm water, drained and de-seeded
(all available from Cool Chile Co. stall in Borough Market)

When handling so many chillies, I definitely recommend using rubber gloves. Thin doctor's ones work best, but Marigold kitchen gloves will do. They can be slightly cumbersome but will protect your fingers just as well.

Wash and slit the jalapeno chillies in half lengthways. Remove the seeds and large membranes or ribs that hold them in place. Peel the garlic and roughly chop both the garlic and chillies. If you are using guajillo chillies, remove the stems and seeds after soaking and roughly chop as well. Transfer the garlic and chillies to the bowl of a food processor or blender. Measure the caraway, coriander, and cumin seeds into a non-stick frying pan. Turn the heat on to low and gently toast the spices until fragrant, about 45 seconds to 1 minutes should be enough. Scatter the spices over the top of the chillies and garlic. Purée until you have a nice paste. Add the tomato purée, red wine vinegar, and enough olive oil to loosen the mixture. Water can also be added to loosen the paste further. You want the texture to be thick enough to hold its shape whilst still suitable for dipping. Season with sea salt and freshly ground black pepper.

Cook's note The ingredients that add a 'smoky' element of taste to harissa are more Arab-Andalusian in origin. North African harissa tends to be more fiery and elegant without the added smoke. I like the addition of the guajillo chillies, but if you are looking for an earthy element to match the elegant fiery heat without smoke try black cumin seeds instead of regular cumin seeds and prepare in the same way.

SQUID BRAISED IN RED WINE WITH SAFFRON RISOTTO

A walk-away dish, as my old chef would call it, is one that takes little time to prepare and yields fantastic results. Gutsy flavours and fruity red wine are lightened up with the addition of orange zest and juice, making the dish perfect for any time of year. Chilli, fennel and orange are natural partners with saffron – a flavour combination which will most certainly transport you to the Costas. [SLB]

Squid

Preparation time 15 minutes, once the squid is cleaned, 10 minutes to get the ingredients together for the risotto

Cooking time 1 hour 45 minutes

Serves 4–5

Season Blood oranges are in season in January through early March. Fresh squid is also available at this time of year, but the fish is at its best from September to November.

1 kg squid, uncleaned weight
1 tblsp plain flour
1 onion
2 leeks
1 large fennel bulb
1 small red jalapeno chilli
4 garlic cloves
Sea salt
1 tsp fennel seeds
1 tsp coriander seeds
2 bay leaves
350 ml fruity red wine
1 orange, blood when in season
Freshly gound black pepper
A handful of fresh parsley

RISOTTO

1 tblsp extra virgin olive oil
15 g unsalted butter
2 round shallots, or 1 banana shallot
1 leek
2 garlic cloves
250 g risotto rice
A pinch of saffron (0·3–4 g)
750 ml stock (preferably homemade fish stock, but chicken or store bought will do)
75 g Pecorino Romano or Parmesan

Preheat the oven to 170°C / 325°F / gas 3.

For tips on preparing squid please see page 235. Cut the body into rings and the flaps into strips. Leave the tentacles whole. Dust with flour and set aside.

Peel and finely dice the onion. Cut the leek in half lengthwise and rinse under cold running water. Cut the leeks into thick slices. Remove the outer layer of the fennel if it is bruised and damaged; otherwise, it should be washed. Remove any bushy fennel fonds from the top and save for later. Finely dice the fennel and set aside. Place a large heavy casserole over a medium flame and add the chopped vegetables. Drizzle with olive oil and cover with a tight fitting lid. Cook for about 5 minutes or until the vegetables are softened and slightly translucent.

In the meantime, wash, halve and de-seed the jalapeno chilli and chop it finely. Peel the garlic and crush together with the fennel seeds and coriander seeds in a mortar with a pinch of salt. Remove the lid of the casserole and add the garlic mixture and the chopped chilli. Once the dried spices have filled the kitchen with their aroma, add the squid and toss it around the pot, allowing it to really mingle in with the aromatic vegetables and spices for 1 minute.

Add the bay leaves and pour in the red wine. Wash the orange, cut it in half and tuck in amongst the squid mixture. Season well and bring to a simmer. Cut out a piece of parchment just larger than the circumference of your casserole and place on top of the squid and vegetables. Secure the lid over the parchment and transfer to a preheated oven. Braise slowly for 1½ hours.

After an hour has gone by, begin to prepare the rice. Heat the oil and butter in a shallow pan or casserole. Peel the shallots and finely mince. Cut the leek in half lengthwise and rinse under cold running water. Cut into thick slices. Add the shallot and leek to the oil-butter and cook for 3–5 minutes or until softened. Peel the garlic and work into a paste with a pinch of salt in a mortar. Add the garlic to the shallots and leeks and gently fry to release the flavour. Once fragrant, add the rice and stir to coat it in the vegetable mixture. Pour over ⅓ of the stock (preferably at room temperature or warm) and bring to a boil. Sprinkle over the saffron and gently stir into the rice. Reduce the heat and cook, uncovered, for about 25 minutes. As the stock is absorbed into the rice, add another ⅓. After the second addition, start to add the remaining stock little by little, tasting and checking the texture of the rice.

As soon as the squid has finished cooking, wash and roughly chop most of the parsley, save a few sprigs for garnish. Fold the parsley through the braised squid and taste for seasoning. Grate the Pecorino Romano or Parmesan and add along with a good pinch of sea salt and black pepper.

To serve, spoon the saffron rice onto plates and top with braised squid. Garnish with remaining sprigs of parsley.

Cook's note Both the squid braise and the saffron can be made ahead of time. The squid will keep for a day in your refrigerator. Bring up to room temperature before transferring to a warm oven to heat through. The rice can be cooked ahead of time but adding only 500 ml of stock (about ⅔ the quantity of the liquid). Transfer rice from the casserole to a baking tray. When ready to cook, spoon the rice back into the cleaned casserole and bring up a simmer with remaining stock. Cook until *al dente* and serve.

CURE-ROASTED HAKE
WITH RATATOUILLE

Hake is a highly underrated fish. With a delicate buttery flavour, flaky texture and similar bone structure to cod, it is a near perfect sustainable substitute.

Home curing is a great way to increase the longevity or 'sell-by dates' of fish purchased from the market. Curing works especially well with delicate flaky fish, such as hake. By firming up the flesh before cooking it tends to hold together with more structure for serving.

I love this sauce-like, roasted ratatouille. By cooking it in the oven the vegetable juices are concentrated and intensified but still have a bit of a bite in the end. Try to substitute the suggested ratatouille vegetables according to season or personal taste. Favourites of mine have to be pumpkin and okra. Whilst sweet pumpkin flesh melds effortlessly with sharp tomatoes and sweet basil, stretching Summer into Autumn, okra has an unparalleled taste and texture providing viscosity and shine to the ratatouille. [SLB]

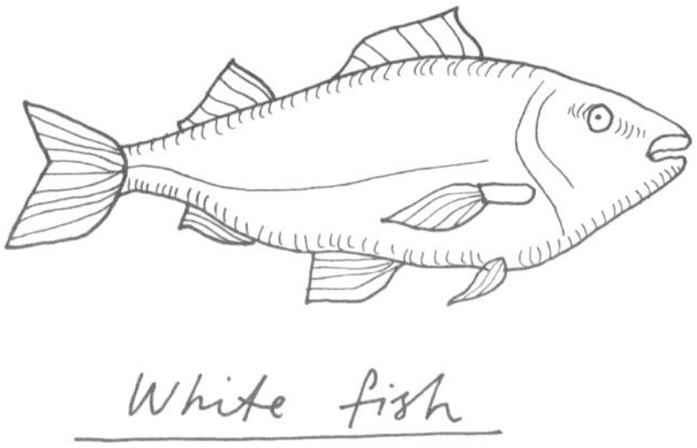

Preparation time 6 hours to overnight for salting the fish

Cooking time 1 hour

Serves 4

Season Hake is in season from late October until March

Hake fillets (600–800 g)
3 tblsp coarse sea salt
1 tblsp caster sugar, additional pinch for the ratatouille
½ tsp dried oregano or marjoram
½ tsp freshly ground black pepper
1 medium aubergine
3 medium courgettes
300 g cherry tomatoes
2 red peppers
3 tblsp extra virgin olive oil
20 g fresh basil leaves
½ tsp sea salt
4 heads of garlic
Ciabatta bread for serving

White fish

Advance preparation: the fish can remain in the salt cure for up to 3 days.

Begin by cleaning and drying the fish with paper towels. Run your fingers along the length of the fish to make sure there are no remaining bones. Mix the salt, sugar, oregano or marjoram and black pepper, then rub the fish flesh with the mixture. Place in a shallow glass or ceramic baking pan and cover. Leave to cure for at least 6 hours, but preferably overnight.

Preheat the oven to 180°C / 350°F / gas 4.

When ready to cook, wash the aubergines, courgettes, cherry tomatoes and red peppers and cut into an equal-sized dice. I like to leave them quite chunky, about 2–3cm in size, so the vegetables retain their integrity. The vegetables should turn into more of a chunky ragout rather than ratatouille. Toss the vegetables in the olive oil and place them in a roasting tin. Wash the basil. Remove the leaves, slice them thinly or tear into small pieces and fold them into the vegetables. Sprinkle with a pinch of sugar and season with sea salt and black pepper. Place in the preheated oven and cook for 50 minutes to an hour. When you put the vegetables into the oven prepare the garlic by slicing the top of the garlic head off to expose all the cloves. Drizzle with olive oil, wrap in foil and place in the oven alongside the vegetables and cook for 50 minutes to an hour as well.

After the vegetables and garlic have been cooking for 45 minutes, prepare the fish and ciabatta. Pour away any marinating juices from the fish which may have collected in the pan. Rinse off the salt mixture from the fish and pat dry with kitchen paper towel. Slice the ciabatta and slide it into the oven alongside the vegetables and garlic. Heat a frying pan over a medium flame. Rub a little oil into the fish flesh and skin. Depending on how the fish has been cut, you may have 'hake steaks' or you may have more of a fillet shape with one end of the fillet thicker than the other. If you have steaks, cook for 4 minutes per side. If you have fillets, sear, skin side down for 4 minutes, flip over and place in the hot oven for an additional 8–10 minutes.

Remove the garlic parcel from the oven and squeeze the garlic cloves into a small bowl. Crush into a paste and smear on the lightly toasted ciabatta. To serve, spoon a mound of hot vegetables into the centre of the plate and top with pieces of fish. Serve the roasted garlic crostini alongside.

MUSSELS IN CIDER WITH TOMATO, CRÈME FRAÎCHE AND DIJON MUSTARD

Mussels are one of the easiest weeknight suppers. They are sweet tasty morsels from the sea that are made for sharing, which always results in a convivial meal to be had by all. A few years ago a customer mentioned to me that they were her favourite dish for Boxing Day every year. She said it was a quick and easy 'hot' option to have on hand for those who didn't want turkey and bacon sandwiches. I couldn't agree more. To many people's surprise mussels can be purchased well ahead of time. They keep very well in the refrigerator for up to 5 days. However, they do like a very specific environment: they must be kept moist with a damp tea towel or wet newspaper. They should be left un-cleaned with their 'beards' intact in a sieve resting in a bowl with a few ice cubes, rather than stored in an air-tight container or water. Finally, they must be kept well chilled. The less they are disturbed the longer they will keep quite happily.

This has to be one of my favourite recipes in the book. The combination of sweet-salty mussels with deliciously dry New Forest Cider is my idea of heaven. Even though I do love the small threads of shallots dotted throughout the mussel broth, I have at a pinch gone without. I have also substituted basil for thyme and parsley with similar success. [SLB]

Preparation time 45 minutes for cleaning and soaking the mussels

Cooking time 10–12 minutes

Serves 2 as a main course, 4 as a starter

Season Mussels are at their best September through December but are reasonably available throughout the year

1 kg mussels
2 tblsp sea salt, for soaking the mussels, plus additional for the broth
60 g unsalted butter
6 shallots
3 garlic cloves
3 large sprigs fresh thyme
¼ tsp freshly ground black pepper
400 ml tomato passata
480 ml cider
1 level tblsp Dijon mustard
2 rounded tblsp crème fraîche
15 g fresh parsley leaves

Mussels & clams

Clean the mussels under cold running water. Leave them to soak for half an hour in a large bowl with plenty of salted water. Scrape off barnacles and pull off the hairy beards. Discard any mussels with broken shells. Most of them will be closed: if any are open, give them a squeeze. If they don't close shut, then throw them away.

Heat the butter in a wide deep saucepan with a tight fitting lid over moderately high heat until foaming subsides. Peel and cut the shallot in half. Then chop the shallot into thin slices. Peel and crush the garlic with a little salt in a mortar. Then add, along with the shallots, to the hot butter. Stir to coat in the warm butter and cook gently until the shallots start to soften and become translucent.

Wash the sprigs of thyme and blot dry with kitchen paper. Pull off the leaves and give them a rough chop to release their flavour. Then add to the pan along with a pinch of sea salt and the black pepper, stirring to coat. Slowly pour in the tomato passata and cider and bring to a gentle boil.

Add the cleaned mussels and cook; covered, stirring occasionally, until mussels open, 4–6 minutes. Remove from the heat. Discard any mussels that remain unopened after 6 minutes.

Wash the parsley and blot dry with kitchen paper. Chop the leaves and fine stems of the parsley and set aside. Stir together the mustard and crème fraîche in a small bowl. Then add, along with the chopped parsley, to the hot tomato broth and whisk until combined.

Divide the mussels amongst warm bowls and ladle the sauce over them. Serve with a leafy green salad and lots of crusty bread.

QUICK MEDITERRANEAN FISH STEW WITH MUSSELS, COLEY, ALASKAN POLLACK OR HAKE

The fish in this dish resemble cod and haddock in terms of texture but are all sustainably fished. Coley, also known as saithe or 'pollock' (which comes from its scientific name Pollachius virens), unfortunately suffers from a greyish toned flesh. This, however, is masked beautifully in the delicious tomato broth. You can use any of these similar-textured fish or a combination of the three.

The depth and flavour in this recipe comes from the mussel juice, so no fish stock is needed. White wine and tomatoes form the base of the soup, while a unique blend of spices gives it a real kick. If you have a sweet pepper or leek lurking in your refrigerator, either or both would be a welcome addition.

When you are in the mood to be fancy, polish this stew off with an old-fashioned rouille for a classical taste of Marseille. [SLB]

Preparation time 10 minutes, plus 30 minutes for soaking the mussels

Cooking time 25–30 minutes

Serves 6–8

Season Mussels, coley, hake and pollack are all at their best from November to March

1 kg locally grown mussels
Sea salt
4 garlic cloves
2 tsp coriander seeds
2 tsp fennel seeds
1 fennel bulb
1 large red onion
2 tblsp olive oil
2 x 440 g tins chopped tomatoes
500 ml white wine
750 g coley, Alaskan pollack or hake fillets, skin removed
4 sprigs fresh mint
4 sprigs fresh coriander

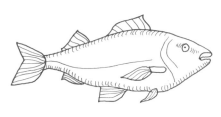

White fish

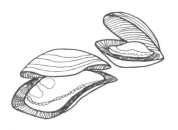

Mussels & clams

Clean the mussels by scraping off any barnacles and pulling off their hairy beards. Cover them in plenty of cold water and sprinkle with about a tblsp of salt. Leave to sit for 30 minutes at room temperature.

Peel and crush the garlic with a little salt in a mortar. Add the coriander and fennel seeds and work into a rough paste bruising the seeds slightly.

Remove the green fronds from the fennel (if there are any) and set aside. Remove the outer layers, if bruised, and discard. Wash and chop into quarters and using the tip of your knife to cut out the bitter core from each quarter. Cut into a fine dice and set aside. Peel the onion and chop into fine dice as well.

Heat the olive oil in a large pan over low heat. Add the onion and fennel, stirring to coat in the oil. Cover and allow the vegetables to cook for 5 minutes or until they become soft and translucent. Add the garlic, fennel and coriander seed paste. Fry gently for approximately 30 seconds, then promptly add the tomatoes to prevent them from burning. Bring this mixture up to a simmer. Allow the flavours to mingle for about 10 minutes to create a poaching liquid for the fish fillets.

Place the mussels in another deep frying pan with a tight fitting lid or casserole and pour in the wine. Cover and bring up to a simmer. Steam the mussels for about 6–8 minutes or just until they start to open. Remove the mussels from the heat. Pick out and discard any unopened ones. Drain the cooking liquid through a sieve and reserve. Taste the mussel juice and add to the tomato mixture. Keep the cooked mussels in a warm place.

Slice the fish into small pieces, about 5·5cm in size. I usually cut the fish on the angle with the natural direction of the flesh as it will hold together better when cooked. Gently lower the fish into the tomato mixture and poach for about 10 minutes. Wash and finely chop the leaves from the fresh herbs and add both to the stew.

Arrange the mussels in a large serving dish or into large individual shallow bowls, ladle the stew over the top to gently the warm the mussels through. Serve with good crusty bread and a green salad.

CARPET-SHELL CLAMS
CHICKPEA AND PARSLEY PASTA
WITH PRESERVED LEMON

Everyone can always use another pasta recipe. This particular flavour combination is given a sophisticated twist with the addition of fresh plump clams. The lemon has a zesty restorative quality whilst chick-peas nourish. Combined with parsley and sheep's milk cheese, the flavours in this dish transport us to the south-western Mediterranean. Serve with a lovely tomato, cucumber and kalamata olive salad with lots of fresh dill or possibly Chargrilled Cornish Sardines (page 245).

Preserved lemons can be purchased in most supermarkets these days but they are extremely easy to make. Halved unwaxed lemons can be packed with sea salt in a glass jar and covered with lemon juice. Spices can be added, such as cloves, peppercorns and coriander seeds to give a more Safi Moroccan flavour. Mature the lemons for a month in the refrigerator. If you have time on your hands and a glut of lemons, it is a worthwhile thing to do. If not, just buy them, but make sure you don't substitute pickled lemons as they are an entirely different product.

Carpet shell clams also go by the names palourde and vongole veraci. True carpet shells are about 3 cm–5 cm in width. The smaller carpet shells are generally more yellow in colour (vongole gialle or yellow carpet shells) but any size will do for this recipe. I mentioned the use of 'cooked' chickpeas below. You can use either tinned chickpeas or dried which have been soaked overnight and cooked until softened. Using dry chickpeas definitely takes the spontaneity out of the dish but they are worth it. Try the recipe both ways, but I doubt you will go back to the tin once you have tasted the nutty-earthy flavour of freshly cooked chickpeas.

Timing is important in this recipe. Make sure you have everything ready at the start. Preparation and cooking times given below are generous. Once you have been through this recipe once, you will be throwing it together in the time it takes to boil the pasta! [SLB]

Preparation time 30 minutes to soak the clams, 5–10 minutes to prep the remaining ingredients

Cooking time 10–15 minutes (the clams and pasta can be cooked at the same time)

Serves 4

Season Carpet shell clams are available throughout most of the year. But avoid their spawning season of May through September.

1·5 kg carpet shell clams
Sea salt
400 g dried spaghetti
  (or your favourite shape of pasta)
120 ml olive oil
  (plus an extra drizzle for stirring)
½ a lemon
2 preserved lemons (rind only)
250 g cooked chickpeas
150 g Pecorino Romano or Sardo cheese
Fresh parsley or baby spinach
Freshly ground black pepper

Prepare the clams for steaming as described on page 235.

Place a large pan of salted water on the stove and bring it to the boil. Cook the pasta according to the manufacturer's instructions minus 1 minute. Drain and set aside.

Squeeze the lemon. Pour the olive oil and lemon juice into another saucepan, large enough to accommodate the cooked pasta comfortably.

Remove the preserved lemons from the jar. Pull out and discard the fleshy interior. Rinse the lemon rind under cold water to get rid of some of the salt. Thinly slice the preserved lemon rind and add to the olive oil and lemon juice in the saucepan, along with the chickpeas.

Grate the cheese and set aside. Wash the parsley or spinach and blot dry with kitchen paper. If you are using parsley, roughly chop the leaves and fine stems only. Have both the cheese and parsley or spinach ready to add at the last minute.

Put the prepared clams into a large pot and pour in 120 ml water; cover, and steam until the shells partially open, about 3–4 minutes. Drain the clams through a sieve but save the cooking liquid. Transfer to a measuring jug and allow any grit to settle to the bottom. Carefully pour the clam cooking liquid into the pot with the olive oil. Bring the mixture up to a simmer over a medium flame. Sift through the clams in the sieve and discard any that have not opened.

Add the drained pasta along with the clams to the pan containing the clam juice and olive oil mixture. Sprinkle in the parsley (or spinach) and toss to coat. Add about half the grated cheese. Mix to incorporate. Season with plenty of freshly ground black pepper.

Spoon into warmed bowls and garnish with the remaining cheese plus a drizzle of olive oil.

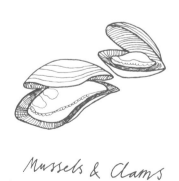

Mussels & Clams

SHELLSEEKERS

Darren Brown *Bovington, Dorset*

In terms of what he does, Darren Brown is easily the most
extraordinary trader in the market. When you meet him, however, he doesn't seem extraordinary at all, but simply exceptionally cheerful and likeable. He spent five years in the Navy and
thoroughly enjoyed it, mainly because of the camaraderie which,
even now, a decade later, he says he still misses. That's the kind of
person he is – at least, until the conversation turns to dredgers.

Darren collects the scallops he sells not with a trawler, in the
usual manner, but by diving. He started out as a chef (he was at
college with Mark Hix) but then joined the Navy at least partly
in order to learn to dive. He keeps his boat in Lulworth Cove,
near Bridport, a small C-shaped bay with high promontories
which is far better known as a tourist destination than as a base
for fishermen. The path down to the beach is lined with cafés
and restaurants, and on the day of our visit, a hot Tuesday in July,
everywhere was full of people, some sipping tea or soft drinks,
some eating scones or rock-cakes, others simply sitting on the
beach enjoying the sun. A few (plus one or two dogs) were
swimming. Apart from those serving in the cafés, Darren and
his assistants seemed to be the only ones not on holiday.

The team's procedure is as follows. Three of them go out in the boat, often cruising six or seven miles along the coast, and Darren and his fellow-diver Andy put on wet-suits with two diving-packs each on their backs. The packs are filled with air containing forty per cent of oxygen, as opposed to the normal twenty per cent, which helps them to withstand the pressure of the water and prevent a condition known as 'the bends'. They dive carrying four large nets each. The nets have air-bags attached to them: when the divers have filled them with scallops, they blow up the bags from one of the packs on their backs which sends them up to the surface, where they are picked up by the third

Grading the catch

member of the team. When all the nets are full or after an hour and a half, when their air supply runs low, the team returns to the Cove to sort through their catch.

The scallops are graded with a measuring-iron into five sizes, ranging from 100 to 130 mm. They are then packed into fine nets, sealed, and thrown back overboard. In theory, as they live off plankton in the water, they can stay alive indefinitely, but Darren says that they should be used within three or four days or they become stressed (which raises the question of how aware scallops or oysters, or indeed any other fish are of their fate: see Edward Lear, *The walrus and the carpenter*). The numbers the team takes may be tiny by commercial standards but sound hugely impressive to me: that day, in two dives, Darren and Andy had collected 160 dozen, *ie* nearly 2,000.

Although he dives all the year round, the visibility under water when the weather is bad in the winter is sometimes virtually nil, 'and if you can't see, you can't work'. In the autumn and winter months, therefore, he puts on a second hat and shoots venison on a neighbouring estate, Creech Grange: Jamie Oliver takes a carcass a week. (In this instance, the deer are not fallow, as on page 62, but Sika, another small non-indigenous breed.) The clams and other fish and shellfish on his stall are caught or collected either by him or two or three other local fishermen.

After nearly ten years of successful diving around the Cove, he now faces a problem: West Bay, one of his best-stocked scallop-grounds, has been discovered by a trawler using dredging-nets, which capture not only scallops but some fifteen or so other species, most if not all of which the fishermen don't want. It also ruins the sea-bed for a long time to come. His indignation rises and crashes like a tidal wave in a calm sea. 'Dredgers should be banned!' he exclaims with momentary but passionate fury. 'They completely wreck the marine environment!' I know that everyone reading this book will wholeheartedly agree.

BOUILLABAISSE

This is truly a special occasion dish. My parents started making it with friends a few years back. Everyone gets a job; whether it is making stock, red pepper aioli, croutons or soup preparation and this wonderfully fragrant soup is all the tastier for it. I'm not sure if it is the wine consumed during preparation, or if it is a genuine sense of accomplishment amongst family and friends for creating such a fantastic feast together which sets the tone, but I can assure you it is always a jubilant one!

This is not a difficult dish to prepare but there are quite a few components. Take a little time to go over the entire recipe before starting. The fish stock and all the aromatic vegetable preparation can be done well ahead of time, leaving only the fish to cook on the day. I have chosen fish in season during the winter months but please substitute appropriate seasonal fish throughout the year. [SLB]

Preparation time 30 minutes to soak the mussels, during which time you prep the fish, vegetables, red pepper aioli, and crostini

Cooking time 25–30 to make the soup

Serves 8–10

Season The fish in this recipe are in season during the winter months November through January

RED PEPPER AIOLI

2 red peppers
2 medium eggs
1 garlic clove
1 tsp mustard
1 tblsp red wine vinegar
300 ml extra virgin olive oil
Sea salt

CROUTONS

1 baguette
1 tblsp olive oil
1 garlic clove

1 kg mussels
Sea salt
450 g hake
450 g sea bream
2 carrots
1 onion
2 celery stalks
3 tsp olive oil
4 garlic cloves
400 g baby potatoes
1 tsp saffron threads
1 tblsp fennel seed
2 litres fish stock preferably homemade
2 tblsp Pernod
3 x 440 g tins of crushed tomatoes
450 g large prawns
Fresh parsley

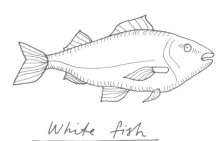

White fish

Mussels

Preheat the oven to 150°C / 300°F / gas 2.

Begin by preparing the aioli. Blacken the skin of the peppers by charring over a gas flame. Transfer to a baking tray and place in the pre-heated oven. Cook for 10 minutes or until the peppers start to collapse. Remove from the oven and allow to cool. Peel and de-seed the peppers and finely chop or purée them into a fine sauce. Set aside. Separate the eggs, peel and crush the garlic to a smooth paste. Combine the yolks, mustard, vinegar and crushed garlic in a bowl. Stabilise the bowl on a damp tea towel. Start to whisk in the olive oil slowly – do this 1 tblsp at a time. Build up the emulsion and when it starts to get a bit thick you can add the olive oil more quickly. The end result will be a thick yellow mayonnaise with a sharp garlic flavour. Taste for seasoning. It will probably need a bit of salt and pepper. If you prefer you can use store bought mayonnaise with the additions of peppers, garlic, mustard and wine vinegar. Keep cool until ready to serve.

Peel and halve the clove of garlic. Slice the baguette into largish croutons and toast in the preheated oven for about ten minutes or until a little golden brown. Once toasted, remove them from the oven, drizzle with olive oil and rub with the garlic.

Clean the mussels by soaking in salted water for 30 minutes. Scrape off any barnacles and pull off the hairy beards. Skin and fillet the hake and sea bream. Slice, with the grain of the fish, into bite-size pieces. Set the fish aside in a cool place.

Peel the carrots and remove the brown papery skin from the onion and transfer to a pan large enough to accommodate all of the fish, vegetables and stock. Drizzle with olive oil, cover and cook. Work the garlic into a paste with a little salt in a mortar. Wash the baby potatoes and cut into 1 cm cubes. Add the potatoes, along with

the garlic, saffron, and fennel seed to the pan. Coat all the ingredients in the flavoured oil. Add the fish stock, Pernod and tomatoes. Bring to a boil. Then simmer for 10 minutes.

Add the slices of hake and bream and poach them gently for another 10 minutes. Peel the prawns and de-vein if necessary and after 8 minutes, add them to the pot and cook for the remaining 2 minutes.

Put the clean mussels into another pan with a bit of water to help create some steam. If you have any leftover wine, substitute wine for the water. Turn on the heat and cook for about 8 minutes, just until the mussels open their shells. Once they are open, remove them from the heat. Discard any mussels that fail to open. Set the cooked mussels aside. Reserve the juice from the steamed mussels by straining them through a sieve and collecting the juice in a pan or a bowl. Taste the mussel juice for seasoning and pour into the soup for added flavour being careful to avoid any grit which may have accumulated at the bottom of the bowl.

Wash the parsley. Chop the leaves and stir into the bouillabaisse. Ladle the fish soup into bowls and garnish with the mussels. Top with a garlic crouton and a dollop of red pepper aioli.

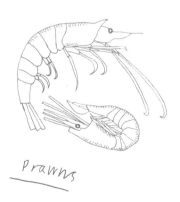

Prawns

SCALLOP AND SWEETCORN CHOWDER WITH SMOKED STREAKY BACON

This is a hearty full-flavoured soup that takes less than half an hour to prepare and cook. Although the dish has been embraced by the Americans, chowder dates back to the early 1700s with references in south western England and the coast of Brittany. The fishermen who worked the waters would place a large pot (chaudiere, in French) over a hot fire and cook whatever was left of the day's catch with stock, milk and a little bread. Englishmen would eat a hearty, nourishing dish of 'jowter' at the end of a hard day at sea.

As hinted above, the true essence of making chowder is to use what is readily available (as with all great fish stews). This particular combination is a favourite of mine, with the natural sweetness of the scallops emphasised by the sweet corn and then balanced with smoky bacon. Serve with some beautiful greens from Fern Varrow's stall at Borough and fresh focaccia from Flour Power. [SLB]

scallops

Preparation time 15 minutes

Cooking time 17–20 minutes

Serves 4

Season Scallops are in season from late
    July until December. English sweetcorn
    is in season from late July until the end
    of August.

600 g sea scallops, with roe
4 thick slices, about 50 g,
    of smoked streaky bacon
1 tblsp unsalted butter
1 large onion
1 large waxy potato
2 large sprigs fresh thyme
1 tblsp plain flour
480 ml full-fat milk
1 bay leaf
½ tsp sea salt
Freshly ground black pepper
Grating of nutmeg
3 raw sweet corn cobs, or enough for 200 g
    kernels (tinned will work but it is
    definitely better with fresh sweet corn)
1 tsp olive oil (for frying roe)
Curly parsley for garnish

Begin by preparing the scallops. Take them out of their shells as described on page 235. Scallop muscles are tough and need to be removed before cooking. They are opaque in colour and located on the side of the scallop. Some scallop muscles have been removed before purchase but it is still worth checking as the muscle and scallop flesh cook at different rates and the muscle takes on an unpleasant chewy texture. The roes are the large orange sack sometimes attached to the scallop. Cut between the scallop and the roe and reserve the roe for garnish.

Using kitchen scissors, remove the rind and slice the bacon in to thin strips. Place them in a 2 litre casserole or saucepan over a medium heat. Add the butter and cook until the bacon begins to crisp and brown. Once tinged golden brown around the edges, use a slotted spoon to transfer the bacon to a plate lined with kitchen paper and set aside.

Peel and finely dice both the onion and potato. Gently lower the vegetables into the hot butter and bacon drippings. Sauté until the onions become slightly translucent and softened. Using a wooden spoon, gently rub the bottom of the casserole to help work any browned bits of bacon into the mix.

While the onion and potato are cooking, wash and remove the leaves from the thyme sprigs. Roughly chop the leaves to lightly bruise and release their fragrance. Scatter them over the onions and stir to incorporate. Sprinkle over the plain flour and stir to combine with the butter and bacon drippings. Cook for a minute to make a roux and cook out the raw flour flavour. Slowly pour the milk into the roux, stirring as you go. A large whisk may be helpful at this point to reduce the risk of lumps. However, I have found that a spoon works fine as long as you have a little patience when pouring the milk and stir

continuously. Add the bay leaf and season with salt, freshly ground black pepper and a grating of fresh nutmeg.

Remove the corn kernels from the cobs by slicing down the cob, turning the circular cob into a square. Then make four more cuts to remove the pointed corners. Don't worry if some of the kernels are smaller or slightly mashed as it adds a nice variation in texture to the finished chow-der. Fold the sweet corn kernels into the soup and bring the whole mixture up to a simmer, cooking gently for 5 minutes.

Slice the scallops into quarters, or in half if they are small. Add to the pot cook for 3 minutes.

While the scallops are cooking sauté any orange roes (which you removed earlier) by placing a small frying pan over a medium flame. Measure a tsp of olive oil and gently lower the roe in the pan. Remember not to overcrowd the pan as that will result in a 'steamed' instead of a sautéed roe. Lightly brown on both sides.

Wash the parsley and blot dry with kitchen paper. Finely chop the leaves and thin stems. Fold half of the parsley into the chowder and save the rest for garnishing. To serve, ladle the chowder into deep bowls and top with the lightly browned roe and some parsley.

Cook's note For the sake of speed, we have used flour and milk. However, for authenticity's sake and for a slighter stew, try substituting half the milk for fresh fish stock and adding breadcrumbs to thicken the chowder at the end of cooking rather than using flour to make a roux.

SCALLOP CEVICHE
WITH PASSION FRUIT

This is a non-traditional version of ceviche in which the fish is lightly poached, and then marinated. Although, it can be prepared in the traditional way with a straight marinating of the fish in the passionfruit and lime; the acids in the recipe will cook the fish. However, this is a good technique to follow for those who cannot eat raw fish. [SLB]

Preparation time 25 minutes, plus 1 hour for marinating

Cooking time 1 minute poaching

Serves 6

Season Scallops are in season from late July until December

900 g scallops
Sea salt
5 large passion fruit,
    or enough to give 120 ml pulp
5 limes, or enough for 120 ml juice
½ tsp sea salt
1 garlic clove
2 small fresh chillies (ideally, Aji Amarillo
    from Turnips' stall at Borough)
1 medium red onion
2 sprigs fresh parsley
2 sprigs fresh coriander
Extra virgin olive oil
3 ripe avocados

Poach the scallops in plenty of salted water until just cooked through, about a minute. Drain and rinse with cold water. Slice the scallops in half and put in a glass bowl.

Cut the passion fruit in half and remove the pulp. Purée the pulp in a food processor for a few seconds and then drain through a sieve. Squeeze the limes and pour the juice over the scallops. Fold in the passion fruit pulp and set aside. Peel the garlic and work into a paste with the salt in a mortar. Wash and halve the chillies; remove the seeds and white ribs. Finely dice and add them to the scallops, along with the garlic. Refrigerate the scallop mixture for an hour.

Whilst the fish is chilling, peel, chop and finely dice the red onion. Wash the parsley and coriander and blot dry. Finely chop the leaves and fine stems of the herbs and just before serving fold in along with the chopped onion. Add a drizzle of olive oil. Halve the avocados and remove the stones. Spoon the ceviche into the centre of the avocado. Serve immediately.

GRILLED SCALLOPS IN THEIR SHELLS WITH HAZELNUT CORIANDER LEMON BUTTER

This is a great 'fresh from the market recipe' when I'm tired of carrying bags that are undoubtedly heavier than I had intended them to be; I never seem to be able to go to the market for just one or two things. Nevertheless, the flavoured butter here can be made well in advance and frozen until needed. You can prepare the scallops as described on page 235 when you get home or have the fishmonger do it for you. Slice off 'chips' of flavoured butter and grill for an instant and elegant dinner.

The combination of hazlenuts and coriander happens to be a favourite of mine but don't be afraid to substitute nuts and herbs. Just keep the proportions the same. Almonds mixed with parsley is a good alternative as is cashews and lemon balm. Look to Inside-out beef burgers (page 120) for inspiration on flavoured butter combinations. [SLB]

Preparation time 1 to 2 hours for the butter to soften plus 20 minutes

---

Cooking time 10 minutes

Serves 4 as a starter

Season Scallops are in season from late July until December

50g hazelnuts
15g fresh coriander
2 lemons (or enough for 2–3 tblsp juice)
125g unsalted butter, softened
12 scallops in their shells
Sea salt
Freshly ground black pepper

Preheat the oven to 200°C / 400°F / gas 6.

Place the hazelnuts on a baking tray and into the preheated oven. Cook for 5–8 minutes to toast them gently. Remove when their skins darken and start to flake off. Rub the nuts in a tea towel to remove the skins. Once skinned, put them in the bowl of a food processor. Pulse them into coarse crumbs. Then, wash and roughly chop the leaves of the coriander. Put them in the bowl of a food processor with the hazelnuts. Squeeze 3 tblsp of lemon juice. Add the softened butter and lemon juice to the processor and switch on and off to bring the mixture together.

Cook's note If you don't have a food processor, you can chop up and mix all the ingredients by hand.

Season the hazelnut butter with salt and black pepper. The butter can be prepared well in advance and frozen for up to a month.

Preheat the grill to its highest setting. Make sure the scallops are opened and loosened from the base of their shells. For tips on scallop preparation see page 235. Put a teaspoon of butter onto each scallop and place on a baking tray. Slide into the oven under the grill and cook for 3–4 minutes maximum. Serve straight away.

Cook's note Why not try substituting the lemon hazelnut butter with lemon anchovy caper and tomato butter from Inside-out beef burger (see page 120).

SEARED SCALLOPS WITH SPICY SWEET POTATO FRITTERS

These are crispy delicious little morsels that are great as a starter or could even be served as a canapé. Don't try to substitute tap water for the fizzy in the sweet potato fritters. The carbonated water lifts the batter to create almost a tempura texture and a perfectly light serving vessel for the sweet scallop. There are a number of ways to dress or garnish this dish but sometimes it is hard to beat simple crème fraîche which not only tastes great but secures the scallop in place when serving. [SLB]

Preparation time 20 minutes

Cooking time 15–20 minutes

Serves 4 as a starter, 24 as a canapé

Season Scallops are in season from late July until December

1 small or ½ a large red jalapeno chilli
235 g sweet potato
8 spring onions
25 g fresh coriander
60 g plain flour
½ tsp sea salt
1 medium egg
125 ml fizzy water
60 ml vegetable oil
12 scallops
Sea salt
Freshly ground black pepper
2 tblsp olive oil

GARNISHES
Watercress or rocket
1 lime
Sweet chilli sauce
    (homemade or store bought)
Crème fraîche

Preheat the oven to 160 °C / 325 °F / gas 3.

Begin by making the sweet potato fritters. Wash the chilli and cut it in half. Remove the white ribs and seeds and finely chop. Transfer the chilli to a medium sized mixing bowl and set aside. Scrub the sweet potato under cold running water to get rid of any grit and grate using the largest hole on your box grater or with a food processor. (I leave the soft peel on for both added nutrition and texture). Combine the sweet potato with the chilli. Peel the outer layer of the spring onions and remove the root end and discard. Slice into thin rings and add to the bowl. Wash, blot dry and finely chop the leaves and fine stems of coriander and fold into the sweet potato. Sprinkle over the flour and season with a pinch of salt. Crack the egg into the bowl and pour in the fizzy water. Give a few strong swift strokes to bring the mixture together.

Heat a frying pan over medium–to–high heat and, add the vegetable oil. Cook in batches, dropping a tablespoonful of batter into the hot oil at a time. Cook for two minutes per side or until golden brown. Continue cooking the remaining fritters adding a little extra oil as necessary. Transfer the cooked fritters to a baking tray and keep warm in a moderate oven.

Put scallops into a bowl and drizzle with olive oil. Season with sea salt and black pepper and toss to coat. Heat a non-stick frying pan over medium-to-high heat and cook the scallops for 2½ minutes. Flip and cook for another 30 seconds.

Wash and blot dry the watercress or rocket. Quarter the lime. Arrange a few sprigs of watercress or rocket on the plates. Place three sweet potato fritters on each and top with the seared scallops. Spoon ½ tsp of crème fraîche over the scallops with a drizzle of sweet chilli sauce. Serve with wedges of lime.

PAN-SEARED SCALLOPS WITH GINGERED TOMATO SAUCE AND FRESH OREGANO

The inspiration for this dish comes from Paris. Friends took us to a small café which served the most fragrant fish soups and fish quenelles in fresh sauces. My untrained eye marvelled at the chalky-white sausage in front of us. Not knowing exactly what it was I popped it into my mouth nonetheless. The 'sausage' shaped quenelle was sweet with white-fleshed fish, salty from the sea and held together with rich cream yet still deceptively light. The lovely red sauce on the plate made a striking contrast to the chalky white quenelle.

Shellseekers' scallops are beautifully white and have bright orange roes. I couldn't bring myself to blitz them in a processor to make quenelles, but the inspiration for the dish is the same. Caramelised scallops rest on a bed of lightly cooked tomatoes infused with ginger and fresh oregano. The addition of ginger, gives a pleasant astringent heat that complements the tomatoes' acidity. Don't forget the sea salt before serving: it is imperative to the overall taste. The shells are not only wonderful cooking implements, they also work as practical serving dishes. [SLB]

Preparation time 12–15 minutes to make the sauce

Cooking time 5 minutes for the scallops

Serves 4

Season Scallops are in season from late July until December

250g cherry tomatoes
2 sprigs fresh oregano
2 tblsp extra virgin olive oil
1 tsp freshly grated ginger
12 Shellseekers' scallops in the shell
1 rounded tsp unsalted butter
Black Pepper
Sea salt
Crème fraîche or double cream (optional)

Begin by washing and quartering the cherry tomatoes. Wash the oregano and blot dry with kitchen paper. Remove the leaves from the stems and chop it finely.

Heat a large frying pan over a medium flame with the olive oil. Peel and grate the ginger and add to the frying pan, along with any ginger juices which may have accumulated on your cutting board. Immediately add the chopped oregano and once the herbs become fragrant, after about 30 seconds, toss in the quartered tomatoes. Cook for 6–7 minutes, or until the juices released from the tomatoes have reduced slightly. Add a good pinch of black pepper and sea salt to taste.

Open the scallops and release from the shell as described on page 235. Cut away the opaque muscle that connects the scallop to the shell.

Heat the unsalted butter in another frying pan over a medium high flame. After the butter has melted and the sizzling subsided slightly, add the scallops to the hot pan and cook for 2½ minutes. Flip and cook for 30 seconds .

While the scallops are cooking, spoon 1 tblsp of sauce into each rounded scallop shell. Discard the flat shells or save for another use. Once the scallops are cooked, place one into each sauced shell. Top with a ½ tsp of crème fraîche or double cream if you are using it. Sprinkle over the coarse sea salt and serve.

Cook's note If you worried about overcooking the scallops while you prepare the shells, spoon the sauce into the half shell before you melt the butter. Arrange the sauced shells on a baking tray and keep them warm in a moderate oven while you cook the scallops.

CLAMBAKE FROM DORSET

The history of clambakes is steeped in tradition and folklore with stories from the sea. A clam bake begins with an open fire on the beach. Stones are pre-heated for a number of hours. After which time, the stones are placed in a hole dug into the sand and fresh sea-weed is piled on top. The best seaweed to use has small pockets that burst open during cooking to create salt-water steam. In the tradition of the great bouilla-baisse, clam bakes utilise whatever the day's catch left the fisherman. All kinds of shellfish are layered on top of the seaweed and then the pit is covered with a thick tarp sealing in steam allowing the shellfish to open. Sweetcorn, potatoes and a cured Portuguese sausage called linguica are traditionally incorporated into the clam bake. Native American tribes were some of the first people to start the tradition of 'baking clams' on the shores of Martha's Vineyard. The tradition was brought to Europe by the fishermen of Portuguese descent who fished off the coast of New England.

Most of us don't have access to a beach. Nor do we always want to heat stones over a fire before we begin cooking. This version of a 'clambake' brings this traditional method of cooking outside back into our kitchens and celebrates the Dorset coastline without getting any sand in your clams. Of course you can use any shellfish you like, but the Shellseeker Stall at Borough harbours the essence of a true clam bake. All the fish are locally caught by divers or line caught direct from the sea, no trawlers to be had here.

The recipe below calls for onions and leeks, which create a bed at the bottom of the pot to steam the shellfish. If you can get your hands on some 'monk's beard' or samphire seaweed, substitute it for the onions and leeks. Both seaweeds will need to be washed well and the tough stems removed before cooking. [SLB]

Preparation time 45 minutes

Cooking time 35 minutes

Serves 6–8

Season October and November are the best months for the shellfish called for in this recipe

500 g mussels
2 tblsp sea salt, for soaking the mussels
500 g scallops in their shells (about 12)
300 g waxy salad or new potatoes
2 Dorset lobsters, about 600 g in weight, 2 brown crabs, about 900 g, cooked or live (see *Cook's note*)
500 g kielbasa or other lightly smoked pork/beef sausage
1 large onion
2 large leeks
2 tblsp olive oil
½ tsp freshly ground black pepper or a little more
350 ml white wine
250 g unsalted butter for serving
1 lemon

Start by cleaning the mussels. Leave them to soak for half an hour in a large bowl of salted water. Scrape off any barnacles and pull off the hairy beard. Discard any mussels with broken shells. Most of the mussels will be closed: if any are open, give them a squeeze. If they don't close shut, then throw them away.

Ensure the scallops are opened, cleaned and ready for cooking (see page 235). Save the scallop shells for garnishing the serving platter.

Place two saucepans on the stove, one large and one small. Make sure the large one can fit the lobsters comfortably. Fill the two pans with water and bring to a boil. Add the potatoes to the smaller one and cook for 12 minutes. Drain and set aside.

When the large pan of water comes to a boil, gently lower in the lobsters. The shells will turn a pinkish-red colour after a few minutes. Bring the water back to the boil and continue cooking for 7 minutes in total. Using tongs or spatulas remove the fish from the pot and set aside.

While the lobster is cooking, loosen the crab-meat by tapping the underside of the body. With the hard shell towards you, stand the crab up and pull the body apart using your thumbs to help separate. Twist off the gill flap and tail and discard. Twist off the legs. Using a sharp knife, split the body down the centre and scoop out the meat. Set aside.

Slice the sausage diagonally into 3 cm chunks and set aside. Peel the onion and cut it in half. Slice the leek in half lengthwise. Rinse the leek under cold running water to remove any hidden grit. Chop both the onion and leek into thick slices. Place a large stock pot (preferably 6–8 litres) over a low flame. Add the olive oil, along with the onions, leeks, and sausage. Cover and cook for 8–10 minutes until vegetables are soft and translucent.

Remove the pot from the heat and begin to layer the ingredients on top of the onion mixture, starting with the potatoes, sprinkled with 1 level tsp sea salt and 2 pinches of black pepper, fol-lowed by the lobsters. Pour over the wine and cover with a tight fitting lid and cook for 4 min-utes. Drain the mussels from the salted water and rinse thoroughly. Remove the lid from the pot, be careful to avoid the escaping steam and scatter mussels over the top of the lobster.

Cover and continue cooking for 7 minutes. Remove the lid for the last time, and add the crab legs and the scallops. Save the body meat (which will probably be quite a small piece) for later. Cook for 4 minutes, just to set the scallops and to warm the cooked crab through.

While the clambake is cooking, melt the butter in a small saucepan ready for serving. Place a large serving platter in a warm oven in preparation for supper. The clambake should now be done. To check that it is ready test to see if the potatoes are soft, the mussels are open, and the scallops opaque. The lobsters should be cooked from the additional parboiling at the start. Lift the lobsters from the pot and transfer to a cutting board. Using tongs for this makes for much lighter work. Also, the tongs enable you to shake the lobster a little to remove any muscles or scallops that may have attached themselves during cooking. Remove the tails from the lobster and crack the claws of both the lobster and crab. Add the reserved crab meat to the pot and spoon the scallops, mussels and potatoes to the pre-warmed platter. Top with lobster tails, claws and crab legs.

Cut the lemon into 6 wedges. Taste the broth/onion mix and check the seasoning. It may need some more black pepper. Spoon the broth over the fish on the platter. Serve with the melted butter for dipping and lemon wedges. Serve with plenty of fresh crusty bread to help mop up the juices.

Cook's note I've chosen to use cooked brown crabs to help reduce the shellfish preparation after the clambake is cooked. Brown crabs can be bought live and cooked as for the lobsters above. 4 minutes should be enough to kill the crab so you can portion the legs and remove the body meat. Then add, as directed above with the scallops to warm through.

HERRING – TWO WAYS

There are many different ways to preserve herring. Matjes and Schmaltz are two examples. Matjes herrings are preserved in brine so they only need an hour to soak before proceeding. Matjes, means 'maiden' and the matjes herring are made with female fish that have not spawned. Schmaltz herrings are more like salt cod, the fish are preserved whole with the innards in tact in salt and then weighted down to extract some of their juices. Therefore, if you opt for this variety you must increase the soaking time to overnight in the refrigerator; they require a little longer to plump up and to reduce their salt content. Once filleted, skinned and soaked, the herrings can be eaten straight away or simply served with a squeeze of lemon and dollop of sour cream. Below are two of my favourite ways to dress herring. [SLB]

CURRIED PICKLED HERRINGS

Preparation time 10–15 minutes, plus 1 hour to overnight soaking

Cooking time 7 minutes to boil the eggs

Serves 2 as part of a main course

Season Fresh herring are in season from late May until early September

3 eggs
4 Matjes or Schmaltz pickled herrings
1 small red onion
4 tblsp mayonnaise, homemade or store bought
4 tblsp sour cream
2 tsp curry powder
1 lemon
Sea salt
Freshly ground black pepper
Parsley for garnish

Soak the herrings for 1 hour if you're using Matjes herrings or overnight if you're using Schmaltz.

Bring a small pan filled with water to the boil. Lower in the eggs and cook for 7 minutes. Rinse under cold water, peel and cut into slices. Wash the parsley.

Cut the soaked herrings into small pieces. Then layer them with the eggs in a shallow glass or ceramic bowl. Peel and finely chop the red onion. Sprinkle it over the top of the eggs and fish. In another small bowl, mix the mayonnaise with the sour cream and curry powder. Squeeze half the lemon. Add lemon juice, salt and pepper to taste. Pour the dressing over the herring and garnish with snipped parsley leaves.

SHERRY HERRING

Preparation time 1 hour soaking,
   plus minimum 6 hours marinating

Cooking time nil

Serves 2 as part of a main course

Season Fresh herring are in season from
   late May until early September

oily fish

4 Matjes pickled herrings
Milk to cover
4 round shallots
15 g dill
½ tsp allspice
1 to 2 tsp sugar
60 ml dry sherry
190 ml tomato juice
Sea salt
Freshly ground black pepper

Soak the Matjes herrings in milk for an hour
to remove some of the salt from the brine.
Once soaked, drain the milk and discard. Cut
the herrings into 2·5–5 cm pieces and place in
a container large enough to hold them.

Peel and finely chop the shallots. Wash the dill,
remove the fronds from the stem and chop them
finely. Combine the shallots and the dill with the
herring. Sprinkle over the allspice and 1 tsp
sugar. Pour over the sherry and tomato juice.
Mix thoroughly to combine. Taste and add more
sugar if needed. Cover and refrigerate for 6
hours or overnight before eating.

Västerbotten cheese and boiled potatoes would
make welcome accompaniments to both of these
dishes as would crusty bread and salad. Produced
in Northern Sweden Västerbotten cheese has a
dry texture similar to a young Parmesan Regiano
or an aged cheddar. Keens cheddar with it's
mildly tangy, sharp bite would be a good
substitute.

OYSTERMAN

Richard Haward *West Mersea, Colchester, Essex*

Whereas Lulworth Cove in Dorset (see page 266) is a Mecca for holiday-makers, West Mersea, on the Blackwater estuary, is a leading yachting centre. There is no beach nor, so far as we could see, any cafés (although there are at least two oyster bars) and the town is straggling, unpretentious, and in most respects completely unremarkable – and likeable for that reason. If you follow the road along the shore as far as it goes, however, you are confronted by a veritable city of boats. There are so many that looking across from the end of the road, the masts look like a solid wall.

Richard met us outside his oyster-bar-cum-store-room, The Company Shed, and whisked us off in his fishing-boat on what

at first seemed like a tour of all that is newest and smartest in yacht design. I am bad at judging distances, but the trail of boats, moored in a curve along the channels of deeper water, must have continued for over a mile. As we went past, Richard said rather drily that he didn't think some of them were ever used – and indeed, if they were all taken out at the same time there would be a traffic-jam worthy of the M25. At the end of the line of boats is Richard's oyster bed. It is marked by a series of poles and a small, rusty rack which until recently he used for farming rock oysters. However, these are so plentiful naturally that he doesn't need to farm them and so has decided not to use it any more.

Although he doesn't cultivate any of his oysters, Richard is very anxious to stress that he regards himself as a farmer rather than a fisherman. He isn't catching fish in the wild: he owns the lease for seven acres of the estuary and rents three or four more. The shore belongs to the Crown and is normally communal: in his case, however, leasing was possible because years ago the Mersea oyster traders formed a co-operative, of which he is a member, and bought the rights to the oyster beds in order to deter poachers from rival centres such as Whitstable. The co-operative's original headquarters was a long wooden building which still stands in a conspicuous position on an off-shore island.

As a farmer tends his land, Richard looks after his stretch of estuary with great care. Every year in late June to early July, he cleans the sea bed by dragging old chains over it to give the oyster-spawn a suitable surface on which to settle. It takes native oysters, who are round and flat, about five years to grow big enough to sell. They are less robust but in terms of content much larger, meatier, and more distinctively flavoured than rock oysters, who are oval, with thick, frilly shells. The rock oysters, however, are cheaper (40p–70p each as compared to 50p–£1·70) and, whereas natives can be taken only when there is an 'r' in the month, the rock oysters are available all through the year.

We didn't see any natives from the boat because they stay under water, but I was amazed to learn that an apparently inanimate bank of pebbles actually included a rich harvest of rock oysters, which (unlike natives) can withstand out-of-water changes of temperature without hardship. If I were prepared to risk the fact that they hadn't been purified, I could have disembarked and collected our dinner in a bucket.

However, rather than picking them up by hand, Richard gathers all his oysters with a small dredging-net, putting back young

ones (which, unlike non-shellfish, are completely unharmed by the experience) and taking the opportunity to remove starfish, which suffocate oysters by wrapping their tentacles round their shells. Once landed, his catch is transferred to racks in The Company Shed and left for forty-two hours while water cleansed by ultra-violet rays is trickled over it. Like scallops, oysters feed by filtering plankton out of the sea-water: over the forty-two hours, anything toxic that they might have imbibed will be excreted.

Richard takes about 2,000 rock oysters a day and, in season, around 1,500 natives, most of which are wholesaled. He keeps some for the bar in The Company Shed, formerly run by his wife and now by his daughter, but apart from a few other local customers, Borough is his only retail outlet.

As a final reassuring thought for those who are uneasy about eating live creatures, Richard reckons that the oysters probably die not during the actual act of consumption but when severed from their shells. I'm not entirely convinced, but I certainly hope he's right.

Along with Herdwick sheep and Morecambe Bay shrimps, Colchester native oysters are also boarded on the Slow Food Ark of Taste.

Opposite and right Shipping and sorting the dredge's catch

OYSTERS ROCKEFELLER

Oysters Rockefeller was first made at a restaurant called Antoine's in New Orleans, Louisianna in 1899 when there was a shortage of French snails. The original recipe has never left the Antoine family, who still serve it today. Many restaurants around the globe claim to have uncovered the secret recipe, but none have ever truly got it right. All we know is that the oysters are enrobed in a vibrant, rich creamy green sauce, which some think comes from the addition of spinach, capers and parsley; employees of the restaurant however, say that this is not so.

Our attempt at this classic dish is a streamline version for modern palates which allows the subtle flavours of the oyster to shine through. Out with the rich cream sauce and in with a simple herb butter. This is a perfect recipe for someone who has yet to appreciate all that oysters have to offer. [SLB]

Preparation time 1–2 hours for the butter to soften plus 20–30 minutes for sauce and time for shucking the oysters

---

Cooking time 3 minutes

Serves 4

Season Rock oysters can now be obtained throughout the year but are usually better outside their spawning period which is in the summer. Richard Hayward says that the best months for eating them are just before spawning, in March, April or May.

16 rock oysters
1 kg coarse rock salt for grilling
6 sprigs parsley
3 spring onions (green parts only)
Fresh celery leaves (optional if available)
4 sprigs of tarragon
4 sprigs fresh chervil
140 g unsalted butter
85 g white breadcrumbs
2 tblsp Pernod
Dash of Tabasco sauce
Sea salt
Freshly ground black pepper

Shuck the oysters as described on page 234. You can have your fishmonger open the oysters for you. However, once you get the hang of it, it is quite easy to do at home. Also, once open they need to be consumed within two hours and more often than not with open oysters, whilst travelling home the lovely oyster 'juice' is lost.

Pour the rock salt over the base of a sturdy baking tray. Embed the oysters in the salt to hold them in place. Preheat the oven grill to its highest setting.

Wash and chop all the herbs, leaves only, until there are no distinguishable leafy bits. This can be done in a food processor but may bruise the leaves and produce an army green coloured rather than vibrant green butter. Transfer the herbs to a medium-sized bowl. Add the softened butter and breadcrumbs. With the back of a spoon, press the ingredients into the side of the bowl to mix them together. Loosen the mixture with 2 tblsp of Pernod (or Herbsaint if you are lucky enough to have it). Season with salt, pepper and a dash of Tabasco.

Dot equal amounts of herb butter on each oyster. Place the tray under the preheated grill and cook for 3 minutes or until the edges of the oysters begin to curl. Don't leave as they overcook quickly and become rather chewy. Serve immediately.

Cleaning up the catch

BARBECUED ROCK OYSTERS
WITH TWO SAUCES

With their gentle briny flavour of the sea, oysters beckon to be paired with something spicy, sweet or acidic. With few ingredients, these sauces are quick to prepare. The flavours in each sauce are clear so the rock oyster flavour isn't masked.

Barbecuing oysters is a great way to introduce opening an oyster to a novice: by barbecuing you avoid 'shucking' the oyster which can lead to many a cut hand and/or fingers. It is imperative to get your barbecue hot, and you must have a cover. If you don't have a covering for your grill, then simply open the oysters as described on page 234 and enjoy them with the sauces. If you are nervous about opening oysters in front of family or friends, remember that they can be opened up to two hours before eating. Just make sure that the oyster-juice stays inside and keep the fish well chilled.

The sweet wine dipping sauce is a variation on a classic mignonette. The other is typical 'cocktail sauce' from the States which I've given a lift to with a smoked chilli powder from the Cool Chile Co. [SLB]

Preparation time 20 minutes,
   plus extra time for shucking if you're
   using a lid-less barbecue

Cooking time 4–5 minutes for grilling the
   oysters

Serves 2

Season Rock oysters can now be obtained
   throughout the year but are usually better
   outside their spawning period, which is in
   the summer. Richard Haward says that the
   best months to eat them are just before
   spawning, in March, April and May.

12 rock oysters
500g rock or sea salt for serving

SWEET WINE, LIME & CORIANDER SAUCE
60ml shaoxing rice wine or mirin
90ml rice or white wine vinegar
1 unwaxed lime
2 spring onions
4 sprigs fresh coriander

Pour the wine and vinegar into a small bowl. Wash and grate the zest of the lime, making sure that you only remove the bright green peel, not the white pith. Squeeze the lime and add, along with the zest, to the wine mixture. Peel off and discard the outer layer and slice the spring onions into thin rings using both the white and green parts. Wash the coriander, chop the leaves only and fold into the mixture, along with the spring onions. Chill until ready to serve.

ANCHO CHILLI, HORSERADISH
   ## & TOMATO SAUCE
1 tblsp prepared horseradish
2 tsp ancho chilli powder
   (from the Cool Chile Co.)
4 tblsp good quality ketchup

This is as easy as it gets. Try to seek out a good ketchup. The Isle of Wight Co. has a gorgeous smooth yet piquant version or you might even consider making your own, as it keeps extremely well and is a fantastic use for a surplus of tomatoes at the end of the summer. Mix the prepared horseradish and ancho chilli powder into the ketchup. Chill until ready to serve.

To barbecue the oysters

If you are using a gas barbecue, heat to a 'hot' setting. If you are using charcoal, make sure that you have a lid, and heat the coals until they are just starting to get a good grey ash coating. Place the oysters directly onto the grill rack. Close the lid and cook until all of the oysters have opened or popped, about 4–5 minutes. If any don't open, transfer them to a platter and use an oyster knife to pry them open.

Pour rock salt onto two dinner plates. Tuck the oysters into the salt and serve with the sauces alongside. Both of the sauces can be made ahead of time but they are at their best when fresh. If you do want to make the sweet lime and coriander sauce combine all of the ingredients apart from the spring onions which should be added just before serving.

Richard Haward – Oysterman;
on Mersea Island and at the
Market stall

OYSTERS DRESSED FOR DINNER, N'AWLINS STYLE

Travelling to New Orleans and not having a Po'Boy is like going to Paris without having had a baguette. It is a rite of passage and every restaurant has its own version. The legend of the Po'Boy started during the 1929 street-car drivers' strike. Two brothers Bennie and Clovis Martin started handing out free sand-wiches for the 'poor boys' made from leftovers. The abbreviation of 'po' comes from the pronunciation of 'poor' with a southern American accent.

The original sandwich has inspired many versions with roast beef, ham, all forms of crustaceans, with oysters being the best. All Po'Boys come 'dressed', which means it's got all the trimmings: lettuce, may-onnaise, dill pickles and mustard. The addition of tomatoes is a contentious issue. Some food historians include them in the fixings and some don't. I've added them to our salad as I think they are a good acidic addition to help balance the flavour.

Traditional rock oyster Po'Boys are packed with oysters, usually 9 or 10 per sandwich. Serving rock oysters to a crowd can be fairly pricy, so I have taken the theory and inspiration behind the sandwich and given it my own de-constructed twist, resulting in a gorgeous salad packed with the 'fixins' without the hefty price tag.

The preparation for this salad is in the cooking of the oysters, so the rest of the ingredients are kept pretty simple. Think crisp lettuce with juicy toma-toes, sweet onions and tart dill pickles topped with cornmeal or polenta crusted oysters and a garlicy-Dijon aioli dressing. Also, you can use store bought mayonnaise instead of aioli should you prefer. [SLB]

Preparation time 30 minutes

Cooking time 10 minutes

Serves 2

Season Rock oysters can now be obtained throughout the year but are usually better outside of their spawning period, which is in the summer, Richard Haward says that the best months to eat them are just before spawning in March, April and May.

100 g crisp lettuce leaves, preferably little gem or good iceberg
1 large beefsteak tomato
1 small red onion
4 small dill pickles
2 medium eggs
1 tblsp Dijon mustard
1½ tsp red wine vinegar
150 ml good extra virgin olive oil
1 garlic clove
1 small baguette
Good tomato ketchup (optional)
6–10 rock oysters
100 g plain flour
100 g polenta
Sea salt
Freshly ground black pepper
Cayenne pepper (optional)
Sunflower oil for frying

Organisation is paramount to this recipe. Have the salad ingredients prepared and arranged, and make the aioli before you begin frying the oysters. You want them hot, which will be a nice contrast to the cool salad.

Wash and dry the lettuce. Wash and slice the tomato and arrange the slices on top of the lettuce. Peel the onion and cut it into fine half-circle slices. Using your fingers, break up the layers of the half circles. Sprinkle in between the tomato and lettuce. Chop the pickles into very fine dice and scatter over the onions.

Separate one of the eggs. Make the aioli by combining one egg yolk, Dijon mustard and red wine vinegar together in a small bowl. Whisk the mixture to thicken it slightly. Begin to pour olive oil into it in a slow, steady stream, the slower the better. It should take about 7 minutes to achieve a nice thick homemade mayonnaise. Peel the garlic and crush to a paste in a mortar and fold gently into the thickened mayonnaise.

Cut the baguette into thick slices and toast it lightly either in a dry frying pan or in the oven. Once a light brown crust is achieved, remove it from the oven and spread with a thin layer of tomato ketchup. Set aside.

Shuck the oysters as described on page 234.

Crack the remaining egg into a medium bowl and beat lightly to break it up. Have the flour and polenta on separate plates near to the egg. Season the flour and polenta with salt, black pepper and cayenne if you have some. Place a frying pan over medium heat with a good coating of sunflower oil. Heat until the pan sizzles when sprinkled with a fleck of water.

Dredge the oysters in the flour, then egg, and then into the polenta. Make sure that you let any surplus egg drip off before dipping the oyster into the polenta. Place the oysters into the hot oil and cook for about 45 seconds per side. Don't worry if they don't take up too much colour, it is more important to not over cook them. Drain on a plate lined with paper towels.

Top the baguette slices with hot oysters and place it next to the composed salad. I usually end up trying to fit all the salad components on top of the baguette and sticking the lot together with a dollop of aioli. The challenge is always fun, always messy and always delicious.

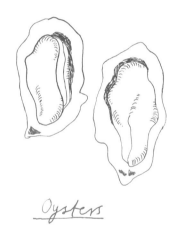

Oysters

APPLEBEE'S FISH

Graham Applebee *Stoney Street, London SE1*

Graham Applebee is different from the other people featured in
this book because he isn't a producer but a restaurateur and fishmonger. Some of his stock comes from Billingsgate but some is
sent directly, *eg* farmed salmon from Loch Duart, in Scotland, and
line-caught mackerel and sea bass from Cornwall. As much
of his fish as possible is line-caught because, quite apart from the
issue of sustainability, it's in better condition than fish caught in
nets, as his manager, David Wilson, described it: a fish struggling
in a net 'loses its shine' rather in the same way as stressed meat
becomes tough.

Neither Graham nor David were fishmongers before Graham
opened the shop. They met working for a group of Italian restaurants in The City: Graham was the buyer and David the manager.
As buyer, Graham went to Borough for vegetables and as the market developed saw that it offered a promising opportunity. Why, I
asked, did they choose fish? 'Why not?' said David. 'There are very
few fish shops and the fish in the supermarkets – well, I wouldn't
want to buy it.'

After twenty years in the restaurant trade, he declares that
he'll never, ever go back. 'Restaurants kill you! I've got children: I
never saw them. The hours are very long and unsociable.' He also
hated the pressure. 'You have to cater for 160 people in the space
of three hours.' He's been at Borough for two years and loves it.
'Here – it's good fun. If you have a passion for something, of
course you enjoy selling it.' His ambition is to open a shop of
his own. Graham on the other hand already has a restaurant in
Wanstead and is hoping to start another next door.

Since opening Applebee's, Graham has developed strong opinions on the issues currently surrounding fish. He believes that the
future lies in fish farming – by which he means responsible fish
farming, carried out in an environmentally-friendly way and
where the fish have plenty of space. He also believes that the issue
of fish food, which at present is fish and thus further depletes
natural resources, will soon be settled by the introduction of a
non-fish alternative.

In the meanwhile, however, he says that he feels perfectly
justified in selling all kinds of seafood, whether scarce or not,
because the fishmonger is too far down the food chain to be

Graham Applebee
in the Stoney Street shop

relevant. By the time the fish have been caught, it's too late: effective action is needed at the fishing end. He is emphatic in his condemnation of the quota system, which he sees as pointless because the use of nets makes it impossible to control the number of fish taken, at least with any accuracy: even with the best of intentions, therefore, all the fisherman can do is to throw back the excess.

On the day of my visit, his stock included red mullet and red snapper, monkfish, turbot, Dover and lemon sole, cod, John Dory, mackerel, wild sea bass, wild sea trout, wild salmon, live langoustine, clams, scallops, and prawns. The sea bass was from Guernsey, where cold, deep water gives the best possible fish; like the farmed version, the wild salmon, was from Scotland. In general, they only stock Scottish salmon. 'Scottish is best,' declared David. 'Salmon from Canada and Alaska are noticeably different. They have darker, softer flesh which we don't prefer.'

Graham gave me a piece of wild Scottish to try and I can vouch not only for its wonderful taste but its firm, smooth, fine-grained, virtually oil-free texture. He does sometimes stock bream and gurnard (which aren't on the threatened list) but they don't sell well. He says that most of his customers pay lip-service to sustainability but in the end they buy the sort of fish they're used to and know they like.

In the belief that part of the difficulty is that people don't know what to do with lesser-known fish varieties, we have given you recipes in the hope that if you try them, they'll become favourites too.

FISH STOCK

Please make fish stock. Vicious rumours of lingering fish smells permeating the walls of your kitchen are false. Fish stock is quick and easy, and well worth the effort. The most difficult part is looking down the face of a fish to rinse its gills. If you can get over that you are already halfway there.

Fishmongers are usually pretty happy to give fish frames and heads away as long as you give them a bit of notice. The good thing about Borough is that they are usually filleting and cutting up fish all day with plenty of good stock items around. So head down early to put in your request, grab a coffee and by the time you finish I bet they will have enough fish bits and pieces for you to take home. [SLB]

Preparation time 10 minutes

Cooking time 50 minutes

Serves Makes about 2 litres of fish stock

Season All ingredients available year-round

1·4 kg fish heads and frames
    (any type of fish will do but try to have
    a mix of both oily and white fish)
2 onions
2 carrots
2 celery sticks
1 fennel bulb
Olive oil
4 garlic cloves
1 tsp saffron
2 bay leaves
1 orange
Pinch of red pepper flakes
375 ml dry white wine
2 litres water
1 tsp sea salt

Wash the fish frames and fish heads. Make sure that you wash out any blood from the gills of the fish heads. Peel and chop the onions and carrots. Wash and chop the fennel and celery. Transfer the vegetables to a large pot and add a little olive oil. Peel the garlic and smash it with the side of your knife. Wash and halve the orange. Add the garlic, saffron, bay, half orange and red pepper flakes to the vegetables. Layer the heads and fish frames on top of the vegetables. Pour in the wine and cover the pot. Allow the fish to steam for about 15 minutes.

Pour in 2 litres of water and bring to a simmer. Once the stock is bubbling gently, simmer for another 15 minutes. Then turn off the heat and infuse for another 15 minutes. Drain, season with sea salt, and cool to room temperature. Freeze in small pots or use straight away.

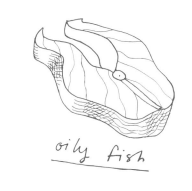

oily fish

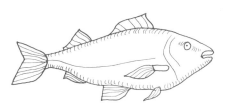

White fish

CRABCAKES WITH SUMMER HERB AIOLI

This is a luxurious fish cake using only white crab meat. You can use a mixture of both white and brown for an equally delicious, although slightly different, finished product. Brown crabmeat is slightly more salty with a finer texture. Taste before seasoning either by cooking a dessert spoonful before shaping the rest of the batter or dipping your finger into the mix. Feel free to change the flavours of the aioli according to your own taste buds and the time of year, a few of my favourite additions include: curried coriander, saffron, and roasted garlic or garlic leaf with a splash of sherry vinegar. [SLB]

Preparation time 10 minutes, plus minimum 1 hour chilling

Cooking time 25 minutes

Serves 4

Season Fresh crabs from the English coastal waters are in season from May until October

---

Half a sweet red pepper
4 spring onions
1 garlic clove
450 g fresh, white lump crabmeat
25 g unsalted butter
1 egg
4 tblsp homemade or prepared mayonnaise
1 tblsp Dijon mustard
2 tblsp breadcrumbs for the crab cake mix
Sea salt
Freshly ground black pepper
4 tblsp chopped fresh herbs
    (parsley, chervil, sorrel, basil, dill)
1 to 2 cups fresh breadcrumbs,
    toasted, for coating the cakes
4 tblsp clarified butter (see Goose rillettes
    recipe on page 107), or vegetable oil
Summer Herb Aioli (recipe follows)

Make sure you assemble the crab cakes a few hours ahead so they have time to chill before cooking.

Wash and finely dice the pepper. Peel and finely slice the onions. Peel and mince the garlic. Gently pick over the crabmeat to check for any bits of shell and cartilage. Melt the butter in a medium-sized frying pan. Once the foaming has subsided, add the finely diced red pepper, spring onion and garlic. Sauté the vegetables until slightly translucent but not browned, about 5 minutes. Remove from the heat and allow to cool slightly.

Lightly beat the egg. In a large bowl mix the crabmeat with the egg, mayonnaise, Dijon mustard and 2 tblsp breadcrumbs, and season with salt and pepper. Wash and finely chop the fresh herbs. Vary the combination depending on what you have in your pantry, garden or refrigerator. However, try to stay with 'soft' herbs such as those listed above and shy away from the more woody herbs of rosemary and thyme. Once the vegetables are cool, combine with the crabmeat mixture and fold in the freshly chopped herbs.

Have ready the remaining breadcrumbs on a small plate. Shape the crabmeat mixture into 8 small cakes and coat in the breadcrumbs. Place on clean plate and continue with remaining crabmeat mixture. Chill for 1–2 hours to allow the cakes to firm up. While the crab cakes are chilling, make the Summer Herb Aioli.

When ready to cook, add 2 tblsp clarified butter to a large frying pan over a medium high heat. Once sizzling, add 4 of the crab cakes. Flip the cakes after about 5 minutes and cook for an additional 4–5 minutes or until nicely browned. Keep warm in a moderate oven while you cook the rest. Serve with Summer herb aioli (recipe follows) and lemon wedges.

SUMMER HERB AIOLI

*For those who don't want to eat raw eggs, add the
fresh herbs, Dijon, and red wine vinegar to commer-
cially prepared mayonnaise and serve as directed.
Although, I'm confident once you try this way of
making mayonnaise you will never go back to store
bought!*

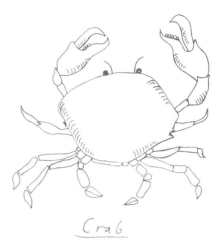

Crab

Preparation time 10 minutes, plus chilling

Cooking time nil

Serves 4

Season Fresh herbs are most vibrant during
the summer – May through August

1 large bunch fresh herbs
   (parsley, chervil, sorrel, basil, mint)
300 ml olive oil
2 medium eggs
1 tsp Dijon mustard or grainy mustard
1 tblsp red wine vinegar
Sea salt
Freshly ground black pepper

Wash and blot dry all the herbs. Pull the leaves
from the stems. Pulse chop them in the bowl of
a food processor. Add half of the olive oil, again
pulsing to combine.

Separate the eggs. In a small bowl mix the yolks,
mustard and vinegar. Season with salt and pepper. Whisk until the mixture is thick and fluffy.
Add the remaining olive oil in a slow steady
stream. Slower is better at this stage, about 1
dessertspoon at a time. Continue with the herb
oil, again in a slow steady stream. The mixture
may loosen, but continue mixing until thick
again. Check for seasoning. Chill until needed.

GRILLED FISH PARCELS
WITH SWEET AND SOUR
DIPPING SAUCE

As well as a lovely main course, these are great as canapés. To make as the latter, thread the parcels onto toothpicks instead of the wooden skewers and cook as instructed below. They are delicious with barley couscous to help soak up some of the sauce. I've chosen hake here, but I have also made this with Applebee's wild salmon and trout with equal success. If you can't find vine leaves at your supermarket, large basil leaves are a good substitute. Basil leaves may not wrap around the fish cube entirely but will look beautiful and taste great. Just be careful when cooking as they will tear more easily and require a slightly less intense heat than fibrous vine leaves. Try cooking them in a hot oven (180°C) rather than under the grill. [SLB]

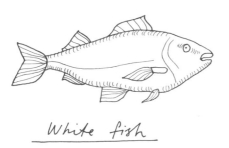

White fish

Preparation time 15–20 minutes to make the sauce

Cooking time 8–10 minutes to grill the fish

Serves 4 as part of a main course

Season Hake is in season from late October until March. Salmon is in season from late February until early September.

2 lemons
   (or enough to give you 120ml of juice)
120g granulated sugar
A pinch of saffron (0.4g)
1 small onion
2 garlic cloves
Sea salt
1 large jalapeno chilli
3cm piece fresh ginger
2 spring onions
15g fresh mint
15g fresh coriander
450g hake fillet
1 unwaxed or organic orange
Freshly ground black pepper
16 vine leaves

Special equipment
4 long wooden skewers soaked in water for half an hour before cooking.

Begin by making the dipping sauce. Squeeze the lemons and heat their juice with the granulated sugar and 2 tblsp water. Bring to the boil and simmer until the sugar is dissolved, about 2 minutes. Once dissolved, add the saffron and set aside to cool to room temperature and infuse.

Whilst the syrup is cooling, peel and finely dice the onion. Peel and work the garlic into a paste with some salt in a mortar. Wash, deseed the chilli and mince. Peel and grate the ginger. Remove the outer layer of the spring onions and slice them finely, using both the green and white bits. Add all the ingredients to the cooled syrup and mix well. Wash and chop the mint and coriander, leaves only, and add to the lemon saffron syrup. Season with salt and pepper.

Check over the hake for any pin bones and skin. Cut into 2·5 cm cubes and set aside. Wash and grate the zest the orange and combine it with a ½ tsp each of sea salt and freshly ground black pepper; sprinkle over the fish.

Wash and dry the vine leaves. Lay a vine leaf flat on the worktop with the ribs of the leaf facing up. Cut out any large pieces of rib from the leaf. If you have large leaves (over 20 cm at its widest point across) cut the leaf in half at the centre rib. Place a piece of the fish in the centre of the leaf or leaf half and fold the two sides of the leaf over the fish and roll up, securing onto a wooden skewer. Repeat with the remaining pieces of fish. Don't worry if all the pointed ends of the leaf are not secured by the toothpick as they will char when cooked under the grill and make for a more visually appealing presentation.

Preheat the grill to the hottest setting. Cook the skewers for 4–5 minutes per side. Serve immediately with the dipping sauce.

SEA BREAM BAKED WITH CAPERS AND OLIVES

Bream has a sweet, firm flesh which is not dissimilar to sea bass. Black Bream has several visible vertical dark bands and a few horizontal pencil-thin golden streaks as its distinguishing marks. Whereas, red bream actually has a reddish tinge to its silvery scales and no vertical black lines. Choose mature bream, anything greater in length than 24 cm, and preferably line caught. Avoid fish during the spawning season of April through to May in UK shoreline waters.

Here we have combined the sweetness of the bream with the salty brine of capers and olives, and with a splash of a good fruity acidic wine. I particularly like a Gros Manseng grape with this dish, but a Sauvignon Blanc would work equally well. [SLB]

Preparation time 7–10 minutes

Cooking time 20 minutes

Serves 2

Season Bream is at its best from June until September

100 g Kalamata black olives (drained weight)
1 rounded tblsp capers
15 g fresh thyme leaves
1 tblsp extra virgin olive oil
2 black or red sea bream, gutted
    (about 1 kg in weight)
100 ml white wine
Freshly ground black pepper
Sea salt

Preheat the oven to 200 °C / 400 °F / gas 6.

Rinse the olives in a sieve, place them on a work surface, and crush them using the palm of your hand. Kalamata olives work particularly well for this recipe as they pit easily. If you can't find them, try another olive that pits well (one good way to find out is to eat one) or purchase pitted ones. Remove the pips from the olives. Give the capers a good rinse, especially if they have been preserved in salt. Remove the leaves from the thyme sprigs and roughly chop to bruise and release their flavour. Combine the olives, capers and thyme leaves together in a small bowl.

Drizzle olive oil onto a baking tray or shallow baking dish just large enough for the fish. Scale the fish (if it hasn't been done for you already) using the blunt side of a butter knife. Hold the fish by the tail over a sink. Scrape the fish from tail to head, away from you. If the fish is slipping out of your hands, dip the finger and thumb you use to hold the fish in salt. This should provide you with just enough grip to hold on to the fish. Using a sharp knife, slash the fish right down to the bone twice on each fillet side.

Scatter half of the olive mixture over the olive oil. Place the fish on top of the olive mixture and sprinkle over the wine. Finish with the remaining half of the olive mixture and a good seasoning of black pepper. Remember you are adding salt in the form of olive and capers so go easy on the salt seasoning. Cover the fish with foil and place in a preheated oven.

Cook for 20 minutes. After which time, remove foil and continue cooking for another 5 minutes.

Serve with boiled new potatoes. There will be some juice in the pan which works as a lovely light sauce.

SALMON FILLETS WITH LEMON AND PARSLEY BUTTER

Really good, farmed salmon, such as Loch Duart, doesn't need more than parsley and the tang of lemon or lime juice to offset the oily nature of the fish.

If you make the parsley butter while the fish bakes, preparation time is effectively nil.

I suggest serving it with baby new potatoes in season, or crushed (as opposed to mashed) floury ones, or champ (mashed with plenty of milk and dotted with spring onions). [SF]

Preparation time A few minutes

Cooking time 11–14 minutes

Serves 2

Season All ingredients available year-round

280–300 g Loch Duart or other salmon, about 2·5–3 cm thick
Sea salt
Freshly ground black pepper
Bunch parsley (enough for 2 heaped tblsp, when chopped)
20 g unsalted butter
1 small lemon

You will need to start boiling the potatoes about 8 minutes before setting the salmon to cook.

Heat the oven to 210°C / 410°F / gas 6.

Carefully wipe the slices of fish with wet kitchen paper and lay them in a baking dish lined with cooking foil. There is no need to skin them because, if you cook the fish skin-side down, the skin will stick to the foil after cooking. Season them moderately with salt (which need not be crushed) and coarsely ground black pepper. Bake for 11–14 minutes just until the fish is opaque all the way through and flakes easily with a fork.

Wash and blot the parsley dry with kitchen paper. Finely chop the leaves, but throw away the lower part of the stems. Put it into a mortar and crush for a minute or so. Add the butter, a little salt and a couple of coarse grindings of pepper, and crush until the butter is soft. Squeeze half the lemon, add 4 tsp lemon juice and continue crushing until it is absorbed.

Spread the butter over the top of the fillets as soon as they are cooked, and serve.

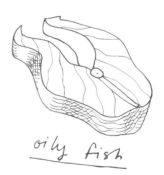

oily fish

PAELLA MAGNIFICA

This, like the bouillabaisse, is another special occasion recipe in my house with all hands on deck. When the dish is made, everyone who is invited to dinner is asked to come early and help with preparations. Family and friends take turns wearing the apron and standing over the hot stove whilst others instruct from the safe distance of the table (which of course has a most delicious pitcher of sangria on it).

The foundation of this dish comes from a recipe by Craig Claiborne, a New York Times food editor for nearly three decades and a true lover of all things to do with food, entertaining and the occasional extravagance. I'm sure he would have approved of our sangria and the convivial time had by all. Don't be put off by the long list of ingredients. The recipe is a 'one-pot wonder', with all the ingredients cooked in the same pot by layering the flavours one on top of the other to create an amazing depth of taste in the finished product. [SLB]

Preparation time 30 minutes,
plus at least 30 minutes marinating
and 30 minutes soaking

Cooking time 55 minutes

Serves 5–6

Season Shellfish is best in the colder months
– November through to late January

1 garlic clove
½ tsp sea salt
1 sprig thyme
¼ tsp ground coriander
½ tblsp white wine vinegar
2 tblsp olive oil
0·6 kg chicken thighs, bone-in, with skin
60 g unsmoked streaky bacon or salt pork
175 g fresh prawns
175 g fresh sea scallops
1 chorizo ring, about 250 g in weight
1 small onion
Pinch saffron threads (0·4 g)
1 tblsp capers
200 g chopped tomatoes in their juice
100 ml white wine
1 pint chicken stock,
   homemade or fresh store bought
250 g Spanish paella or long grain rice
Sea salt
Freshly ground black pepper
400 g jar artichoke hearts in olive oil, drained
4 tblsp fresh or frozen peas
60 g pimentos
10 mussels
10–15 littleneck or carpet-shell clams
25 ml Sambuca
15 g fresh parsley
Lemon for garnish

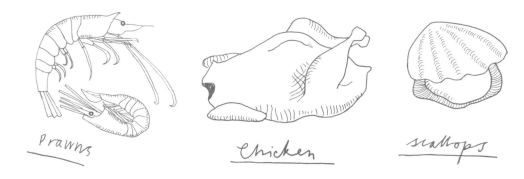

Prawns   Chicken   scallops

Begin marinating the chicken thighs. Peel and crush the garlic with the salt into a paste. Wash the thyme, remove the leaves and add them to the garlic-salt mixture. Roughly chop, then combine with the coriander in a glass bowl that will hold the chicken comfortably. Pour in the white wine vinegar and olive oil. Allow the chicken to marinate for at least 30 minutes at room temperature – any longer and the chicken needs to be refrigerated. This can be done (and in fact is all the better for it) the day before cooking.

Chop the streaky bacon or salt pork into 1cm cubes. In a 4-litre casserole, sauté the pork until the fat has rendered and pork bits have started to brown. Transfer the crispy bits of pork with a slotted spoon to a small bowl and set aside.

Meanwhile, quickly fry the prawns in the pork fat until pink; remove and set aside. Do the same with the scallops, although the scallops should only be 'tinged' brown around the edges, one minute on each side should be enough. Remove and set aside. Try not to stack the scallops as the steam they give off will deglaze those 'tinged' brown bits you worked so hard to achieve.

Remove the papery skin from the chorizo if there is any and slice the chorizo. Fry in the same pan and cook until the chorizo starts to release some of its fat, browning slightly around the edges. Using a slotted spoon, transfer to the small bowl containing the pork bits. There should be about 2 tblsp of fat in the pan. If there is any more, spoon off and discard the surplus.

Brown the chicken in the chorizo fat remaining in the pan. Give yourself a good few minutes to do this properly. You want the skin to have some colour on it. Peel and finely chop the onions while the chicken is browning. Sprinkle the onions and sauté for a few minutes before adding the saffron, capers and tomatoes over and around the chicken. Return the pork bits and chorizo to the pan. Pour in the wine and chicken stock. Season with salt and pepper. Add the rice, along with the artichoke hearts, peas and pimentos. Stir to incorporate all of the ingredients as best you can. Cover, and simmer over a low heat for 30 minutes.

While the paella is cooking, steam the mussels and clams together in another pan with 60 ml of water until they open, about 4–5 minutes. For information on cleaning mussels and clams see page 234. Discard any that don't open after 8 minutes. Remove the mussels and clams from the pan strain the cooking liquid and reserve. Taste the mussel cooking liquid. It should be pleasantly briny and taste of the sea.

After 30 minutes, remove the lid from the paella and check the level of liquid at this stage the rice should have swelled to fill the pan but there should be enough cooking liquid to keep it juicy. Pour in the cooking liquid from the mussels and clams. Be careful not to pour in any grit which may have fallen to the bottom of the bowl or measuring jug. Tuck the scallops, prawns, mussels and clams over the top. Sprinkle over the measure of Sambuca. Cover again and gently heat through for an additional 10 minutes. The paella at this stage can be kept warm for up to half an hour.

Wash and chop the parsley and cut the lemon into wedges. Spoon the paella onto plates and serve with lemon wedges and a sprinkling of parsley.

FISH CURRY

The delicious combination of tamarind and coconut has its origin in the Muslim religion. My first taste of this intriguingly rich yet tart mix was in a beef curry. Religions, with their dietary guidelines, have influenced cuisines from all over the world but what I love about cooking is that every country (or religion for that matter) interprets flavour combinations and ingredients in their own way putting their own unique stamp on a recipe. Here I've taken a Muslim flavour foundation and given it an Indian identity with the use of a dried spice blend.

Tamarind is not an ingredient a lot of us are used to. It has a sour and slightly tart taste. There aren't many ingredients in our Westernised diets that are sour, we tend to utilise acidic lemons and limes more readily than sour fruits, such as tamarind pods and pomegranates. Many Indian restaurants I know of use both lime juice and double cream to enrich dishes. This may possibly be the Western interpretation of a tamarind coconut curry.

Most firm white-fleshed fish work wonderfully with this dish, as do sea trout. [SLB]

Preparation time 15 minutes

Cooking time 15 minutes

Serves 4

Season depends on what fish you use. Hake is in season from late October to March; Sea Bass from May until December; Sea Trout from late March to early July

4 round shallots
2·5 cm piece of fresh ginger
1 red chilli
2 garlic cloves
1 tblsp paprika
1 rounded tblsp coriander seeds
1 tsp cumin seeds
1 tsp ground turmeric
50 g unsweetened desiccated coconut
100 ml coconut cream
1 tblsp olive oil
1 tblsp tamarind paste (mixed with 100 ml water)
600 g fish steaks (about 2·5 cm thick)
Fresh coriander for garnish

Peel the shallots and ginger and slice thinly. Wash and halve the chilli and deseed. Peel the garlic and crush with the side of your knife to release the natural oil. Put the prepared ingredients, along with the paprika, coriander seeds, cumin seeds, turmeric and the desiccated coconut into a food processor. If you don't have a food processor or a blender a pestle and mortar will do, just make sure that you roughly chop the ginger and chilli first. Purée the ingredients into a thickened paste, slowly add the coconut cream and blend thoroughly to combine.

Heat a medium-sized saucepan with a tight fitting lid or a casserole (one large enough to hold the fish in one layer) over a low flame with the olive oil. Add the spice paste and fry gently for 30 seconds, stirring constantly. Once the spices have filled your kitchen with their aroma, add the tamarind water and stir to combine. Bring to a gentle simmer. Season with salt and pepper.

If you can't find tamarind paste, do not worry as the dish is good without it but remember to add the water as it is a necessary ingredient to thin the spice paste.

Using a spatula to help you, slip the fish into the casserole. Bring the spice mixture up to a simmer. Cover and cook, very gently for 15 minutes, turning the fish half way through. If you have a particularly deep casserole it might be a good idea to cut out a piece of parchment paper slightly larger than the circumference of your casserole. Press the parchment down into the casserole nearly touching the fish. This will help to circulate the steam and cook the fish evenly. While the fish cooks, wash the coriander leaves and blot dry with kitchen paper. Roughly chop the leaves and thin stems only. Serve the fish and sauce on a bed of rice. Garnish with fresh coriander.

Cook's note As hinted at in the introduction you could substitute the juice of 1 lime and 100 ml double cream for the diluted tamarind paste and coconut cream. To do so, still add the 100 ml water to the spice mixture along with the double cream but add the lime juice at the end of the cooking.

White fish

PENNE WITH LEMON CRAB, PEAS AND PROSCIUTTO

Fresh crab is absolutely sensational; it's a highly underrated crustacean. The sweet flesh is deliciously juicy and very versatile. The recipe below is one to save for good friends or family, not so much because of the cost of crab meat as the timing of the dish. It is a little tricky getting everything together ahead of time and once the pasta is boiling you have to go with it and eat it as soon as the dish is put together. But boy will you be rewarded! The lemons cut through the rich cream, the salty prosciutto and Parmesan balances the sweet peas and crab meat, whilst mint and chillies give the dish another dimension. [SLB]

Preparation time 10 minutes,
   plus picking crab meat

Cooking time 15 minutes

Serves 4

Season Fresh crabs from the English coastal
   waters are in season from May until
   October

---

100 ml double cream
1 lemon unwaxed or organic
2 dried chillies de arbol
   (available from Cool Chile Co.)
12 thin slices prosciutto
15 g fresh mint
100 g Parmesan, plus extra for garnishing
1·25 kg undressed crab (yielding about 200 g
   white and 100 g brown meat)
340 g dried penne
200 g fresh peas

It is essential to have all ingredients ready before the pasta starts cooking. So, measure out the cream, grate the zest of the lemon and squeeze the juice. Measure out the peas. Chop the dried chillies and remove the prosciutto from any packaging. Wash and remove the leaves from the mint, stack them up and have them ready to be thinly sliced. Grate 100 g of Parmesan and set aside for use later on. Have bowls or plates warm and ready for service.

Pick over the crab meat according to instructions on page 235. Bring a large pan of salted water to the boil and cook the penne *al dente* according to the packet's instructions, usually about 10 minutes.

While the pasta is cooking place a small saucepan on the stove to gently warm the cream. Once the cream has scalded or formed a little skin on top, turn off the heat, fold in the crab meat and set aside.

During the last 2 minutes of cooking the pasta, toss the peas into the pasta pot. After the 2 minutes have passed, drain the pasta through a sieve, reserving about 120 ml of pasta cooking liquid.

Add the lemon juice to the cream-crab mix along with the lemon zest. Chop the mint leaves and sprinkle them over the cooked pasta, along with the chopped dried chillies and Parmesan. Spoon the hot, lemony crab meat over the pasta and toss to coat. Add the reserved 120 ml of pasta cooking liquid and heat gently over a low flame.

Spoon into warm bowls and top with pieces of prosciutto and a few large shavings of Parmesan.

SCOTTISH LANGOUSTINES
WITH ROASTED GARLIC AIOLI

These days, Borough Market can be a wonderfully exhausting place. Crowds can get to the best of us on occasion so it is good to have a few recipes on hand that can provide tasty sustenance after a busy day. This is the prefect throw-together solution for such occasions and it can be put together with minimal effort and preparation. The ingredients below are for two. However, you may have a little aioli left over which is always good with a roast chicken the next evening. 'Turnips', one of the vegetable traders, sells wild garlic leaves in late spring. If you are lucky enough to find the long soft green leaves, slice them thinly as you would basil, and fold into the aioli just before serving for a fresh, mild garlic flavour. You can substitute store bought mayonnaise for the aioli; just add the roasted garlic, lemon juice, Dijon mustard and chives to the purchased version and season to taste.
[SLB]

Preparation time 20 minutes

Cooking time 6 minutes, plus additional
    30 minutes for roasting the garlic

Serves 2

Season Scottish langoustines are best in
    the summer – June, July and August, wild
    garlic leaves are in season in late spring.

Large head of garlic
150 ml olive oil plus a drizzle for the garlic
1 medium egg
½ lemon
1 tsp Dijon mustard
Fresh chives or wild garlic leaf
    (enough for 2 tblsp when chopped)
Sea salt
Freshly ground black pepper
12 Scottish langoustines
2 tblsp dry sherry
1 tsp dried oregano

Preheat the oven to 200°C / 400°F / gas 6.

Begin by making the roasted garlic aioli. Slice the top off the garlic, drizzle with oil, and wrap in foil. Bake in the preheated oven for 30 minutes, then set aside to cool. This can be done well ahead of time. You can even freeze roasted garlic purée which is great to have on hand to flavour soups or stews as well as aioli. Separate the egg. Squeeze the lemon to give you 2 tblsp of juice. Combine the egg yolk, lemon juice and Dijon mustard in a small bowl. Whisk until thickened and frothy. Then, in a slow steady stream start to pour in the olive oil, whisking to emulsify the mixture as you go. After about 7 minutes the emulsion should be thick and creamy. Slower is better at the start, once the mayonnaise starts to thicken you can add the olive oil a tablespoon at a time.

Squeeze the whole head of garlic to push the cloves through the cut-off tops into a small bowl. Mash the garlic cloves with a fork. Wash and finely chop the chives and fold them into the mixture, along with the mashed garlic. Season with salt and pepper to taste. Cover and refrigerate until needed.

Preheat your grill to its highest setting.

Slice the langoustines in half lengthwise, straight through the head leaving the claws in tact. Arrange on a baking tray (cut side up) and season with salt and black pepper. Sprinkle with the sherry and dried oregano. Place the langoustines under the preheated grill and cook for 3–4 minutes or until the flesh turns an opaque milky white. Serve straight away with aioli, plenty of napkins and finger bowls!

OVEN ROASTED WILD TROUT WITH CHERRY TOMATOES

Trout are long, thin, speckled fish ranging in colour from silvery-grey (rainbow) to brown (brown trout). They vary in size from 15–50cm and weigh anywhere from 225g to 2kg. Pink-fleshed sea or ocean trout, the migratory form of the species, have a slight peachy-apricot toned flesh. All trout have a firm, yet creamy texture and are fantastically high in good-for-you mono- and polyunsaturated fats.

After shopping all morning at the market and laden with heavy bags of food, sometimes all you want when you get home is a very simple recipe that you can throw together quickly. This is one of them. When you roast a whole fish in the oven there is hardly any preparation at all. The cooking time will vary according to the size of your fish. For gutted fish allow 15 minutes per 500g of fish in a hot oven. [SLB]

Preparation time A few minutes to gut the fish if necessary, plus 10–12 minutes to prepare the salad

Cooking time 25 minutes

Serves 2

Season Fresh sea trout is in season from late March until early July

---

1 whole rainbow, brown or sea trout
   (about 500g), gutted
250g cherry tomatoes
2 tblsp good extra virgin olive oil
Sea salt
4 small courgettes
Freshly ground black pepper
1 lemon
3 sprigs of fresh dill
100g feta cheese

Gut and scale the fish, if necessary, according to the instructions on page 236.

Preheat your oven to 220°C / 420°F / gas 7.

Find a shallow, oven ready, ceramic dish large enough for the fish to fit snuggly. Ideally, you want the fish and tomatoes to lie in the dish in one even layer. It is better to have the fish and tomatoes slightly snug and overlapping than spread out on a large baking tray.

Rinse the cherry tomatoes and place them in the dish. Season with salt, pepper and a little drizzle (about 1 tblsp) of olive oil. Place in the oven and cook for 10 minutes. During this time the tomatoes should begin to burst, or at least the skins will crack and juice will start to seep out.

After 10 minutes, remove the dish from the oven. Push the tomatoes to the side and place the trout in the centre. Drizzle with more olive oil and sprinkle a little sea salt over the skin. Return the dish to the oven and cook for about 15 minutes if you have 500g of fish. As always, you want your fish to flake easily.

While the fish is cooking, prepare the salad. Wash the courgettes and, using a potato peeler, shave them into ribbons. Season with salt and pepper. Squeeze half the lemon. Pour the over the juice and drizzle with 1–2 tblsp olive oil. Pull the fronds from the dill stems. Pile them up on your chopping board and run a sharp knife over them to roughly chop and bruise them slightly; fold into the shaved courgettes. Remove the feta from its brine and crumble over the top.

Mound the salad into the centre of serving plates and top with large pieces of flaked trout. It is always easier to remove the top fillet (and usually that one is the prettier portion). However, to get to the bottom fillet, remove the fish frame, from tail to head. Then you can get a spatula under the bottom fillet and lift it from the baking dish. Spoon some of the tomatoes and their juices over the top of each portion before serving.

WEEKNIGHT LINGUINE
WITH PRAWNS, CHILLI BASIL
AND CHERRY TOMATOES

This dish is probably made once a week in our house. The joy comes from the quick preparation and tantalising combination of flavours.

This is a 'two-pan' supper: one pan to boil the pasta and one to prepare the sauce. By the time you boil the pasta the sauce is done! Applebee's prawns are truly wonderful and you want to savour every morsel. If you'd like to jazz up the recipe for a special occasion, peel the prawns, wash the shells and secure them in a wrapped-up piece of muslin. Add this to the pan of water when you are boiling the pasta. Drain and reserve a ladleful of cooking liquid. Before you add the prawns to the sauce, add the cooking liquid and reduce until slightly thickened. It is tricky to incorporate this step but it does add another dimension to the dish.

A friend described this recipe as 'substitution friendly.' So, feel free to change the shape of the pasta, the herbs or the type of shellfish; the combination of scallops with fresh ginger and cherry tomatoes on a bed of papardelle is equally tempting. [SLB]

Preparation time 15 minutes

Cooking time 10 minutes

Serves 4

Season Prawns are normally available year-round, but their peak season is from September to November

---

450 g prawns
4 garlic cloves
Sea salt
4 small dried red chillies (chile de arbol – available from Cool Chile Co.)
400 g cherry tomatoes
75 g–100 g Parmesan
400 g linguine
2 tblsp extra virgin olive oil
15 g basil leaves

Place a large pot of water over a high flame; cover and bring to the boil. While you are waiting for the water to boil, peel the prawns and remove the back vein by running a knife down the back of the prawn tail, this exposes the vein and makes it easy to remove.

Peel and crush the garlic with a little salt in a mortar. Wash the chillies and cut them in half. De-seed them if you wish (by doing so you will remove a fair portion of the heat) and chop them very finely. Wash and quarter the cherry tomatoes. Set them aside. Grate the Parmesan and have ready for service.

Once the water is at a rolling boil add the dry pasta and a good dash of salt. If you are using the prawn shells wrapped in muslin, add them to the pan now. Cook for one minute less than indicated on the back of the package.

Meanwhile, pour the olive oil into a frying pan and place it over medium heat. When warm, add the garlic and chillies and cook until fragrant, about 30 seconds. Add the cherry tomatoes and cook for 5–6 minutes or until they start to burst and break down. Add the prawns and toss to coat in the tomato mixture. This sauce gives a light coating to the pasta and doesn't insulate with a thick sauce.

In preparation for service, it is a good idea to warm the serving plates in the oven. Wash and blot dry the basil. Remove the leaves from the stems and chiffonade or tear the basil leaves into small pieces. Fold them into prawn and tomato mixture. Drain the pasta, and if you wish reserve a ladleful of the pasta cooking liquid. Add to the pasta sauce and reduce down a bit to concentrate the flavours.

Return the pasta to the pan, pour the sauce over it and toss well. Serve in large warm bowls with plenty of grated Parmesan.

HERB CRUSTED HALIBUT WITH FENNEL AND ORANGE SALAD

Halibut is a fish to watch and be wary of. Ask your fishmonger if it is Black, Atlantic or Pacific halibut. Pacific halibut is best. While it may be sourced from a distance, Pacific stocks are well managed by the International Halibut Pacific Commission, which applies strict harvesting conditions. Stocks of Black and Atlantic, on the other hand, are generally low and catches are still decreasing despite efforts to change fishing methods.

This recipe marries the fish with a beautiful combination of flavours: the briny olives paired with the sweet acidity of the citrus and a crisp liquorice back note from the fennel. Watercress and tarragon brighten the salad with a bitter, herbal base.

Halibut is a juicy, fleshy fish that benefits from being cooked with its skin, not only for insulation from the hot pan, but to hold the fish together for presentation.

This is a great supper to get you through the late winter months on the cusp of spring. If you cannot find blood oranges at the market, substitute slices of a jaffa or juicing orange (peel and all) for the segments below for a bitter-sweet addition to the salad. [SLB]

Preparation time 20 minutes, plus 4 hours marinating

Cooking time 10 minutes

Serves 6

Season Avoid Pacific halibut during its spawning season, between November and January

6 x 2·5cm thick halibut fillets, about 140 g each
3 large sprigs thyme
3 sprigs fresh parsley
1 unwaxed and/or organic orange
1 tblsp extra virgin olive oil, plus an additional 200 ml extra virgin olive oil
Sea salt
Freshly ground black pepper
2 round shallots, or 1 banana shallot
1 tblsp white wine or cider vinegar
2 blood oranges, or 2 unwaxed oranges
180 g (drained weight) pitted green olives
1 generous tsp runny honey
2 fennel bulbs
200 g watercress
40 g fresh tarragon

Using damp kitchen paper, blot the fish clean with a few swift strokes. Wash the sprigs of thyme and parsley. Remove the leaves and roughly chop to lightly bruise and release their flavour. Transfer to a glass or ceramic bowl large enough to accommodate the fish comfortably. Wash the orange and grate the zest. Add to the bowl, along with 1 tblsp of the olive oil and a good seasoning of salt and pepper. Cover and marinate the fish in the refrigerator – any amount of marinating will be beneficial, but at least 4 hours is ideal.

Peel and finely dice the shallots and place in a medium-sized bowl with the vinegar and a pinch of salt. Using a sharp knife remove the skin of the blood oranges and cut into segments or slices. Roughly chop the olives and gently fold them into the shallot-vinegar mixture, along with the orange segments. Drizzle over the honey and season well with black pepper. Remove any bruised outer leaves from the fennel and wash thoroughly under cold running water. Trim the top, saving any fennel fronds, and cut the bulb into quarters. Slice the fennel into thin slivers through the core.

Don't worry if some of the edges of your quarters fall apart. Add to the bowl and drizzle over 180 ml olive oil to coat. Wash and trim the watercress, tarragon and any fennel fronds, and dry thoroughly with kitchen paper. Keep this separate from the fennel orange salad until ready to serve.

Preheat the oven to 180°C / 350°F / gas 4.

Remove the fish from the refrigerator. Heat a large oven-proof sauté pan over high heat for a minute or two. Drizzle the remaining 20 ml olive oil onto the skin side of each fillet and place the oil-side down in the pan. Cook 3–4 minutes or until the skin is nicely browned. Carefully, flip the fish over (always flipping away from you so you

avoid splashing hot oil on you) and continue cooking for another 7–10 minutes in the preheated oven.

To serve, divide the watercress and herbs among the plates. Top with sautéed halibut, preferably skin-side up, and spoon on a generous portion of the orange salad, either on the top or tumbling off the fish to the side.

Cook's note When pan-frying fish the first side you put into the preheated pan should be the side of the fish you serve to your guests. This is because the first side cooked will be going into a clean pan thus will have a cleaner caramelised crust.

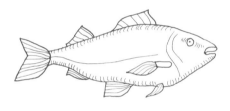

White fish

RAZOR CLAM, CHORIZO AND TOMATO STIR FRY

This recipe is technically a stir fry, but you do have to par-cook the clams first. It is, however, one of the quickest and tastiest recipes I know. If you ever have the opportunity, try to dig for razor clams yourself. They are slippery little suckers and great fun to catch! Their speed at evading your capture depends on a number of things: the size of the clam, the consistency of the sand and finally the temperature. Razor clams are cold-blooded organisms. Lower temperatures make the clam sluggish and slow whilst warmer temperatures make them faster. In other words, if you are gathering them in July and August, you had better be fleet of foot! Razors dig into the sand by extending their foot or 'digger' below their shell and then turns the foot perpendicular to its body to anchor itself. It then pulls itself down to the anchored foot.

A good trick is to locate their blow-holes in the sand. By blocking their blow-hole, you can force them to return to the surface. Local adventurers have used foods such as Worcestershire sauce, Tabasco, English mustard to lure razor clams to the surface. They don't like the salt and heat in such sauces, so if you spray or drip one of these condiments into their hole, within a few minutes you should see the tips of razor clams rising to the surface.

I love to pair Pays d'Auge Fromages' delicious chorizo with the razor clams. It has a visibly lower fat content than most chorizo and a slightly spicy chilli flavour that cuts through the rich meat. Pays d'Auge can be found at Borough on Fridays and Saturdays. If you can't get to Borough, try Portobello Market: they have a stall on the same days in between Elgin and Blenheim on Portobello Road. [SLB]

Preparation time 30 minutes for soaking the razor clams

Cooking time 15–18 minutes

Serves 4

Season Razor clams are easier to catch in the colder months, thus they are available in greater numbers from November to February

16 razor clams
120 ml white wine (or water)
1 chorizo ring (usually 250–300 g, a little more or less is fine)
1 tsp olive oil
250 g cherry tomatoes
2 garlic cloves
1 chilli de arbol (or ½ tsp dried chilli flakes)
A good pinch of sea salt
15 g fresh parsley

Razor Clams

Soak the razor clams as described on page 235.

Once soaked, rinse in plenty of cold water. Place the wine in a heavy-based saucepan which has a tight-fitting lid. Bring to the boil and lower in the razor clams. Cover with the lid and cook for about 2½ minutes. Check to see if most of the shells have opened. If so, strain through a colander reserving the cooking liquid in a measuring jug or a small bowl. Discard any clams that haven't opened. Remove the flesh from the shell and cut into 2·5 cm pieces.

Cut the chorizo in half and run a knife down the length to loosen the skin. Peel off as much of the casing as you can. Cut each half into half again and finely slice. Set aside.

Heat olive oil in a large frying pan. Add the chorizo and cook until it starts to render its fat. There won't be very much fat, but if there is more than 1 tblsp, remove and discard any extra.

Wash and halve the tomatoes and set them aside. Peel and crush the garlic in a mortar with the chilli and a pinch of salt. Add to the frying pan. Once fragrant, about 30 seconds, add the cherry tomatoes. Cook until the chorizo has a tinge of gold around the edges and the cherry tomatoes start to caramelise and break down.

Scatter the sliced razor clams over the top and toss to coat in the tomato-chorizo mix. Taste the razor clam cooking liquid, it should have a lovely lightly salty flavour with a touch of acid from the wine. Gently pour the cooking liquid over the tomato-chorizo mix, leaving behind any residual sand which may have accumulated at the bottom of the bowl, and fold through. Wash the parsley and blot dry with kitchen paper. Finely chop the leaves and thin stems and sprinkle over the top. Serve with a green leafy salad, plenty of bread to soak up the juices. Wash down with a cold beer.

Cook's note For a more substantial main course try tossing in ⅔ of a tin of washed and drained chickpeas. This classic combination of big flavours also works well with prawns (sautéed directly in the chorizo, garlic, and chilli or with small carpetshell clams steamed separately as above.

Sausages & sausage meat

BROWN & FORREST*

Michael Brown *Hambridge, Somerset*

Michael Brown and
Jesse Pattison beside the smoker

I was particularly eager to meet Michael because I've served his smoked eel in one guise or another every Christmas and for just about every party I've given for the last fifteen years or so. It's not only delicious but even when presented very simply, just with brown bread, it lends a feeling of luxury to the entire meal.

Standing looking very lean and fit in his Somerset smoke-house, where stacks of beech and gnarled apple branches were waiting to perfume his products, Michael told me about the strange life-cycle of the European eel, which is as remarkable as that of salmon. It is believed to swim all the way to the Sargasso Sea to spawn. The larvae spend their first three years of life drifting back across the Atlantic in the Gulf Stream. They can evidently smell, or in some other way sense the proximity of fresh water, which enables them to find their way into all the river systems of

Europe as far north as Norway. Eels are extraordinarily long-lived: unless raised on eel-farms, in which case they reach adult size in only two years, they take ten to fifteen years to mature – and even then don't stop growing. They can live to be as old as 100, by which time they might be very big indeed (it has been claimed that the Loch Ness monster is an eel). Another fact of life (or rather death) about them is that, like shellfish, they deteriorate very rapidly once they have been killed, which helps to explain why they are easier to buy smoked than fresh. Unsmoked, they have to be sold live.

Michael started out collecting elvers from the river Parrett in Somerset and selling them on to eel-farms, which at that time, in the 1970s, were a flourishing industrial side-line (very large quantities of heated water, however, are needed and they were discontinued here after a few years). After a time, he began to catch adult eels on the Somerset Levels.

The eels are caught in triangular traps with open backs which used to be made of wicker, like baskets. As they swim down-stream on their way back to the Sargasso Sea, they enter the open side and in a fast-flowing river can't swim strongly enough to go against the current and escape.

Initially, all his eels were bought and smoked by the Dutch. It soon occurred to him, however, that rather than selling them direct, he might try smoking them himself. His early efforts were discouraging. He tried a recipe for cold-smoking, the method traditionally used for salmon and other fish in Britain, but found that in the case of eels it didn't work. Then a friend introduced him to a smokery in Augsburg, Germany, where he discovered that the secret is to hot- rather than cold-smoke, which not only smokes but cooks the item in question. The smoking is much faster (eels take only an hour and a half) and the end result is moister and more succulent. The Germans suggested smoking over beech but when he returned to Somerset, Michael decided to try using local apple wood as well. The soft sweetness of the apple has become a hallmark of the entire Brown & Forrest range.

He opened his smokehouse in 1981. Since then, his business has never looked back. After perfecting eel, he added salmon, some of which is hot- and some cold-smoked; then he started on chicken, and then trout. He now has a list which includes sweet-cured Orkney herring fillets, Craster kippers, duck, lamb, bacon, salami, Parma-style ham, traditionally cured Cheshire ham, wild boar sausages, venison, garlic, and many other items.

The smokery is on the site of a former farm. In 1994, he converted one of the barns into a shop. Five years later he opened a restaurant which, given that the farm is on the outskirts of a not-very-large village near nowhere, is amazingly successful. Last year it served 15,000 lunches, ie nearly forty-eight covers a day (it shuts on Sundays and in the evenings but offers tea, coffee, and cakes up to 4·30pm). As one would expect, most of the items on the menu are smoked, but you can end your meal with a pudding such as Eton Mess or (Michael's favourite) Golden Syrup Bread-and-Butter Pudding. The dining-room is hung with exhibitions by local artists which change every month.

By now, Michael has several major contracts, notably with the Tate Modern, which he gained as a result of the Market. Until recently, Borough was very important to his business, but of necessity it has become less so of late because he currently has no London stallholder. This means that he either has to come himself or send one of his smoking team, which he can only manage once a month. However, if you miss him you can always use his mail-order service (see page 330).

* In case you're wondering, Forrest is simply an old friend of Michael's whose name Michael uses to make a good title for the business. In 2007 Michael sold the business to Jesse Pattison.

Right Checking the smoked duck breasts
Opposite A rack of freshly smoked eels

TORTIGLIONI WITH SMOKED EEL AND CELERIAC

My notes after making this for the first time read: 'Not positive enough. Try bacon instead of eel.' So I did, and found that whereas with eel the flavours add up to more than the sum of their parts (which was why I followed it through), the bacon killed the dill and tasted like — just bacon. The answer turned out to be to use more eel and serve the dish warm or cool rather than hot. The flavours really do work together — I'm tempted to say, creatively. Sour cream and dill point up the richness of the eel, spring onions add pungency and the celeriac contributes an unexpected note of sweetness. [SF]

Preparation time 25–30 minutes (celeriac is notoriously hard to peel – but remember, I'm slow)

Cooking time 20–25 minutes

Serves 2 for a main course or 4–5 as a first course

Season Celeriac is in season September–April. Smoked eel is available all the year round, although at its best in September and October

Small bunch (18–20g) dill
5 spring onions
1 small root celeriac
3 tblsp extra virgin olive oil, preferably fruity
Sea salt
Freshly ground black pepper
½ tsp whole black peppercorns
150g tortiglioni or similar large pasta pipes
2 largish or 3 small garlic cloves
2 heaped tblsp sour cream plus a little extra for serving
175–185g smoked eel

Skinning an eel with a spoon

Wash, blot or shake dry, and pull the leaves from the dill: take care not to mistake the smaller stems for leaves (they look much the same but are tough). Finely chop. Trim off the top of the onions, leaving about 5 cm at the lower end, including the white part. Remove the outer layer and root, and slice finely.

Heat the oven to 200°C / 400°F / gas 6.

Peel the celeriac. The skin on some roots is ridged and uneven, with little inlets and curlicues which mean that you have to cut quite deeply. You may also find that after peeling, the root is smudged with earth from the skin and needs washing (it may also discolour on exposure to the air, but so far as this recipe is concerned, it doesn't matter). When it is clean, chop 200 g of it into 2 cm squares. Cover the bottom of a baking tray with 1½ tblsp of the oil and roll the squares in it so that they are coated on all sides. Spread them in a single layer, preferably not touching each other, season lightly with salt and freshly ground black pepper and roast for 20–25 minutes, until they are soft and tinged with gold.

Set a large pan of water to boil for the pasta. Peel the garlic, slice and then roughly crush it in a mortar with the whole peppercorns. Leave it on one side. Look at the instructions on the packet of pasta and time the pasta to be ready at the same time as the celeriac (De Cecco tortiglioni, which I recommend, takes 12 minutes). Bring the water to a rolling boil, sprinkle in a good pinch of sea salt and add the pasta. Start timing it when the water returns to the boil.

While the pasta cooks, warm the remaining 1½ tblsp oil over medium heat in a wok or deep pan large enough for the pasta and all the other ingredients. Add the garlic and peppercorns from the mortar and stir-fry for a few seconds, until the aroma rises. Add the sliced onion, stir and remove from the heat.

Start testing the pasta at least two minutes before it is due to be ready. As soon as it is soft enough to eat but still with plenty of bite, remove it from the heat and drain it in a sieve or colander. Turn it into the pan with the garlic and onions and toss. Add the dill and toss gently. As soon as it is ready, add the celeriac and toss again. Leave it to cool for a few minutes while you shred the eel removing any bones. Do this unevenly, leaving some quite large pieces. Toss it lightly rather than thoroughly, taste and if you like add a few flakes of salt and/or more pepper. Fold in the cream. Then, serve with a small dollop of extra cream on top of each portion. Plate up and eat immediately.

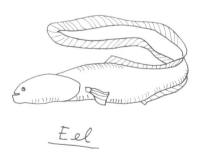

Eel

SMOKED EEL PEARL BARLEY RISOTTO WITH WATERCRESS

Wakame is a dried seaweed used to infuse soups and rice dishes in Japan. Here we are using it to infuse the stock as it adds a pleasant salty background flavour to the dish as well as a taste of the sea. You can find it in most health food stores. Barley is as delicious a grain to cook as risotto. The glutinous quality of barley is similar to that of Arborio rice. However, the nutty texture and flavour put this recipe in a class of it's own. [SLB]

Preparation time   10 minutes

Cooking time   40 minutes

Serves   4

Season   Eel is at its best in September
        and October

600 ml chicken stock (preferably homemade
    but store bought will do)
2 pieces wakame or kombu seaweed
    (optional)
2 sprigs fresh thyme
300 g smoked eel fillets
140 g pearl barley
2 tblsp olive oil
1 small onion
1 carrot
2 garlic cloves
125 ml white wine, at room temperature
Sea salt
Freshly ground black pepper
30 g watercress
4 tblsp grated Parmesan

Risottos are generally best when made with warm stock. The shock is just too much for the rice or barley grain when cold stock is added to a pan of hot rice or barley. The shell usually seizes and toughens, taking a lot longer to soften and transform into a luxurious dish. So, begin by placing a small saucepan over a medium flame. Pour in the chicken stock and lower in the seaweed. Wash the thyme and blot dry with kitchen paper. Add the thyme to the stock and bring the mixture up to a gently simmer.

Meanwhile, trim and remove the skin from the smoked eel. Run your fingers along the fillet to feel for stray bones and cut them away. Flake the fillets into 1 cm pieces (roughly) and set aside.

Begin making the risotto by placing the barley in a heavy-bottom saucepan over a medium heat without any butter or oil. Gently toast for 5 minutes or so. Toasting the grains will not only intensify the colour, but add depth of flavour to the finished dish. Transfer to a small bowl and set aside.

Heat the olive oil in the same heavy-bottomed saucepan. Peel and finely dice both the onion and carrot. Add both the vegetables to the hot oil and cook for 5 minutes, stirring frequently, until translucent and soft but not brown. Peel and crush the garlic with a little salt into a paste with a pestle and mortar. Add to the saucepan with the vegetables and sauté until fragrant, about 30 seconds. Add the barley and cook, stirring, for 1 minute. Try to coat each grain of toasted barley with the garlicky aromatic oil.

Pour the wine over the barley and vegetables. Bring to a simmer, stirring, until it has nearly evaporated. Turn the heat down to medium-low and add a ladle of hot stock to the barley mixture and cook, stirring occasionally, until the liquid has been absorbed. Add another ladle of stock and continue cooking and stirring until it too has been absorbed. Repeat this process until all or most of the stock has been used and the barley is *al dente* – this will take about 30 minutes. Season with salt and pepper.

While the barley cooks, wash the watercress and blot dry with kitchen paper. Pick over the leaves and remove any tough stems. Remove the pan from the heat and fold in the smoked eel, Parmesan and the watercress, so that the watercress only wilts slightly. Check the seasoning one last time and serve immediately.

Cook's note For an equally delicious variation try adding lightly sautéed mushrooms to the recipe. Blot about 425–450g of mixed mushrooms clean with damp kitchen paper. Roughly chop and sauté separately in a frying pan with a little butter and fold into the barley risotto at the end.

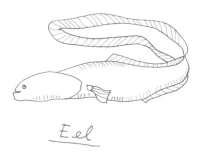

Eel

SMOKED SALMON AND FRESH GOAT CHEESE PIZZA WITH DILL

These make a great change to the typical tomato-based pizza toppings. Cooking instructions below are for indoors, but these pizzas are fantastic when cooked on the barbecue. Just make sure you have a fine meshed grill rack so that the pizza dough cannot slip through. To barbecue the pizza, pile the preheated charcoal over one quarter of the area of your barbecue but before you do this ensure you preheat the whole grill rack. Place the dough on top of the preheated grill rack and arrange your toppings on the dough. Using tongs to rotate the pizza dough over the 'hot spot' will help control the rate at which the pizza cooks and you won't end up with a burnt bottom. [SLB]

Preparation time 15 minutes,
   plus 1 hour for the dough to rise

Cooking time 10–12 minutes

Serves 2 hungry people or as part of a
   barbecue – makes 2 x 10 inch pizzas

Season All ingredients available year-round

PIZZA BASE

180 ml warm water
2½ tsp commercial yeast
200 g plain flour and extra for dusting
4 tblsp corn-meal
2 tblsp wholemeal flour
½ tsp sugar
2 tblsp olive oil,
   plus additional for oiling bowl
1 tsp sea salt

TOPPINGS

15 g fresh dill
2 small leeks
300 g soft goats' cheese
4 tblsp crème fraîche
10 slices smoked salmon

Preheat the oven to 200 °C / 400 °F / gas 6.

Stir together the water and yeast in a small bowl. Let it stand until foamy, about 10 minutes.

In a large bowl combine the flour, corn-meal, wholemeal flour and sugar. Once the yeast has started to foam, add the water to the flour along with the olive oil and salt. Stir together until the mixture becomes a soft dough. Knead on a floured surface, incorporating more flour as necessary to prevent the dough from sticking, until it is smooth and elastic, about 5 to 10 minutes. Put the dough into a deep, oiled bowl and turn to coat with the oil. Let it rise, covered with plastic wrap, in a warm place for 1 hour or until doubled in bulk.

Once doubled, punch the dough down with your fist. Form the dough into 2 balls.

Wash the dill and leeks thoroughly and blot dry. Remove the dill leaves from the stems and finely chop. Cut the leeks in half lengthwise and thinly slice them. Set both ingredients aside until ready to assemble.

Roll out each ball of dough to about 8 mm thick. Brush the tops with olive oil. Divide the goats' cheese into four portions, 2 for each pizza as we are going to sandwich the salmon with the goat cheese and crème fraîche. Crumble one portion of goats' cheese over each pizza, leaving about 12 mm around the edge. Dot each pizza with 1 tblsp of crème fraîche and sprinkle with the chopped leeks and fresh dill. Bake in the preheated oven for 8 minutes.

Remove the pizza from the oven and arrange the smoked salmon evenly over the top. Cover with the remaining goats' cheese and crème fraîche and drizzle lightly with olive oil. Bake for another 8 minutes. Serve with a green salad. A lightly oaked or even unoaked chardonnay would be perfect with the smoked salmon.

SMOKED TROUT AND PEAR SALAD WITH HORSERADISH CREAM

Smoked fish is an essential ingredient in my kitchen. We almost always have either smoked trout or mackerel in our refrigerator as it is quick to prepare, has an extremely satisfying flavour and a meaty texture. This salad is fantastically flexible. Substitute mackerel for the trout, or even quince for pears. Roasted radicchio is a perfect alternative accompaniment to the watercress. Use the recipe as a guideline — but keep the principal flavours the same: peppery watercress, sweet pears and smoky fish. The dressing is versatile and delicious with most kinds of fish. [SLB]

Preparation time 5 minutes to make the dressing and assemble the salad

Cooking time 5–10 minutes to sear the pears

Serves 4

Season Fresh sea trout is in season from late March until early July, smoked trout is available throughout most of the year

1 lemon (enough juice for 2 tblsp)
120 ml double cream
½ tblsp prepared horseradish (or fresh grated if you are lucky enough to find it. The greengrocer, Turnips has it in early April)
4 sprigs fresh dill, plus extra for garnish
1 rounded tsp grainy mustard
⅛ tsp cayenne pepper
2 firm pears, unpeeled
Freshly ground black pepper
2 bunches watercress
255 g smoked trout
Sea salt

Squeeze the lemon. Whisk the cream with the horseradish and 2 tblsp of lemon juice. Wash the dill, then remove the dill fronds from the stems and finely chop. Fold the dill and the grainy mustard through the horseradish cream. Season with cayenne, salt and pepper and set aside.

Heat a large oven-proof frying pan over medium heat. Quarter the pears and sear on both of the exposed flesh sides until golden. Put the entire frying pan into the oven and roast until the pears are soft. If you have very ripe pears it may not be necessary to put them in the oven.

Wash the watercress thoroughly and blot dry, then pile it in the centre of each of 4 plates. Set 2 roasted pear quarters on each plate. Flake large pieces of trout around the pears and spoon on some of the horseradish dressing. Garnish with the remaining dill sprigs and serve.

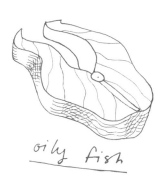

oily fish

KIPPER SALAD, WHISKEY SAUCE, WITH CRÈME FRAÎCHE AND DIJON MUSTARD

The kipper was invented by John Woodger at Seahouses in Northumberland about 1843. This invention coincided with the development of the railway network which allowed large quantities of fresh fish to be moved rapidly from one place to another. A new way of smoking fish came into being at this time; to better reveal their flavour the fish were mildly smoked and dried with minimal salt. As a result of the widespread availability of fresh and lightly smoked fish, the popularity of heavily salted and smoked products dwindled.

The Old English word kippian, meaning 'to spawn', has various possible origins the Icelandic word kippa meaning 'to pull or snatch', the Danish word kippen meaning 'to seize or snatch' or the English kipe which describes a basket used to catch fish are all possible parallels. Another theory traces the word kipper to kip, a name given to the small beak a male salmon develops during the breeding season. We're not sure where the name comes from but we do know that a kipper is a whole fish that has been split from head to tail, gutted, salted, and smoked. It is usually a herring, but traditionally a kipper can be any fish found in great numbers and caught during its spawning period, such as salmon. Spawning fish were not as tasty but their great abundance seemed a terrible thing to waste, when caught, they are salted and smoked to improve flavour and preservation.

This is the ultimate recipe for those who need the 'hair of the dog that bit them'. The morning after a decadent evening needs a gentle start with a good dose of Omega-3's and a little help from the Scots (or the Irish) to get you on your way. [SLB]

Preparation time 10 minutes

Cooking time 3–5 minutes

Serves 2

Season Kippers are available year-round. while May is the prime season for English Watercress

---

100 g (1 bunch) watercress
30 g unsalted butter
1 lemon
2 kipper fillets (up to 4 depending on how hungry you are)
30 ml Irish Whiskey or Scotch Whisky
3 tblsp double cream or crème fraîche
1 level tsp Dijon mustard
Sea salt
Freshly ground black Pepper

Wash the watercress thoroughly and blot dry with kitchen paper. Pick over and remove any large stems and discard. Arrange the salad leaves over the plates and set aside.

Put the butter into a frying pan and heat over a medium flame until it sizzles and subsides. Juice the lemon and measure out 1 tablespoon and set aside. Add the kippers to the warm pan and fry gently for one minute. Turn the heat down to low and add the whiskey and cream. Gently turn the fish over in the warm sauce. Tilt the pan to one side to pool the sauce. Work the Dijon into the sauce with the back of a spoon. Taste for seasoning.

Spoon the kippers on top of the watercress and serve. You can finish with an equal amount of crème fraîche instead of double cream if you like, but make sure that you only use half as much lemon juice.

Cook's note Whiskey is a Kipper's match made in heaven and there are endless variations on how these two can be paired together. For those who may not need a gentle start to the day try mashing 4 juicy prunes with a half of a small de-seeded chilli in a mortar. Add a peeled clove of garlic and an equivalent sized piece of peeled fresh ginger and work into a rough paste. Add to the frying pan with the whiskey working it into the sauce with the back of a spoon. Omit the lemon juice, cream and mustard.

SMOKED EELS WITH CELERIAC APPLE SAGE ROSTI AND REMOULADE SAUCE

Smoked eels are a dream to have in the kitchen as they are so easy to prepare. The most labourious part of this meal is the prepping and cooking of the rosti. I've presented the eels here as a light main or starter but they work equally well as canapés. Instead of making two large rosti, pinch about a tablespoon of the potato mix between your fingers and place into the hot frying pan. The recipe below makes about 8–10 small bites.

It is also worth noting that I have also made the remoulade sauce with equal parts of low fat yoghurt, cream cheese and mayonnaise with equally good results. The sour cream is definitely more luxurious but the yoghurt-cream cheese combination will work in a pinch. [SLB]

Preparation time 15–20 minutes

Cooking time 11–14 minutes

Serves 2

Season Eel is at its best in September and October

1 lemon
1½ tblsp sour cream
1½ tblsp mayonnaise
1 tsp Dijon mustard
½ tsp prepared horseradish
½ tsp sea salt
Freshly ground black pepper
Piece of celeriac
    (enough for 115 g, after peeling)
1 small potato
    (enough for 115 g, after peeling)
1 small cooking apple
4 large leaves sage
30 g unsalted butter
2 tsp extra virgin olive oil
150 g smoked eels for serving
Parsley for garnish

Preheat the oven to 180 °C / 350 °F / gas 4.

Cut the lemon in two. Set aside half for garnish and squeeze the other half.

To make the remoulade, mix the sour cream, mayonnaise, Dijon mustard, horseradish and lemon juice together in a small bowl. Season with salt and pepper and set aside.

Peel and grate the celeriac, potato and 60 g of the apple, either with a box grater or with a food processor. Transfer to a small bowl. Wash the sage leaves. Stack them on top of one another and slice as thinly as you can. Add to the bowl and fold into the celeriac mixture. Season with salt and pepper.

Heat an oven-ready non-stick frying pan over a medium flame. If you don't have an oven-ready frying pan a baking tray will work too, but allow it to preheat in the oven while you are frying the rosti. Melt the butter and oil together in the pan. Divide the grated celeriac mixture into two, squeezing out any excess liquid and, once the foaming has subsided in the pan, place the two portions in it side by side. Make sure there is enough room in between the rosti as well as around the edges of the pan. Cook the rosti for 2 minutes each side and transfer the frying pan to a preheated oven and continue cooking for 7–10 minutes. Or if you are using a baking tray, transfer the rosti to the preheated baking tray and place in the oven. Cook as directed.

Wash the parsley. Remove any skin from the eels, and run your fingers over the top to check for bones. Transfer the rosti to warm plates and top with a small dollop of remoulade sauce. Arrange a few flakes of smoked eel over the top. Garnish with parsley and lemon wedges.

SMOKED EEL POTATO CROQUETTES WITH CARAMELISED PEAR SAUCE

These little fritters are delicious on their own, but I like them even better with a fruity aioli. Smoked eel has a luscious texture and smoky flavour which is not far from a good streaky bacon.

This is a Spanish-influenced recipe with very English ingredients. These croquettes can be deep fried, as per traditional croquettes, or shallow fried with a thin coating of oil in the pan. Just make sure that, if you fry them in a lightly oiled pan, you shape them into patties rather than quenelles so they cook evenly. Smoked eels are a little tricky to sell to someone who hasn't grown up with them, but this recipe will win over your toughest critics. [SLB]

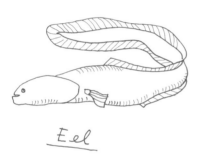

Eel

Preparation time 35 minutes

Cooking time 10–12 minutes

Serves 4 (makes 16 quenelles)

Season Eel is at its best in September and October

CROQUETTES

500 g baking potatoes

450 g smoked eel

Horseradish (or prepared) – enough for 1 tblsp when grated

2 medium eggs

1 tblsp plain flour, plus additional flour to coat croquettes

about 100 g day-old bread for breadcrumbs

500 ml–1 litre sunflower oil for frying

CARAMELISED PEAR SAUCE

1 ripe pear

Knob of butter

1 garlic clove

Sea salt

Freshly ground black pepper

1 tsp runny honey

150 ml extra virgin olive oil

Bring a medium-sized pan of water to the boil. Add the potatoes with the skin on and cook until they can be easily pierced with a knife, about 20 minutes. Drain and allow to cool.

Remove the skin from the eels and run your fingers up and down the fillets to check for any pin bones. Shred the meat into fine pieces and place in large mixing bowl. Peel the horseradish and the cooled potato. Grate the horseradish. Transfer the potato to the bowl with the eels and add the horseradish; crush with a potato masher to mix the ingredients together. Add one of the eggs and sprinkle over the flour. Give the mix a good stir to combine all the ingredients. Shape the fish mixture, using two spoons to make 'quenelle'-like shapes. The mix should make 16 quenelles. At this stage the croquettes can be refrigerated or cooked straight away.

Make the sauce first as you want to have every-thing ready once the croquettes are cooked. Wash the rocket and parsley and blot dry with kitchen paper. Heat a large frying pan over a medium flame. Cut the pear in half and remove the core with a small spoon or a melon baller. Add the butter to a pan and when it is sizzling add the pear halves, cut side down. Cook for 3 minutes or until golden brown on the cut side. Once caramelised and brown, flip the pears over and place them in a hot oven and cook until a knife can be inserted easily. Set aside to cool.

Peel and crush the garlic with a good pinch of salt, about ¼ teaspoon, and some coarsely ground black pepper in a mortar. Transfer to a small bowl and add the honey. Blitz the pear in a food processor, skins and all. If you prefer a smoother paste, you can remove the skins but the little bits they create in the sauce add a kick of sweet pear flavour.

Add the crushed garlic to the blitzed pear and begin pouring in the olive oil in a slow, steady stream. The mixture will thicken quickly from the sugar in the pear. Set aside until ready to serve.

Remove the crust from the bread and grate into breadcrumbs either with a box grater or in the work bowl of a food processor. Crack the other egg into a small bowl and beat lightly to break up the yolk. Have two side plates (one for the additional flour to coat the croquettes and one for breadcrumbs) near the egg bowl.

Heat a large casserole with the sunflower oil (the sunflower oil should be about 5 cm deep) to about 165–170 °C / 330–340 °F. Use a ther-mometer to measure the heat. If you don't have one, tear off a piece of bread and carefully lower into the hot oil. If the bread dances around in the hot oil with bubbles enveloping the piece of bread, the oil should be up to temperature. Remember when you add the croquettes to the oil the temperature will drop, so don't over crowd the casserole.

Dredge each quenelle in flour and then dip into the egg. Allow some of the egg to drip off before rolling it in breadcrumbs. Using a slotted spoon lower the quenelles into the hot oil – do this in batches of three or four, carefully adding each quenelle into the oil individually. Cook until golden brown and remove from the oil, draining on paper towels.

Serve the croquettes with some rocket and parsley leaves, possibly with a squeeze of lemon and a small bowl of caramelised pear sauce on the side.

Cook's note The croquettes can be cooked ahead of time and crisped up in a hot oven before serving. I've also made these with an equivalent amount of sweet potatoes instead of baking potatoes, which worked equally well.

Appendices

APPENDIX 1:
CONTRIBUTOR BIOGRAPHIES

Sarah Freeman

It is with great sadness that we must report that Sarah Freeman died in December 2007, shortly after the first publication of this cookbook in October of that year. Happily she was aware of the praise lavished on the book and of particular pleasure to her was the book's choice by Sheila Dillon as the Radio Four Food Programme's Cookbook of the Year.

Sarah Freeman was born at the beginning of the Second World War, when she said that she ate better then than perhaps at any other time in her life. Her parents had moved to the countryside and grew in their garden all the fruit and vegetables that they could possibly eat, and also reared pigs and chickens.

Every evening a delicious dinner was cooked by a local woman, Mrs Jackson, because Sarah's mother hated cooking. Mrs Jackson taught Sarah traditional British cooking skills, probably better than any cookery school. Sarah later spent time in France theoretically learning the language but actually learning French culinary skills, again with ingredients grown on the premises. Boarding school and Oxford were good examples for her of why someone should study cookery, as she would have starved had it not been for cheese, for which she developed a life-long love. She started her working life as an editor, finally becoming arts editor for *Harpers & Queen*. When her daughter, aged about six, complained to the nanny that 'the day never starts until mummy comes home' she felt compelled to leave her work and started to write books.

Her first was *Isabella and Sam: the story of Mrs Beeton*, the idea of which came to her because *Queen* magazine had been founded by Isabella Beeton's husband, who was a brilliant and innovative publisher. This was followed by *Mutton and oysters: a study of Victorian food*, a series on cookery for students and, more recently, *The real cheese companion*, a survey of the best handmade British and Irish cheeses, for which she visited over one hundred farms and dairies. She also wrote *The best of modern British cookery*, a new edition of which was published in 2006.

Over the last few years she was also deeply involved in the international Slow Food movement, and the director of a Slow Food project to save foods threatened by modern conditions, as well as being UK advisory editor and a regular contributor to its magazine, which was published in seven languages.

Sarah Leahey-Benjamin

Sarah Leahey-Benjamin started cooking while at university where she spent many more evenings cooking with friends rather than studying in the university library. After university Sarah funded her days as a cancer researcher at Harvard Medical School by working in restaurants at night. Four years later she jumped ship to take up an apprenticeship as a chef and worked full time in restaurants learning everything from stocks and sauces to pastry. She travelled extensively throughout Europe which helped to form the basis of her belief that the best food is regional and seasonal and settled in Britain with her English husband. Her recipes are both richly layered and personally presented providing a cultural context.

Sarah teaches a variety of cooking classes at Divertimenti Cookery School in both Knightsbridge and Cambridge as well as at Books for Cooks in Notting Hill. In addition to teaching, Sarah has spent the last few years building up a consultancy and wholesale business marketing seasonal British chutneys, jams, and cakes supplying restaurants and delis.

Sarah was interviewed and featured in the *Sunday Telegraph Stella Magazine* in May 2007.

George Nicholson

George Nicholson's photography has been shown at three solo exhibitions; 'Painting with Light' in 2003; 'Made in Southwark – a photographic celebration of the hand', in 2004; and 'Black & Light' in 2006.

His photographs have been used to illustrate a number of publications on London's urban fabric, including *Vision for London* in 1992; *Rivers of meaning* in 1996; and *River calling*, in 2002 and *Made in Southwark* – also published by Civic Books.

George has been a leading figure in the renaissance of the Borough Market in his role as Chairman of the Trustees. He is a board member of Coin Street Community Builders, and Company Secretary to The National Retail Planning Forum. Through the London Rivers Association, since 1997, he has led a team from the UK working with the Government of West Bengal on the revival of the Kolkata waterfront.

Catherine Dixon

Catherine Dixon has worked as a freelance designer since graduating from Central Saint Martins College of Art & Design, London. Clients include Penguin Books, Laurence King and C H Beck. She was part of the D&AD award-winning team also nominated for the Design Museum's Designer of the Year in 2005 for Penguin's Great Ideas series. As a writer she is a regular contributor to *Eye*, has worked on the website publiclettering.org.uk and co-authored with Phil Baines the book *Signs: lettering in the environment* in 2003. She completed her PhD in typeform description at CSM in 2001 since when she has continued to pursue typographic research interests, now alongside her position as Senior Lecturer in typography.

Emma Lofstrom

Emma Lofstrom is a Swedish illustrator currently based in London, where she is working on a freelance basis while pursuing her MA studies in Communication Art & Design at the Royal College of Art. She was nominated for the V&A Student Illustrator of the Year 2006, while still an undergraduate at Central Saint Martins, and also received a Highly Commended for her book jacket design in the Penguin Design Award 2007. Clients include the Stockholm Culture Festival, *Rubbish* magazine and Southwark Playhouse.

Tobias Steed

Tobias Steed has been involved in various forms of publishing for over thirty years, spanning numerous genres from academic to travel, kids to cooking, in print and online.

In 1988 he co-founded the award-winning Compass American Guides illustrated travel series that he sold in 1992 to Random House in New York, where he subsequently spent time as Director of New Media. After returning to Britain to work across the various News International newspaper, online and other publishing interests, Tobias became a published author himself with *Hollywood cocktails*, now translated into seven languages. Tiring of the politics of the big corporation, Tobias once again embraced the peculiarities of the small business entrepreneur and founded Can of Worms Enterprises in order to facilitate his involvement in a variety of undertakings in the creative industries and which this co-operative publishing project expounds so well. More information on the activities of Can of Worms can be found at: www.canofwormsenterprises.co.uk

APPENDIX 2: CONTACT INFORMATION

Civic Books is deeply appreciative to the traders who gave their time to be interviewed for this book. They would of course be delighted to serve you in the Market, but should you wish to make contact otherwise their details are listed below. For a listing of all the traders in the Market please visit our web site:
    www.civicbooks.com
or the Borough Market's own web site at
    www.boroughmarket.org.uk.

Applebee's Fish | Graham Applebee
Stoney Street, London SE1 9AA
07990 578883

Brown & Forrest | Jesse Pattison
Bowdens Farm, Hambridge, Somerset TA10 0BP
01458 250875
info@smokedeel.co.uk
www.smokedeel.co.uk

Denhay Farms | Amanda Streatfeild
Broadoak, Bridport, Dorset DT6 5NP
01308 458963
www.denhay.co.uk
sales@denhay.co.uk

Farmer Sharp | Andrew Sharp
Diamond Buildings, Pennington Lane,
    Lindal in Furness, Cumbria, LA12 0LA
01229 588299
info@farmersharp.co.uk
www.farmersharp.co.uk

Farmhouse Direct (3–4) | David Kitson
Long Ghyll Farms, Brock Close, Bleasdale,
    Preston PR3 1UZ
01995 61799
info@farmhousedirect.com
www.farmhousedirect.com

Furness Fish and Poultry | Leslie Salisbury
Stockbridge Lane off Daltongate, Ulverston,
    Cumbria LA12 7BG
020 7378 8899
furnessfish@yahoo.com

Gamston Wood Ostriches | Susan & James Farr
Gamston Wood Farm, Upton Retford,
    Nottinghamshire DN22 0RB
01777 838858
sue@gamstonwoodfarm.com
www.gamstonwoodfarm.com

The Ginger Pig | Timothy Wilson
Borough Market, Southwark Street, London SE1
020 7403 4721
gingerpig@btconnect.com

Northfield Farm Ltd | Jan McCourt
Northfield Farm, Wissendine Lane, Cold Overton,
    Oakham, Rutland LE15 7QF
01664 474271
jan@northfieldfarm.com
www.northfieldfarm.com

Oysterman (Richard Haward Oysters)
Richard Haward
The Company Shed, 129 Coast Road, West Mersea,
    Colchester CO5 8PA
01206 383284
richard@oysters.u-net.com
www.richardhawardsoysters.co.uk

Seldom Seen Farm | Robert Symington
Seldom Seen Farm, Billesdon,
    Leicestershire LE7 9FA
0116 2596742

Shellseekers | Darren Brown
Sika's Rest, Lytchett Lane, Bovington, Dorset BH20
07074 104607
shellseekers@talk21.com

Sillfield Farm | Peter Gott
Sillfield Farm, Endmoor, Kendal, Cumbria LA8 0HZ
015395 67609
enquiries@sillfield.co.uk
www.sillfield.co.uk

West Country Park Venison | Peter Kent
Keyethern, Hatherleigh, Okehampton,
    Devon EX20 3LG
01837 810028
peterkent999@hotmail.co.uk

Wild Beef | Richard & Lizzie Vines
Hillhead Farm, Chagford, Devon, TQ13 8DY
01647 433433

Wyndham House Poultry | Lee Mullet
2–3 Stoney Street, London SE1 9AA
020 7403 4788
wyndhamhouse@aol.com

APPENDIX 3:
THE PLEASURE OF FOOD

The enjoyment of food is a multi-sensory experience. There are many fine organisations, markets and individuals who campaign vigorously for the type of issues that this book has only touched upon: sustainability, provenance, care and of course taste.

Here are just a few you might find interesting or helpful. All of the links are available by visiting this book's supporting web site at www.civicbooks.com:

Slow Food
    www.slowfood.com
    In the UK: www.slowfood.org.uk
Slow Food is a non-profit, eco-gastronomic member-supported organization that was founded in 1989 to counteract fast food and fast life.

Radio Four *The Food Programme*
www.bbc.co.uk/radio4/factual/foodprogramme.shtml
Sheila Dillon presents *The Food Programme* on Radio 4. It broadcasts at the following times: Sunday 12·30–13·00 (rpt Monday 16·00–16·30).

National Association of British Market Authorities (NABMA)
www.nabma.com
The voice of local authority markets, NABMA has promoted the interests of its local authority members for the past 80 years.

The National Farmers' Retail & Markets Association (FARMA)
    www.farma.org.uk
FARMA is a co-operative of farmers, producers selling on a local scale, and farmers' markets organisers.

Soil Association
    www.soilassociation.org
The Soil Association is an environmental charity promoting sustainable, organic farming and championing human health.

Emporion: Association of Best Foods and Traditional Markets of Europe
    www.emporiononline.com
EMPORION aims to support the identity and culture which flourishes in markets.

Marine Conservation Society
    www.mcsuk.org
    www.fishonline.org
MCS is the UK charity dedicated to caring for our seas, shores and wildlife. The MCS Fishonline website provides current information on which fish to buy, sustainability issues and which fish to avoid.

APPENDIX 4:
BOROUGH MARKET

For further information, recipes, trader details, shopping lists and other useful tips on using the Borough Market Cookbook please visit our web site at:
www.civicbooks.com.
All the links listed on this page can also be directly accessed through this website.

Visiting Borough Market

The retail opening hours for Borough Market are:
Thursdays: 11am – 5pm
Fridays: 12pm – 6pm
Saturdays: 9am – 4pm

How to get to Borough Market

Train: Located near to the mainline National Rail network and the London Underground (Northern Line – City Branch and Jubilee Line) at London Bridge Station

Bus routes: 17, 501, 521 (Monday – Friday) 21, 35, 40, 43, 47, 48, 133, 149, 343, 381, RV1

Car parking: Free but limited spaces are available next to the Jubilee Market. There are further car parks on the corner of Southwark Street and Southwark Bridge Road, and on Snowsfields.

Further travel information is available from:
Transport for London Journey Planner:
www.journeyplanner.tfl.gov.uk
Transport for London:
www.tfl.gov.uk
National Rail:
www.nationalrail.co.uk

If you can't visit in person visit the Borough Market online at: www.boroughmarket.org.uk

The Borough Market is a Registered Charity: 1076940
8 Southwark Street, London, SE1 1TL
+44 (0) 20 7407 1002

Other markets around the UK

London Farmers' Markets
www.lfm.org.uk
LFM promotes local and seasonal foods while encouraging sustainable agriculture, traditional animal breeds and heritage fruit and vegetable varieties. It also aims to reduce the gap between rural and urban communities.

Certified Farmers' Markets
www.farmersmarkets.net
A web directory of inspected and genuine farmers' markets around the UK.

Also published by Civic Books:

The Borough Market Book: From roots to renaissance
RRP £19.99 176 pages ISBN 1-904104-90-8

'This book is a beautiful celebration of a way of shopping and eating that proves there's an alternative to the supermarket. With contributions from Borough market stallholders such as Randolph Hodgson of Neal's Yard Dairy and the chefs who shop there, including John Torode, Rose Gray and Antonio Carluccio, it captures the personalities and the produce that make Borough the unique place that it is.'
Olive Magazine

The Borough Market Book celebrates what can be achieved when people, place and politics collaborate to bring to market the highest standards and stands as a clarion call for market's throughout Britain. Reflecting the diversity and quality of the Market itself, the Borough Market Book has been written and photographed by a discerning team of contributors:

Ptolemy Dean has been a Trustee of Borough Market, an architect and a presenter on the BBC televion series *Restoration*. He writes on the history of the market and it's architectural heritage.

Sheila Dillon presents BBC Radio 4's *The Food Programme* and writes on the politics of food.

Henrietta Green is the country's leading expert on Britain's speciality food producers, founded the first Food Lovers' Fairs and writes on the produce available in the Market.

Dominic Murphy is the Green Consumer columnist for *The Guardian* and writes on where the produce comes from.

Jason Lowe has photographed a long list of food books and can be found in the Market on many Saturdays.

Available directly from the Publisher, Civic Books:
+44 (0)20 7708 2942

Index of recipes

Arranged by principle ingredients.

MEAT

Bacon
Good bacon sandwich with oven roasted tomato
    chutney 96
White bean soup with Denhay back bacon and
    rosemary 92
Zita tagliata (pasta pipes) with Denhay bacon and
    Brussels sprouts 94

Beef
Biltong date and cheddar salad with hazelnut sherry
    vinaigrette 87
Casseroled beef provençal 118
Coriander and fennel crusted sirloin salad with hoisin
    vinaigrette 211
Daube of Galloway beef with bacon and Shiraz 50
Inside-out beef burgers 120
Short ribs braised in dark ale with maple syrup 208
The ultimate steak 82
Whiskey espresso marinated steak with chimichurri
    sauce 210
Wild beef bolognese 78
Wild beef braised with rhubarb, honey and saffron
    84

Chicken
All-in-one sandwich 148
Butterflied lemon chicken with polenta and roasted
    tomatoes 152
Charmoula chicken 143
Chicken and mushroom pot pie with parmesan-chive
    crumble crust 140
Chicken dumpling soup 146
Chicken risotto with air-dried ham and peas 156
Chicken with white wine, saffron, pine nuts and
    currants 147
Chicken with wild boar pancetta and perry 138
Label Anglais chicken with basil roasted vegetables
    and Gruyère polenta 154
Pomegranate chicken and bread salad 144
Roast chicken with roast potatoes and bread sauce
    134

Chicken carcass
Roast chicken stock 136

Chorizo
Lentil and chorizo salad with sherry vinaigrette 176

Duck
Seared duck breasts with fresh raspberry vinaigrette
    159
Smoked duck toasts with gingered rhubarb 158

Gammon
Roast gammon with maple bourbon glaze 91

Goose
Left over goose rillettes 107
Roast goose with bread sauce and a choice of three
    stuffings 102

Grouse
Roasted grouse with apples, bacon and calvados 213

Guinea Fowl
Braised guinea fowl with sage and garlic 160

Lamb
7-hour roast leg of lamb with white beans and kale
    178
Grilled butterflied leg of lamb with lemon, dill and
    garlic 114
Herdwick lamb stewed with kidneys and pearl barley
    49
Lamb loin chops with basil and anchovy butter 113
Lamb meatballs braised in a saffron tomato spinach
    broth 115
Little lamb shank pies with Parmesan pastry 116
Roast lamb with chilli date almond pesto 60
Shepherd's pie 206

Lamb's kidney
Quickly cooked lambs' kidney with red-wine sauce
    and rice 204

Mutton
Casseroled mutton with red wine, cassia bark and
    roasted garlic 54
Chez Louisette's mutton stew with Madiran 52
Mutton chops with seasoned yoghurt and fatoush 58
Turkish mutton pizzas 57

Ostrich
Coriander crusted ostrich fillet with cabrales cheese
    196
Ostrich 'oyster' minute steaks 197
Ostrich plum and port casserole 195
Ostrich stew with mushrooms and lemon zest 192
Ostrich stir fry 198

Pheasant
Pot-roasted pheasant with cream and almonds 216

FISH

Extras

Further recipe indexes are available online at www.civicbooks.com.

Printed and bound by Oriental Press, UAE
Printed on 120gsm Sappi Offset, stock manufactured
    in a mill conforming to the ISO14001 environmen-
    tal management standard and FSC certified
Typeset in MT Joanna and Frutiger

Project produced by Tobias Steed,
Can of Worms Publishing in association with:
Art and Design Director Catherine Dixon
Typesetting Woojung Chun
Editorial Director Rachel de Thample
Editorial Assistant Laura Chastney
Production Director Tobias Steed and Catherine Dixon

All interviews were conducted by Sarah Freeman

ACKNOWLEDGEMENTS

Our appreciation is extended to many but in particular to all market traders, shoppers and staff of the market who have given their time for interviews, thoughts and tips.

To Claire Hartten and Simone Crofton for their involvement and enthusiastic support in the original conception of the project.

To Special Blue/Creative Imaging, London for their image scanning.

To Butler, Tanner & Dennis, UK for their colour correction and additional scanning.

George Nicholson's photographs were shot on a Mamiya medium format c 330 and a Leica 111g using Ilford FP4 and FP5 film. Selected images can also be viewed at: www.georgenicholsonphotography.co.uk.

Emma Lofstrom's cover illustration is based on line drawings, turned into a six-layered screenprint to add colours and textures. We would like to congratulate her on her graduation, BA (Hons) from Central Saint Martins College of Art & Design, her nomination for the V&A Student Illustrator of the Year Award 2006 and her commendation from the inaugural Penguin Design Award. More of her work can be viewed at: www.emmalofstrom.se.

This book would not have been possible without the endorsement and support of the Trustees of the Borough Market.

Finally, our thanks go to Robin Knowles and Civic Regeneration, Southwark, London for their continued support for the project.